Jean-Marie Straub &
Danièle Huillet

Edited by Ted Fendt

Österreichisches Filmmuseum
SYNEMA – Gesellschaft für Film und Medien

A book by SYNEMA ☰ Publikationen
Jean-Marie Straub & Danièle Huillet
Volume 26 of FilmmuseumSynemaPublikationen

This book was published with the support of the Goethe Institut.

SYNEMA – Gesellschaft für Film und Medien
Neubaugasse 36/1/1/1, A-1070 Wien

Design and layout: Gabi Adébisi-Schuster, Wien
Copy editors: Alexander Horwath, Regina Schlagnitweit
Cover photo: © Michel Chassat/Viennale
Printed by: REMAprint
Printed and published in Vienna, Austria.
Printed on paper certified in accordance with the rules of the Forest Stewardship Council.

ISBN 978-3-901644-64-1

Österreichisches Filmmuseum (Austrian Film Museum) and SYNEMA – Gesellschaft für Film & Medien
are supported by Bundeskanzleramt Österreich / Kunst und Kultur – Abt. (II/3) Film and by Kulturabteilung der Stadt Wien.

BUNDESKANZLERAMT ☰ ÖSTERREICH

Table of Contents

Jean-Marie Straub and Danièle Huillet in Chicago, 1975, with the
son of Bernard Rubenstein. Photo courtesy of Bernard Rubenstein.

Foreword

Twelve years have passed since the publication of the last English-language book on the films of Danièle Huillet and Jean-Marie Straub, Ursula Böser's nearly unavailable *The Art of Seeing, the Art of Listening*, and it has been twenty years since Barton Byg's seminal *Landscapes of Resistance*. During this time, there have been noteworthy changes in the reception of these filmmakers and their films in the English-speaking world. Many previously unavailable texts, fallen into obscurity or never available in English, have been unearthed, translated and made accessible online and new, original writing continues to appear as Jean-Marie Straub's latest films screen internationally.

Nevertheless, the films, old and new, continue to remain inaccessible. Apart from the hazards and whims of programming, this is certainly also due to the lack of prints with English subtitles and of decent prints in general – the color films from 1969 onward were printed on fast-fading stocks that have retained little of their original vibrancy. And then there is the long-prevailing notion that audiences are not interested in "challenging" or "difficult" films. My personal experience suggests the contrary. Every New York screening of their work I have attended since 2008 – *Too Early, Too Late* at Light Industry – has been well attended, some-times sold out, even when scheduled unusually early in the morning. The traveling North American retrospective that motivated the publication of this book will thus be an opportunity for many filmgoers to discover these films for the first time, hopefully with fresh eyes and ears.

The present volume emerges from conversations that I had with Barbara Ulrich – Jean-Marie Straub's closest collaborator since Danièle Huillet's death in 2006 – when she was in New York in February 2014 to assess the quality of the old U.S. distribution prints. We agreed that what was needed was a book to fill a variety of gaps, something comprehensive and foundational dealing with each film and aspect of Huillet and Straub's diverse and extensive body of work. Rather than being interpretive or theoretical, proffering *the one way* to view the films, we felt, instead, that the emphasis should be on facts and details, a kind of Straubian dictionary. A "Huilletian" dictionary is perhaps the better expression, though.

One of France's leading Straub-Huillet scholars, Benoît Turquety, once proposed that if there is a "Huilletian" form of writing, it would be defined by Danièle Huillet's affinity for precise information: her filmography of their work from the 1970s that includes details on budgets, shooting dates, film stocks and camera models, her lengthy annotations of their assistant Gregory Woods' work journal from the production of *Moses and Aaron*, her corrections of Straub's statements in post-screening discussions, clarifying a date, title or name. This catalogue is an attempt at something of that nature.

Claudia Pummer's comprehensive essay that opens the book and my own essay on the distribution and reception of the films in the Anglo world provide an overview of each film, Straub-Huillet's working methods and how they have been considered and discussed over the years. A lengthy interview by François Albera conducted in 2001 follows, delving into Huillet and Straub's interwoven and inseparable beliefs regarding filmmaking, politics and life. Straub-Huillet's collaborators elaborate further on their working methods. Three shorter pieces – by John Gianvito, Harun Farocki, and Jean-Piere Gorin – offer distinct ways of engaging with Straub-Huillet from a filmmaker's point of view (indirectly encompassing yet another filmmaker's portrait of "the Straubs," a film by Pedro Costa). Finally, the most detailed filmography to date and a selected bibliography of English-language criticism as well as a selection of previously unavailable photographs, letters and other documents chronicling Huillet and Straub's filmmaking as well as their relationship to North America round out the book.

I owe Barbara Ulrich my deepest gratitude for initiating this project, her encouragement and perseverance throughout and for answering many, many questions along the way.

I would like to thank Alexander Horwath for bringing the book under the auspices of the Austrian Film Museum and seeing it through to completion with great passion within a very short period of time.

I am also greatly indebted to the many people who have helped me research and assemble this book; among them, Straub and Huillet's collaborators, the technicians and actors who responded to my questions with love and enthusiasm; Gregory Woods and Bernard Rubenstein who shared their time, memories and photographs; Dan and Toby Talbot for access to their personal archive of correspondence; the Columbia University Rare Books and Manuscript Library, for access to the New Yorker Films and Dan Talbot papers and providing facsimiles; Bruce Jenkins, Jonathan Rosenbaum, Thom Andersen, Tom Luddy and George Robinson for the invaluable information they provided about Straub and Huillet's reception and time spent in the United States; Klaus Volkmer, the Munich Film Museum and Rudolf Thome for helping locate rare materials and films; Monica London and Barton Byg for their translations as well as Sally Shafto, Marie-Pierre Duhamel and Bernard Eisenschitz; the Goethe-Institut, which has provided generous support; and Gabi Adébisi-Schuster for turning a large array of materials into a beautiful book.

And, finally, I would simply like to thank Danièle Huillet and Jean-Marie Straub for their films.

Ted Fendt, January 2016

Claudia Pummer

(Not Only) for Children and Cavemen

The Films of Jean-Marie Straub and Danièle Huillet

For half a century, Danièle Huillet and Jean-Marie Straub collaborated on more than two dozen German-, French-, and Italian-language films, most of them adaptations of European art, music and literature. Among them are dramas by Hölderlin and Corneille, music by Bach and Schoenberg, a poem by Mallarmé, political essays and letters by Rousseau, Mahmoud Hussein, and Friedrich Engels, as well as novels by Kafka and Heinrich Böll, Cesare Pavese and Elio Vittorini. The duo which is widely referred to as Straub-Huillet, is often considered to be part of a particular strain of radical political avant-garde filmmaking that developed in the 1960s and 70s. In this context, Straub-Huillet are typically mentioned alongside European filmmakers such as Jean-Luc Godard, Jean-Pierre Gorin, Alexander Kluge, Chantal Akerman, Peter Gidal, Marcel Hanoun, Miklós Jancsó, and Harun Farocki. While most of them are associated with the political Left, it is above all their non-commercial mode of production and experimental treatment of film form which has determined their status as members of the political avant-garde. In addition, this label owed

much to the programming strategies on the international film festival and art-house circuit as well as to the emergence of cinema as an academic discipline by the mid-seventies, especially on U.S. and British campuses.

Like many other European filmmakers who belong to the generation that came of age right after the Second World War, both Straub-Huillet's political understanding and their creative approach are deeply informed by the historical sensibility of the WWII-era and its aftermath. In this context, the French critic Serge Daney has spoken of a generation of filmmakers for whom "the true birth of cinema" begins in the 1950s "with images of the reality of the camps."[1] Daney particularly highlights Alain Resnais' documentary *Nuit et Brouillard* (*Night and Fog*, 1955). "For the Straubs," he adds, "it's their whole life, it's what they do. Remembering that on the one hand it mustn't be forgotten, and on the other it mustn't be rebuilt."[2] If Resnais' documentary film disclosed unprecedented images in the 1950s, Straub-Huillet's first German-language films attempted something similar ten years later: to openly address the country's continued affiliations with militarism, Nazism, and anti-Semitism. Both films established, in addition, two major themes within their oeuvre: to situate contemporary

---

1 Serge Daney, *Postcards from the Cinema*, trans. Paul Grant, Oxford: Berg, 2007, p. 65
2 Ibid., p. 66

political issues within larger historical and geopolitical contexts and to argue for the necessity of political resistance. Beginning with *Machorka-Muff* in 1962 to *Fortini / Cani* in 1976 to *Europa 2005, 27 Octobre* (*Europa 2005, 27 October*) to Straub's recent solo works *Joachim Gatti* (2009), *La Guerre d'Algérie!* (*The Algerian War!*, 2014), and *Kommunisten* (*Communists*, 2014), many of the films deal explicitly with contemporary political issues. However, they also highlighted the radical implications of films that appeared to be less overtly political. Straub pointed, for instance, to "the political message" of "Hölderlin's communist utopia" that is expressed in their Hölderlin adaptation *Der Tod des Empedokles; oder: wenn dann der Erde Grün von neuem euch erglänzt* (*The Death of Empedocles or When the Green of the Earth Will Glisten for You Anew*, 1986).[3] In the same vein, the duo called Kafka "at heart a realist,"[4] because, as Huillet emphasizes: Kafka describes characters "who appear helpless as they are confronted with something that is difficult to grasp directly, something that is not the 'fate' of the Greeks, but produced by industrial society."[5] These statements attest, for once, to how much attention the two filmmakers dedicate to disclosing an original text's radical or realist underpinnings and, more importantly, the texts' (and their films') continued relevance and currency in contemporary society.

Some of Straub-Huillet's most explicit political statements can be found in notes that are auxiliary to their films. In this vein – and in response to critics who found the film not political enough – Straub called *Chronik der Anna*

Magdalena Bach (*Chronicle of Anna Magdalena Bach*, 1967) his contribution to the fight of the Vietcong against the Americans. Their Schoenberg opera adaptation *Moses und Aron* (*Moses and Aaron*, 1974) begins with a handwritten dedication to Holger Meins, a filmmaker and member of the German Red Army Faction, who died under dubious circumstances in a German federal prison right before the film was released. At the 2006 Venice International Film Festival, the filmmakers released three letters, typed and handwritten by Straub, during the press conference to their Pavese adaptation *Quei loro incontri* (*These Encounters of Theirs*). In these letters, Straub attacked the festival for its creative and political opportunism, especially in the context of the ongoing international war on terror. "I wouldn't be able to be festive in a festival," he writes, "where there are so many public and private police looking for a terrorist. *I* am that terrorist, and I tell you, paraphrasing Franco Fortini: so long as there's American imperialistic capitalism, there'll never be enough terrorists in the world."[6] Straub's recent vidéo-

---

3 "Danièle Huillet und Jean-Marie Straub im Gespräch mit Hans Hurch" [1989] in *Die Früchte des Zorns und der Zärtlichkeit: Werkschau Danièle Huillet/Jean-Marie Straub und ausgewählte Filme von John Ford*, ed. Astrid Johanna Ofner, Vienna: Viennale and Austrian Film Museum, 2004, p. 110

4 Wolfram Schütte, ed., "Gespräch mit Danièle Huillet und Jean-Marie Straub," in *Klassenverhältnisse: Von D. Huillet und J. M. Straub nach dem Roman "Der Verschollene" von Franz Kafka*, Frankfurt: Fischer, 1984, p. 38

5 Ibid., p. 40

6 See Tag Gallagher's translation of the letters: "Three Messages," *Kino Slang*, edited by Andy Rector, September 13, 2006, http://kinoslang.blogspot.com/search?q=Straub+Venice

tract *Joachim Gatti* follows along these lines. Gatti is a French filmmaker and activist who was injured during a protest in Montreuil when a so-called flash-ball gun, fired by police, hit him and lacerated one of his eyes. The short film is only one and a half minutes long and consists of a still shot of a photograph depicting Gatti before the injury. On the soundtrack Straub recites from the preface to Jean-Jacques Rousseau's *Discours sur l'origine et les fondements de l'inégalité parmi les hommes* (*Discourse on the Origin and Foundations of Inequality Among Men*, 1755), a passage in which Rousseau laments that intellectuals have the tendency to distance themselves from – or even turn a blind eye to – the violent protests that take place in the streets. Straub ends the voice-over by adding for himself: "And I Straub, I say to you that it is the police, the police armed by Capital, who kill."[7]

Aside from highlighting a continued commitment to political protest under contemporary geopolitical conditions, the Venice letters as well as the recent vidéotract on Gatti emphasize some fundamental principles of Straub-Huillet's work practice and approach to adaptation. Virtually all of their films rely on the direct quotation of an original text. Entire passages (musical or literary) are recited by way of a performance style that is deliberately devoid of so-called naturalistic or psychological motivations. Many of the original authors they

Joachim Gatti (2009)
Christophe Clavert and Jean-Marie Straub on the set

engaged with were outspoken and active Leftists, including communist writers like Brecht and Franco Fortini; others, however, are widely considered conservative or apolitical, among them the French novelist Maurice Barrès, the Austrian composer Arnold Schoenberg, and the French poet Joachim Gasquet. Straub-Huillet's politics have, in other words, nothing to do with party-affiliation but are rather based on something that registers with the filmmakers as they first read and engage with a text. "It's like a love story," Huillet once put it,

7 For a translated English version of the full text and a link to the film, see "Joachim Gatti, 2009," in *Kino Slang*, edited by Andy Rector, April 4, 2010, http://kinoslang.blogspot.de/search?q=joachim+gatti, np.

"which happens not only when you meet a person, but also when you encounter a text that contains something that seems right."[8] On these grounds Straub-Huillet have developed some unusual alliances throughout their career such as a fondness for filmmakers like John Ford and D.W. Griffith, while openly criticizing contemporaries such as Rainer Werner Fassbinder and Alexander Kluge.

Over five decades, Jean-Marie Straub and Danièle Huillet made films in different places, under various conditions and adapted different kinds of source materials. Each Straub-Huillet film introduces, in this respect, a great number of variations and new elements into a body of work that is typically celebrated (or criticized) for being organized around a set of strict rules and stylistic principles. Even though their work contains a number of signature techniques – among them the so-called *plan Straubien* (or Straubian sequence shot), the casting of non-professional actors, and the use of direct, location sound recording – their work asks us to pay equally close attention to the irregular and unique aspects in each film or, in some cases, in different versions of one and the same film. The most fundamental principle in the duo's oeuvre is therefore not a matter of form or style, but derives from an ethical position that defines how the filmmakers relate to a text, a place, and the people with whom they work. More than merely a personal sentiment, this position belongs in part to the specific critical and creative conditions under which Huillet and Straub emerged as artists in the immediate postwar era in Paris, France.

THE PARIS YEARS AND THE FRENCH NEW WAVE

Straub and Huillet started making films in the early sixties in West Germany, with two short adaptations based on writings by the contemporary German novelist Heinrich Böll, entitled *Machorka-Muff* (1962) and *Nicht versöhnt oder Es hilft nur Gewalt, wo Gewalt herrscht* (*Not Reconciled, or Only Violence Helps Where Violence Rules*, 1964/65). In fact, their first four works, created during a ten-year residence in Munich, were German films. And even though they moved to Italy in 1968, they continued to produce German-language works throughout their career. Due to this, they are often associated with the Young German Film of the 1960s and its successor, the 1970s New German Cinema. Straub-Huillet also continued to receive funding from German federal and state institutions as well as the public television networks.

However, the two French-born filmmakers had already begun their collaboration a decade earlier in Paris. Both in their early twenties, Huillet and Straub met in 1954 at the *Lycée Voltaire* in a film class that prepared students for the entry exam at the national film school *I.D.H.E.C. (Institut des hautes études cinématographiques)*. Only Huillet showed up for the test, yet never completed it: "They showed us Yves Allégret's *Manèges*," she later recalled "and asked us to analyze it. I left my exam book blank, except for three lines in which I said it was scandalous they should show us such a ter-

8 Helge Heberle and Monika Funke Stern, "Das Feuer im Innern des Berges," in *Frauen und Film*, no. 32, 1982, p. 10

rible film."[9] Huillet's outrage is representative of the French New Wave generation's vocal reproach of the established French cinema's so-called "tradition of quality," which was also the subject of François Truffaut's notorious article "A Certain Tendency of French Cinema" (*Cahiers du cinéma*, no. 31, 1954). "At a time when Italian neorealism turned to the street for inspiration," explains Jean Douchet, "French film confined itself to the studio and wallowed in a pessimistic and morose vision of daily life."[10] Instead of turning to the streets themselves, young French film enthusiasts turned to the movie screens for inspiration. The local ciné-clubs played a crucial role in nurturing a new generation of filmgoers and aspiring filmmakers. Aided by a number of cultural institutions, various film clubs had reopened throughout the country since the end of the Occupation. Often accompanied by lectures and discussions, these screenings gave audience members opportunities to discover works from various historical, national, and aesthetic backgrounds.

Until he moved to Paris, Straub had co-organized such a film club in his hometown Metz, La Chambre noire, and in this context made the acquaintance of Truffaut and André Bazin. Both of them were active in the film club movement and attended screenings as guest speakers throughout the country. Already an established critic at the time, Bazin had co-founded *Cahiers du cinéma* in 1951 and became a mentor to a group of young critics who wrote for the journal on a regular basis, among them Truffaut, Jean-Luc Godard, Jacques Rivette, and Éric Rohmer. In addition, Bazin had a profound influence on some of the French New Wave's core aesthetic and critical principles. Based on his appreciation of Italian Neorealism, he favored a new mode of filmmaking that defied classical conventions of cinematic storytelling in favor of an aesthetic structuring of reality "that allows the viewer to see nothing but the event itself."[11] Jean-Luc Godard called him in hindsight the only real critic among the established film critics and historians of the period, and added: "We at *Cahiers* always considered ourselves future directors. Going to ciné-clubs and the Cinémathèque was already thinking the cinema and thinking about the cinema. Writing was already making cinema because between writing and filming there is only a quantitative difference, not a qualitative one."[12]

The concurrence between criticism and cinema, writing and filmmaking, gains special importance in respect to Straub-Huillet's own experiences and explorations as filmmakers. Straub has reported that he wanted to become a film critic at the time, rather than a filmmaker. Yet he appears in the credits to a short film that is often considered an early work of the New Wave movement: Jacques Rivette's *Le Coup du berger* (*Fools Mate*, 1956). The script was co-written by Rivette and Claude Chabrol, who

9 Richard Roud, *Jean-Marie Straub*, New York: Viking Press, 1972, p. 26
10 Jean Douchet, *The French New Wave*, trans. Robert Bonnono, New York: D.A.P., 1998, p. 31
11 André Bazin, "In Defense of Rossellini," in *What is Cinema? Vol. 2*, trans. Hugh Gray, Berkeley: University of California Press, 2005, p. 101
12 Michel Marie, *The French New Wave: An Artistic School*, trans. Richard Neupert, Malden: Blackwell Publishing, 2003, p. 26–27

was also the film's producer. Jacques Doniol-Valcroze, co-editor of *Cahiers du cinéma*, had one of the lead roles, while Godard and Truffaut made appearances as extras. Straub is listed as assistant director, but later downplayed his role by saying, "all I did there was carry valises. I did it because it was a reunion of friends, and they didn't have money to pay for assistants."[13] In the same interview, Straub settles some of the other myths that had come to determine his roots as a filmmaker in France, like his alleged assistant-ships for a number of established French directors, among them, Abel Gance, Jean Renoir, and Robert Bresson. "There have been errors of translation," he clarifies, "at the time when all the films that I'm supposed to have worked on were being made, in fact, I wasn't even living in Paris. I used to hitchhike to Paris often to see movies, and occasionally I would have the opportunity to go into a studio and watch them filming, for an hour or two, or sometimes a day. But it was really just like looking through a keyhole."[14] Nevertheless, before he moved to Paris, Straub had the idea for the Bach project, after reading a short fictional biography by the British writer Esther Meynell, in which the story of Bach's life is told from the perspective of his second wife Anna Magdalena. When he met Huillet in 1954, he asked her if she would help him write the script.

The degree of Huillet's involvement with either filmmaking or the *Cahiers* group during this period remains, in comparison to Straub's, much more obscure. However, her reaction to the *I.D.H.E.C.* entry exam attests to the fact that she shared the French New Wave's overall crit-icism. In addition to this, she had developed an early interest in a particular type of cinema: the making of ethnographic documentaries. Indeed, new approaches to ethnographic cinema, embodied specifically by the filmmaker Jean Rouch and his conception of *cinéma vérité*, provided another important aesthetic impulse for the new generation of French filmmakers. To them, writes Jean Douchet, reality meant "lived experience, immediacy. It burst forth accidentally from the filmed event as it did in real life, revealed itself in Jean Rouch's ethnographic approach as a document that is allowed to speak. In short, it privileged notions of immediate reporting, and a spur-of-the-moment, impromptu, and improvised reality in contrast to the definitive, static, and mummified aspect typical of so many documentaries."[15] This brings to mind Straub-Huillet's *Chronicle of Anna Magdalena Bach* whose title echoes, of course, Rouch's *Chronique d'un été* (*Chronicle of a Summer*, 1961), a documentary he made in collaboration with the sociologist Edgar Morin. Indeed, Richard Roud was one of the first to point to the Bach film's *cinéma vérité* qualities.[16] And yet, the Bach film's *vérité* elements have little in common with the provisional and observational nature that informed most *vérité*-style documentaries in the fifties. In fact, Straub-Huillet's approach calls for a minimization of impromptu gestures

13 Joel Rogers, "Jean-Marie Straub and Danièle Huillet Interviewed: *Moses and Aaron* as an Object of Marxist Reflection," *Jump Cut*, no. 12/13, 1976, p. 61–62
14 Ibid., p. 62
15 Douchet, op. cit., p. 80
16 Roud, op. cit., p. 66

and situations, since most of their scenes are extremely well-rehearsed and planned out beforehand. Thus, where Rouch and Morin's *Chronicle of a Summer* ends on a self-reflexive note, judging the line between fiction and reality to be abstruse, *Chronicle of Anna Magdalena Bach* stages the encounter between fiction and reality unambiguously: the spectator is always able to separate between the two.

Straub-Huillet's films also lack the anarchic exuberance specific to early New Wave cinema. Their films don't share, for instance, the obsession with contemporary youth culture and Bohemian lifestyle and avoid references to consumer culture, popular colloquialism, and the sexual revolution. Their films focus instead on certain literary and artistic traditions that are usually defined as classical or modernist. To be more precise, unlike some of the other New Wave filmmakers, Straub-Huillet refrain from transposing these texts onto a contemporary social setting. The much more somber and mature tone of Straub-Huillet's films recalls rather another group of filmmakers that is either considered a precursor or part of the first New Wave generation: the so-called "Left Bank" group that included Alain Resnais, Chris Marker, and Agnès Varda. However, unlike the Left Bank, which was strongly influenced by the contemporary literary phenomenon of the *nouveau roman*, Straub-Huillet engaged with a much older canon. With some notable exceptions, like Heinrich Böll, Franco Fortini, and (Left Bank affiliate) Marguerite Duras, they adapted for the most part texts written by non-living authors.

Truffaut and Straub, 1954

Nevertheless, Straub-Huillet shared with many New Wave filmmakers a fondness for long-take cinematography, the regular employment of non-professional actors, and a penchant for inserting archival footage and quotidian, documentary scenes into their fictional narratives. And yet, the duo's roots in the French New Wave might be best described in terms of a shared commitment to an ethical position that is summarized by Jean-Luc Godard's statement "tracking shots are a question of morality."[17] In 1954, Truffaut had already articulated something similar in "A Certain Tendency in French Cinema," a piece of criticism that seems highly relevant for a discussion of Straub-Huillet's work since Truffaut focuses in particular on literary adaptations, a practice that not only dominated the French "quality" cinema during the immediate postwar era but that is, of course, equally central to the couple's approach to filmmaking.

In his article, Truffaut attacked the acclaimed "tradition of quality" for its tendency to distort an original author's work. According to him, contemporary French screenwriters and directors edited and added to the adapted material, allegedly to compensate for a work's "un-filmable" passages. In reality, Truffaut surmised, the changes and substitutions occurred, on the one hand, in order to push the filmmaker's own political agenda and, on the other, to cover up his inability to produce film scenes beyond established conventions and ready-made clichés. This so-called realism, Truffaut raged, envisioned human beings "barricaded by formulas, plays on words, maxims, instead of letting us see them for ourselves, with our own eyes."[18] Truffaut's words echo Bazin who once praised Roberto Rossellini for "creating [an] aesthetic structure" that was "better suited" to direct the events in front of the camera than the director: "the structure which Rossellini has created allows the viewer to see nothing but the event itself."[19] Thus, the figure of the auteur Truffaut envisioned in his article is not the dominating artist-genius who leaves his per-

sonal imprint on a generic text that was later associated with the term "auteurism." Truffaut's auteur is an artist who creates new images with the means of cinema without distorting an original text and its author's intention. French screenwriters, Truffaut objected, changed an original text's language, added new scenes, and turned characters into abject beings; "so inordinate is the authors' desire to be superior to their characters that those who, perchance, are not infamous are, at best, infinitely grotesque," he writes.[20]

When Jean-Marie Straub and Danièle Huillet released their first two short films in the early sixties in Germany, a similar conflict played out: their refusal to portray their characters in a judgmental or grotesque way led to strong disapproval among West German critics and audiences.

THE MUNICH YEARS: BÖLL, BACH, AND BRUCKNER

In the fall of 1958 Straub left France to escape imprisonment for refusing to serve in the French military during the Algerian War. A year later, the couple settled in Munich. Straub's exile separated the duo from the just emerging international phenomenon of French

17 Jean-Luc Godard, et.al. "Hiroshima, notre amour," *Cahiers du cinéma*, no. 97, July 1959, p. 5. See also Serge Daney, "The Tracking Shot in *Kapo*," in *Postcards From the Cinema*, pp. 17–35
18 François Truffaut, "A Certain Tendency of the French Cinema" in *Movies and Methods: An Anthology*, ed. Bill Nichols, Berkeley: University of California Press, 1976, p. 232
19 Bazin, op. cit., p. 101
20 Truffaut, op. cit., p. 233

New Wave cinema and aligned them instead with the Young German Film, a movement that coincided precisely with their ten-year residence in West Germany. Since Straub-Huillet lacked the funding that was needed for the Bach film, they decided to make two short films in the meantime. Both *Machorka-Muff* and *Not Reconciled* are based on literary works written by Heinrich Böll, one of the most prolific and respected West German political novelists at the time. Both original works accused the German Federal Republic of having failed to adequately address its National Socialist past. The short story "Hauptstädtisches Journal" ("Bonn Diary," 1957) on which *Machorka-Muff* is based, exposes the continued presence of ex-Nazi officers in the resurrected military apparatus of the German Federal Republic, while Böll's novel *Billard um halbzehn* (*Billiards at Half-Past Nine*, 1959), the literary source for *Not Reconciled,* shows how anti-Semitic sentiments and totalitarian structures informed German social and political institutions well before and long after the period between 1933 and 1945. In addition, it addressed the German people's continued failure to revolt against these conditions. *Machorka-Muff* is certainly one of the first films made in the German Federal Republic after WWII that dealt explicitly with a subject that would eventually preoccupy many New German Films, especially after 1968. As a French citizen who was born in the contested French border region of Alsace, Straub states that he was particularly equipped to make a film that "no German

could make – just as no German was able to make *Germany, Year Zero*, no American *The Southerner* or *The Young One*, and no Italian could have written *The Charterhouse of Parma*."[21]

Machorka-Muff follows the rise of the high-ranking military officer Erich von Machorka-Muff who returns to the West German capital to be rehabilitated in spite of his actions in the German army during WWII and in order to be able to take on a lead role in the Federal Republic's military restoration in the fifties. Even though Straub-Huillet left the plot and dialogue unaltered, West German critics and audiences, especially those on the Left, reacted to *Machorka-Muff* rather negatively. The film was also rejected by the Oberhausen Film Festival.

One of the greatest points of contention was the main character himself. Straub-Huillet refrained from judging the character "from above" and refused to turn him into a caricature. Thus, instead of placing the burden of responsibility onto the individual, Straub-Huillet attempted to reveal the overall conditions that made his actions possible. The actor who portrayed Machorka-Muff (a well-known German journalist who was an outspoken critic of the rearmament politics) delivered his lines with a minimum of affect and pathos, thus making it impossible for the viewer to develop a sense of superiority and condemn him for his actions. Another criticism was Straub-Huillet's tendency to extend certain shots long after the obvious action had subsided, while refusing to add any kind of narrative exposition that would help the viewer to gain an immediate understanding of the plot.

21 Roud, op. cit., p. 29

This became an even greater concern with the release of their second film, *Not Reconciled*. Afraid that another controversy would strain Heinrich Böll's reputation among the German Left, his publisher tried to stop *Not Reconciled*'s distribution. The *Filmbewertungsstelle* (the Federal Republic's official tax-reducing quality-rating agency) also denied the film a quality rating and the film was rejected by the Berlin Film Festival selection committee.

However, back home in France and, especially, among the circle of *Cahiers* critics, the films were received with much greater understanding. Jacques Rivette went so far as to call *Machorka-Muff* "the first film *d'auteur* made in Germany after the war."[22] His review in *Cahiers du cinéma* included, in addition, a translated version of Karlheinz Stockhausen's letter to Straub, one of the few official statements of defense that Straub-Huillet's film received in the German Federal Republic. Stockhausen was, perhaps, the first to notice similarities between the film's temporal structure and the structure of a musical composition.

Machorka-Muff and *Not Reconciled* were among the first films made in West Germany that addressed the country's National Socialist past and the continued existence of militarism and anti-Semitism in the Federal Republic. But the filmmakers' own experiences in France also informed their handling of the subject matter. One sequence in *Machorka-Muff* features, for instance, a selection of archival newspaper clippings from the 1950s and early 60s that focus particularly on the implementation of the military draft within the context of the country's rearmament politics. The issue of the draft is not explicitly addressed in Böll's text. However, by inserting the real newspaper articles, Straub-Huillet recontextualize Böll's short story in light of their own experiences without actually changing the original text; the newspaper sequence stands apart clearly from the rest of the dramatic adaptation.

Archival photographs, newsreel footage, and rear-projected images, are frequently used in this manner, especially in the films Straub-Huillet made in the sixties and seventies. The use of external pictorial or documentary material is by no means unique to their oeuvre, but rather common in new wave and later avant-garde cinemas of the period. *Not Reconciled* and the later *Einleitung zu Arnold Schoenbergs Begleitmusik zu einer Lichtspielscene (Introduction to Arnold Schoenberg's "Accompaniment to a Cinematographic Scene,"* 1972) also make heavy use of archival footage, especially in order to suggest the continued trauma of state-sanctioned discrimination, oppression, and violence. These early Straub-Huillet films recall somewhat Alain Resnais' postwar films such as *Night and Fog, Hiroshima mon amour* (1959), *L'Année dernière à Marienbad* (*Last Year in Marienbad*, 1961), and *Muriel ou le Temps d'un retour* (*Muriel or the Time of Return*, 1963). However, as Straub has pointed out: "Far from being a puzzle film (like *Citizen Kane* or *Muriel*), *Not Reconciled* is better described as a 'lacunary film,'" because unlike these other flashback

22 Jacques Rivette, "Machorka-Muff," *Cahiers du cinéma*, no. 145, July 1963, p. 36

Machorka-Muff (1962)
Erich Kuby, Newspaper sequence

narratives, *Not Reconciled* does little to put the viewer in the position to put the pieces together in the end.[23] Moreover, Straub-Huillet tried deliberately "to eliminate […] any historical aura in both costumes and sets" in an attempt to put "the past […] on the same level as the present."[24] It is worth noting that after *Not Reconciled* they abandoned the use of flashbacks altogether and focused instead on works that followed a linear narrative order.

Quite recently, Straub addressed the Algerian War directly in a short film he made in 2014, entitled *The Algerian War!* Even though the entire film is only two minutes long and consists of only a few shots, it bears certain similarities with the topics involved in their first short films. *The Algerian War!* tells the story of a man who assassinates his lieutenant in an act of belated protest after the lieutenant orders the massacre of Algerian civilians. The action the man takes is the very act that is missing in Germany both before and after the war and that allowed officers like Machorka-Muff to maintain their positions later on. Unlike *Machorka-Muff* which is completely devoid of any signs of rebellion, *Not Reconciled* features two characters that echo the violent resistance of the man in *The Algerian War!* There is, first of all, Johanna who, as a young woman, voices vocal opposition against the German emperor and as an old woman attempts to assassinate a leading politician. Clearly modeled as a spiritual descendant of Brecht's Saint Joan of the Stockyards (hence the film's subtitle *Only Violence Helps Where Violence Rules*, which is a quote from Brecht's play), Johanna's political resistance is con-

tained, however, by locking her away in a mental institution. There is also Johanna's son Robert, who worked as a demolition expert in the army during WWII. After the war he blows up the abbey his father, an architect, had built, as an act of "protest against the hypocrisy which preserved the Cathedral in Cologne […] from bombs while thousands were killed."[25]

As noted, it was in part Straub-Huillet's refusal to provide narrative clarity that led to "the unbelievably hostile reaction of the audience," Richard Roud observed during the Berlin premiere of *Not Reconciled* in 1965.[26] Aside from the aforementioned points of criticism, audiences also mocked the non-professional actors' local accents and their "unusual" intonation that resulted from Straub-Huillet's deliberate effort to avoid naturalistic or psychologically-motivated vocal performances. "The mistakes are frustrating, especially in terms of [Straub's] directing – or failure to direct – the actors," wrote Enno Patalas, the chief editor of the leading West German film journal *Filmkritik*.[27] Patalas' attitude, however, changed markedly with the film's sudden success at various international film festivals abroad, a development that also brought positive attention to the new phenomenon of the Young German Film. Thus, only one year after his initial condemnation of *Not*

23 Roud, op. cit., p. 41
24 Roud, op. cit., p. 40
25 Jean-Marie Straub, Danièle Huillet. *Nicht versöhnt oder Es hilft nur Gewalt, wo Gewalt herrscht* (1964/65). Trans. Danièle Huillet and Misha Donat
26 Roud, *Jean-Marie Straub*, p. 44
27 Enno Patalas, "Nicht versöhnt," *Filmkritik*, no. 9, August 1965, p. 474

Prewar and postwar era in
Not Reconciled (1964/65)

Johanna's assassination attempt in
Not Reconciled

Reconciled, Patalas described the upcoming *Chronicle of Anna Magdalena Bach* most enthusiastically: "Based on Straub's prior achievements with his short film *Machorka-Muff* and, above all […] with *Not Reconciled* […] *Chronicle of Anna Magdalena Bach* can be expected to be one of the most important and most interesting works of the New German Film."[28] Patalas' unconditional praise for a film that was not yet completed included an appeal to the readers of *Filmkritik* to financially support the Bach film. The appeal was also signed by Alexander Kluge and Volker Schlöndorff, the two most acclaimed young German filmmakers at the time.

Yet Straub-Huillet's affiliations lay elsewhere as the personal dedications in the finished Bach film illustrate. They list four names to express their gratitude. The first three were old friends at *Cahiers du cinéma*: Jacques Rivette, Jean-Luc Godard, and Michel Delahaye. The three had not only supported the couple's work during the vicious attacks on the two short films, but Godard, for instance, had invested a substantial sum of money at a time when the Bach project was in danger of falling apart. The fourth person mentioned in the dedication is Peter Nestler, a German filmmaker and one of Straub-Huillet's closest long-term friends and collaborators, who had also helped finance *Chronicle of Anna Magdalena Bach*. In addition to this, Nestler was part of a group of German filmmakers, called the "New Munich Group" that also included the directors Klaus Lemke, Rudolf Thome, Max Zihlmann, and Eckhart Schmidt. What defined this distinct circle of filmmakers, according to Enno Patalas, was

that they worked in part collaboratively and that their work was based on "similar visual motifs, formed by way of similar filmic methods […] and in response to the same historical situation: […] life in the Federal Republic."[29] More precisely, the filmmakers of the New Munich Group shared Straub-Huillet's interest in aesthetic practices that grew out of the French New Wave movement such as Bazin's cinematic realism and a *vérité*-approach to non-fiction filmmaking. There is some evidence that Straub-Huillet had a significant influence on the New Munich Group's aesthetic formation and development. They organized screenings and hosted regular gatherings in their downtown apartment that was conveniently located above a movie theater. In 1995, Rudolf Thome included a tribute to these evenings in his film *Das Geheimnis*: the characters are eating "spaghetti with butter and cheese," apparently the Straubs' signature dish. "After dinner," Klaus Lemke recalls, Huillet and Straub "served real French coffee in their small studio apartment which was completely filled with books, a big bed, more and more books […] as well as an expensive record player."[30] Straub-Huillet's affiliations with the New Munich Group also

28 Enno Patalas, "In eigener Sache," *Filmkritik*, no. 10, November 1966, p. 601
29 Enno Patalas, "Ansichten einer Gruppe," *Filmkritik*, no. 5, May 1966, p. 247
30 Thomas Brandlmeier, "Die Münchner Schule: Zur Vorgeschichte des Jungen Deutschen Films 1962–1968," in *Abschied von Gestern: Bundesdeutscher Film der Sechziger und Siebziger Jahre*, eds. Hans-Peter Reichmann and Rudolf Worschech, Frankfurt/Main: Deutsches Filmmuseum, 1991, p. 58

included a number of collaborations of less an-
ecdotal character. Huillet, for instance, was the
editor of Thome's short film *Jane erschießt John,
weil er sie mit Ann betrügt* (*Jane shoots John because
he's cheating on her with Ann*, 1967/68) and in
1972, Peter Nestler appeared in a lead role in
Straub-Huillet's *Introduction to Arnold Schoenberg's "Accompaniment to a Cinematographic
Scene."* Thus, even though Straub-Huillet left
Munich in 1968, they maintained many of the
friendships and professional affiliations that had
formed during this period. One of Straub's later
films, the 2007 documentary *Itinéraire de Jean
Bricard* (*Itinerary of Jean Bricard*) includes, once
again, a dedication to Peter Nestler who, like
most of the members of the New Munich
Group, remains relatively unknown to audiences both in and outside of Germany.

The Bach film was an ambitious project and
it took Straub and Huillet more than a decade
to complete it. While many independent German producers and public broadcasters saw the
potential market value in a biographical film
about the Baroque composer, they refused to
commit to the terms Straub-Huillet envisioned
for the film. There was, first of all, the filmmakers' insistence on using direct sound. This
included scenes that featured the musical performances which were all to be recorded live
and filmed in one shot, a technically complex
and costly endeavor. Moreover, as they had
done previously, they chose mainly non-professional actors. One of them was the Dutch
musician Gustav Leonhardt who, as some objected, had not only nothing physically in common with the historical Bach but also spoke

with a Dutch accent. Yet Straub-Huillet insisted
on Leonhardt because he was one of the leading Bach interpreters at the time who performed Bach's works on period instruments.
Christiane Lang, the actress who appeared in
the role of Anna Magdalena was also a classi-
cally trained musician. Thus, Leonhardt and
Lang assumed their roles as professional musicians rather than as actors portraying psycho-
logically rounded characters. Like the performances in the two previous short films, the actors
recited their lines matter-of-factly, without any
naturalistic embellishments.

Straub-Huillet's insistence on historical ac-
curacy involved the recreation of the original
musicians' work conditions: for instance, all actors and musicians wore period costumes, including wigs and spectacles (some of them
even with prescription lenses). In addition, they
played musical instruments that were either
original or rebuilt to fit the style of the period.
These creative decisions were motivated by an
attempt to document Bach's life and work as
truthfully as possible without trying to create
the illusion of a dramatic reenactment (as in
most conventional biopics). Straub-Huillet's
commitment to this kind of historical fidelity
prevented the filmmakers from using many of
the original Bach locations, especially the exteriors. Straub had visited most of these places
right after he had left France, often accompanied by Huillet, and the two had found many of
the original cityscapes and buildings so dramat-
ically changed or destroyed that it became impossible to use them for the film. Instead they
replaced them with sketches and drawings of

the original locations from the period. In effect, *Chronicle of Anna Magdalena Bach* has almost no exterior locations. This becomes apparent in a scene where Leonhardt performs with the orchestra in front of a rear-projected image that depicts an archival shot of the Thomas School, a building that was destroyed in 1902. Yet instead of using rear projection in a canonical fashion – to produce a believable simulation of an outside location – the oblique angle and odd spatial dimensions in this shot highlight the artificial construction of the space. Thus, instead of trying to tell the Bachs' story through cinematic conventions, Straub-Huillet attempted to revive the historical scene through the recordings of the musical performances and through the incorporation of archival documents.

This includes, first of all, handwritten sheet music and letters as well as program notes from the period. There are also drawings and prints from the time. And, most importantly, there is Bach's original music. Instead of following a conventional narrative arc, the plot largely follows the chronology of the musical compositions. Each piece that made it into the film is part of a live-recorded performance, filmed in one shot. Huillet has called *Chronicle* "a fictional feature-film with documentary means."[31] The documentary aspect derives from the fact that we see musicians *at work*. In addition, we see musicians who, while playing the original pieces on original instruments, retrace the conditions under which Bach (and his contemporaries) made music together. Bach appears in this scenario as a principal collaborator and co-author within the film because each piece determines the chronology of the plot and the length of the shot. However, Bach certainly does not work alone. Straub-Huillet, of course, select each piece beforehand and make decisions about how to compose, frame, and edit it, in combination with the additional audiovisual material. There is also Gustav Leonhardt who, together with the other musicians, interprets the music and, in doing so, impacts the sound and the duration of each scene or shot accordingly.

The film's title is a nod to Esther Meynell's biographical novel that had initially inspired Straub. However, instead of using Meynell's text as a foundation, Straub-Huillet decided to base the script on original texts authored by the Bach family. Since Anna Magdalena did not leave any written letters or memoirs, her voice-over narration is based on documents written by her relatives (her husband, their sons, and a cousin). The film features, however, a number of original scores that Bach historians have identified as transcriptions produced by Anna Magdalena's hand. Bach also wrote some of the music featured in the film explicitly for her, for she herself was an accomplished singer and pianist. By including these manuscripts, Straub-Huillet incorporate evidence of Anna Magdalena's physical labor into the film. In addition, they point to the collaboration that existed between her and her husband, a relationship that begs, of course, a certain comparison to Straub-Huillet's own personal and professional affiliation. The film, interestingly, maintains a clear

31 Heberle and Funke Stern, op. cit., p. 9

Anna Magdalena at work in *Chronicle of Anna Magdalena Bach* (1967)
Musicians, the rear-projected Thomas School

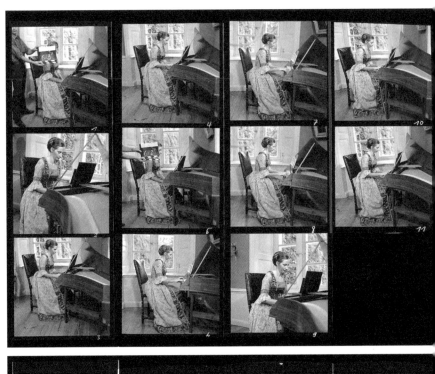

Chronicle of
Anna Magdalena Bach
set photos

spatial separation between husband and wife: Anna's voice – which dominates the oral narration of the film – is exclusively heard off-screen as part of the voice-over, while Bach, in contrast, speaks his lines onscreen. Even when the characters are in the same room, they are mostly depicted in separate shots. They appear in the same shot during some of the musical performances that also feature Lang/Anna singing on screen. In other words, the compositions present a careful arrangement of the couple's personal and professional space that attests at once to the division of labor and the work they produced together. *Chronicle of Anna Magdalena Bach* stands out within Straub-Huillet's oeuvre insofar as it represents their first feature-length project as well as the film "that brought Straub and Huillet together and brought them their widest international recognition."[32] Yet it is perhaps at the same time their most atypical work, due to the fact that it did not originate from a text whose direct quotation served as the film's dialogue.

Der Bräutigam, die Komödiantin und der Zuhälter (*The Bridegroom, the Actress, and the Pimp*, 1968), the last film Straub-Huillet made during the time of their West German residence, emerged from the collaborative encounter between the duo and the Munich Action-Theater, a performance group that included not only the young Rainer Werner Fassbinder, but also the members of the stock ensemble he would later use in his films, among them Hanna Schygulla, Irm Hermann, and actor-composer Peer Raben. While the dialogue for the earlier films had either prosaic or epistolary origins (Böll's texts

and Bach's letters), *Bridegroom* introduced a third type of literary genre into Straub-Huillet's body of work: the adaptation of plays and with it the theatrical or stage performance as a distinct medium. Their brief encounter with the Munich Action-Theater foreshadows Straub-Huillet's later collaborations with the Teatro Francesco di Bartolo in Buti, a work connection Straub maintained until 2011.

The film developed out of a play by the Austrian playwright Ferdinand Bruckner, called *Krankheit der Jugend* (*Pains of Youth*, 1926). The members of the Action-Theater group had asked Straub to direct it and Straub finally agreed, but only after he had cut the text of the original play down to eleven minutes of stage time. The play was performed together with *Katzelmacher*, Fassbinder's first play written for the Action-Theater and the original text for his later film of the same name. The creative encounter with Fassbinder and the Action-Theater provided Straub-Huillet with the narrative core for *Bridegroom* (as well as some of its footage), and it similarly informed Fassbinder's beginnings as a filmmaker. His first feature *Liebe ist kälter als der Tod* (*Love Is Colder Than Death*, 1969) was, like *Bridegroom*, an adaptation of Bruckner's play. In his own film he also reprised his role as the pimp, which he had played under Straub's direction on stage and onscreen. Both *Love Is Colder Than Death* and the following adaptation of *Katzelmacher* (1969)

---

32 Barton Byg, *Landscapes of Resistance: The German Films of Danièle Huillet and Jean-Marie Straub*, Berkeley: California, 1995, p. 51

are also noteworthy because they belong to a period in Fassbinder's career in which he explored similar aesthetics as Straub-Huillet, including a non-naturalistic style of acting and long-take cinematography. Fassbinder dedicated *Love Is Colder than Death* to Straub, as well as Claude Chabrol and Éric Rohmer.

Straub-Huillet's own adaptation of Bruckner's *Pains of Youth* differs significantly from Fassbinder's. Instead of attempting to create a coherent cinematic interpretation of the original play, *Bridegroom* is better described as offering us different takes or variations on the play's main narrative theme centering around social oppression (especially of women) and the possibility of resistance. The film's structure falls largely into three larger segments. It opens with a brief shot depicting a graffiti-inscription Straub-Huillet discovered on the wall in Munich's main post office: "Stupid old Germany, I hate it over here, I hope I can go soon, Patricia." Aside from other connotations, the disgruntled statement seems especially humorous in hindsight as it appears in a film that would, indeed, be the last film Straub-Huillet made before leaving Germany. The shot with the graffiti transitions to an uninterrupted four-minute tracking shot filmed from the position of a car driving alongside a busy street, the Landsberger Straße, at nighttime. Located on the outskirts of the city, the Landsberger Straße was a center for small-scale commerce during the day that turned into a red-light district by night. The camera captures fleeting images of prostitutes standing on the sidewalk waiting for clients to drive by. Both the graffiti and the Landsberger Straße sequence actualize the topics of social oppression and sexual exploitation that are raised in Bruckner's play within a contemporary quotidian setting. The shadowy figures of the women standing and waiting on the sidewalk are frequently interrupted by brightly illuminated shop windows and advertising billboards, meaning that the women's bodies are shown in relation to a larger system of commercial solicitation and commodification. The film's second segment features another long take, but in this case the camera remains motionless, perfectly framing a small theater stage. The shot depicts one of the Action-Theater's original performances of Bruckner's play in its entirety. It retains the documentary character of the first scenes, yet is equally indebted to the medium of theater. The third and final segment features, in contrast, a more conventional cinematic narrative that recasts Bruckner's play in the form of a gangster drama with focus on Lilith and James, a romantic couple struggling to escape Lilith's former pimp in pursuit of a bourgeois life. Even though it is set in a contemporary milieu, the segment fuses documentary and theatrical elements as in the scene in which the couple's marriage vows are filmed in one single shot or by substituting quotations of poetry in lieu of conventional dialogue.

The three autonomous parts of *Bridegroom* encapsulate, interestingly, the three major modes of representation Straub-Huillet were to develop – sometimes separately, but more often in conjunction – during the almost five decades of their collaboration. The first two shots – the graffiti and the street scene – are in-

Above left: Fassbinder and the Action-Theater, *The Bridegroom, the Actress, and the Pimp* (1968)
Theatrical and quotidian life in the film

formed by an ethnographic, documentary approach that is equally central to *Fortini/Cani* (1976), *Geschichtsunterricht (History Lessons*, 1972), *Too Early, Too Late* (1980/81), and, more recently, *Europa 2005, 27 October* and *Itinerary of Jean Bricard*. The recording of the stage production recalls the duo's equally strong investment in theatrical recitals that begins with their adaptation of Pierre Corneille's play *Othon* in 1968 and includes their Hölderlin films and their Pavese and Vittorini adaptations. Straub-Huillet's adaptation of Schoenberg's opera *Von heute auf morgen (From Today Until Tomorrow*, 1996), which was entirely filmed on a sound stage, comes to mind as well. While *Machorka-Muff, Not Reconciled*, and *Chronicle of Anna Magdalena Bach* already contain aspects of both the theatrical and the documentary they remain for the most part heavily informed by the conventions of naturalistic mise-en-scène and editing patterns. But beginning with *Othon*, it could be argued, Straub-Huillet increasingly abandon such strategies of a classical cinematic form.

Only the short film *En rachâchant* as well as the two feature-length films *Class Relations* and *Sicilia!* – all of them filmed in black and white – signal a return to a more conventional form of classical cinematic narration. As noted, this form also dominates the last segment in *Bridegroom* but combines it with a technique that signals another crucial shift in Straub-Huillet's creative approach: the recital of texts from a past literary tradition within an everyday, contemporary setting. The dialogue spoken by the young

couple in the modern setting of a suburban family home consists entirely of quotations from poems written by the Spanish mystic St. John of the Cross in the 16th century, foreshadowing Straub-Huillet's consistent confrontation of classical and modern, quotidian and theatrical, and – in regard to language and translation – of written and spoken text material.

ROME: CORNEILLE AND BRECHT

In 1968, Huillet and Straub left Germany and relocated to Rome, Italy, where they continued to live until shortly before Huillet passed away in 2006. Most of the films they made after 1970 were shot on exterior locations in Italy. "Straub/Huillet often stress that the impetus for a film arises from a feeling for a place: partly as a paraphrase of the French filmmaker Jean Renoir, Straub has defined film (or the 'filmic') as 'a slender dialectic between film, theater, and life.'"[33] This seems especially true for *Les yeux ne veulent pas en tout temps se fermer ou peut-etre qu'un jour Rome se permettra de choisir à son tour (Eyes do not want to close at all times or Perhaps one day Rome will permit herself to choose in her turn*, 1969). *Othon*, as the film is widely known, pushed the aesthetic confrontation between classical material and a contemporary quotidian setting much further than their previous films. Based on Pierre Corneille's tragedy *Othon* (1664), the film was, after four German-language productions, Straub-Huillet's first French-language film and the first to be shot on Italian locations.

Othon, in fact, did not begin with Corneille's text, but with a place that the two filmmakers

33 Byg, op. cit., p. 182

had encountered during their first visit to Rome a few years earlier: the terrace of the Palatine Hill. Most of the film is set on this terrace, which is located in the ancient part of the city and offers a panoramic view onto the modern cityscape below. Dressed in costumes that emulate the ancient Roman period, the actors perform Corneille's dense seventeenth-century verse while everyday life in the modern city goes on around them. Thus, in the film three distinct historical periods and cultural worlds overlap: the period of the ancient Roman empire, the era of the French *Grand Siècle*, and a European capital city in the midst of the twentieth century.

Othon was made specifically with a French audience in mind. However, the majority of the actors who appear in the film are Italians who speak the French dialogue with a noticeable accent, recalling *Chronicle*'s Gustav Leonhardt speaking German with a Dutch accent. However, while casting choices had previously been based primarily on the performer's skills as a musician, the employment of predominantly non-native speakers in *Othon* derived from a deliberate effort to produce the dialogue through a series of obstacles. The actors struggled with the foreign tongue while competing at the same time with the unfiltered environmental sounds around them.

Both the accented language and the use of direct sound differed notably from how dialogue and sound were conventionally treated at the time in the Western European context, especially in Italy. The largest markets in terms of distribution and audience in Europe, Italy,

Germany, and France effectively eliminated the sound of foreign-languages from their movie and television screens. All foreign films were, instead, dubbed into each country's respective language, a technique that not only alters a film's dialogue while replacing one vocal performance with another, but also affects the quality of a film's entire soundscape. A dubbed soundtrack usually lacks the depth, resonance, and vibrancy of direct sound recordings. Particularly in Italy and Germany, but to an extent in France as well, dubbing contributes, in addition, to the idea of a uniform national language devoid of any regional dialects (such as *italiano standard* or the German *Hochdeutsch*). Linguistic standardization, especially in the Italian context, was considered central for the creation of a national identity and the Italian public broadcasting agency RAI played a central role in these efforts after World War II. Jean-Marie Straub's open letter to the Program Manager of RAI 2, entitled "Il doppiaggio è un assassinio" ("Dubbing Is Murder") is, in this regard, especially noteworthy.[34] In short, Straub-Huillet opposed the post-synchronization of on-screen dialogue into another language for their own films.

The duo had various reasons for their resistance to linguistic replacement. "Directors prefer to dub out of laziness," Huillet once argued, because it restricts them in their choice of locations; in other words, not all locations allow for a clean recording of sound during the shooting

---

34 Jean-Marie Straub, "Dubbing Is Murder," in *Writings*, New York: Sequence Press, 2016

Othon (1969)
On the Palatine Hill, in the garden of the Villa Doria Pamphili,
Straub (left) as Lucus (clockwise from top left)

process.[35] The locations on the Palatine Hill and the garden behind the Villa Doria Pamphili (*Othon's* second major location) provided the possibility for clean sound recording of the dialogue, while allowing the environmental soundscape to compete with the actors' voices without drowning them out. Direct sound, in addition, maintains and captures something of the material conditions – auditory as well as visual – that define a particular location at the moment of filming. The sound of a car horn or the steady gurgling of a water fountain in the scenes shot in the Villa's garden invite spontaneous and unfiltered elements into a scene that is otherwise meticulously well rehearsed. Straub-Huillet's films often contain shots that linger on even after the characters have left the frame, a technique that some viewers mistakenly identify as a formal mannerism but that actually serves a precise function, as Huillet who was in charge of editing their films, has emphasized: "You can't edit direct sound as you edit the films you are going to dub: each image has a sound and you're forced to respect it. Even when the frame is empty, when the character leaves the shot, you can't cut, because you continue to hear off-camera the sound of receding footsteps. In a dubbed film, you wait only for the last piece of the foot to leave the range of the camera to cut."[36]

Since Straub-Huillet had little hope that subtitled versions of their films would attract a significant number of foreign viewers, they usually made each film with a specific national audience in mind. *Othon* was "dedicated to the very great number of those born into the French language who have never had the privilege to get to know the work of Corneille," as the film's closing titles state. Moreover, the film aimed at presenting an accented version of Corneille's classical verses in order to reintroduce him to French audiences as a revolutionary writer whose work had lost nothing of its currency. This is also what Marguerite Duras applauded in her review of *Othon*: "All accents are allowed except that of the *Comédie Française* – in other words, the accent of camouflaged meaning, of authority."[37] The French-language text is made "foreign" not only by the strange diction and unusual intonation, but also by the speed with which some of the performers recite the verses. According to Benoît Turquety, "the history of the performers' bodies alters the text, and renews its perception by the spectator."[38] The text facilitates, in turn, the experience in the native-language spectator of hearing a familiar language in a fresh and new way. *Othon*, the classical play, similarly appears in a new light and gains an importance that has more to do with the present than with the past.

Accents, dialects, and foreign pronunciations

35 "Direct Sound: An Interview with Jean-Marie Straub and Danièle Huillet," trans. by Bill Kavaler, in *Film Sound: Theory and Practice*, eds. Elisabeth Weis and John Belton, New York: Columbia University Press, 1985, p. 151
36 Ibid., p. 152
37 Marguerite Duras, "*Othon*, by Jean-Marie Straub," in *Outside: Selected Writings*, translated by Arthur Goldhammer, Boston: Beacon Press, 1986, p. 157
38 Benoît Turquety, "Orality and Objectification: Danièle Huillet and Jean-Marie Straub, Filmmakers and Translators," *SubStance: A Review of Theory and Literary Criticism*, vol. 44, no. 2, 2015, p. 51

have informed the treatment of dialogues throughout Straub-Huillet's body of work. In *Not Reconciled*, for instance, Huillet appears briefly as the young Johanna, speaking two lines with her slight French accent that differs from Martha Staendner, a native German speaker, who plays Johanna as an old woman. Similarly, the actor who plays her husband Heinrich at old age speaks with a recognizable regional Cologne accent, unlike the young actors who portray him as a young and middle-aged man. In interviews Straub has accordingly often referred to Renoir's early sound films as "the most beautiful films in existence [...] not only because they speak so beautifully with southern French accents, but because of the fact that it is original sound."[39]

The act of capturing a performer's accented speech recalls, of course, the filmmakers' own biographical experiences with geographical as well as linguistic displacement. Beginning with the Bach film and especially after their move to Germany, both were forced to articulate themselves as artists predominantly in foreign languages, first German, then Italian. In this light, Straub's own appearance (under the pseudonym Jubarite Semaran) in the cast of *Othon*, as one of only three native French speakers seems noteworthy, suggesting that the two filmmakers' first engagement with a French-language text was a rather personal matter.

This has specific connotations for Straub who was born in 1933 in Metz and spent most of

his childhood years under Nazi occupation. He recalls being forced to learn and speak German as a child. Huillet, on the other hand, did not learn any German until the two started working on the Bach film. She later reported that she learned the language on the basis of the archival material they consulted for the film: Bach's lyrics, his letters, etc. In doing so, one could argue, Huillet experienced German as a language whose "strangeness" operated on multiple levels: aside from being the language of a foreign country, it was also the antiquated German of a different period as well as a dramatic and written language. Furthermore, when Straub-Huillet moved to Italy in 1969, they started writing, speaking and working in Italian and their engagement with Italian authors would be substantial, including the twentieth-century writers Franco Fortini, Cesare Pavese, and Elio Vittorini and, more recently, Straub's adaptation of Dante Alighieri for *O somma luce* (*Oh Supreme Light*, 2009).

Even though Straub-Huillet resisted having their films' dialogue dubbed into other languages, they did produce different language versions of some of their films, among them *Too Early, Too Late, Lothringen!* (1994), and *Cézanne. Dialogue avec Joachim Gasquet* (*Cézanne. Conversation with Joachim Gasquet*, 1989). In these cases, such versions seemed appropriate because the main dialogue took place off-screen as part of a voice-over that could be replaced in its entirety. Thus, instead of simply adding a new audio-track to the visuals, Straub-Huillet created a different film, even though the changes seem minimal. The French-lan-

39 Andi Engel, "Andi Engel talks to Jean-Marie Straub," *Cinemantics* 1, 1970, p. 17

guage version of *Cézanne*, for instance, is 12 minutes shorter than the German-language version, because reciting Gasquet's original text in the German translation produces a longer audio track. In other words, Straub-Huillet adjust the images to match the translation, not the other way around. In the film both audio versions are performed by the filmmakers themselves. In the French version, they speak in their native tongue and in the German version in an accented voice.

In fact, for *Chronicle of Anna Magdalena Bach*, Straub-Huillet had already recorded various voice-overs of Anna Magdalena's narration with women who spoke with different accents in Italian, French, English and Dutch, motivated by the original British distributor who had plans to dub the film. Straub included one of these alternate versions in his recent film *Dialogue d'ombres* (*Dialogue of Shadows*, 2013). The film begins with a segment from the Bach film in which Christiane Lang speaks Anna Magdalena's voice-over in French with a noticeable German accent. Another example of such linguistic displacement also defines Straub's latest collaborations with the German actress Cornelia Geiser in films like *Corneille-Brecht* (2009) and *Dialogue of Shadows*. Geiser speaks the French texts (of Pierre Corneille and Georges Bernanos respectively) with a slight German accent. Similar to the accented spoken discourse of some of the native Italian speakers in *Othon*, her distinct pronunciation demarcates each word, each phrase, in a particular way, thus foregrounding her own distinct verbal encounter with the text. Her relationship to the French text differs from her encounter with Brecht's German text that she reads in the second part of *Corneille-Brecht*. The difference between the two texts occurs not merely on account of their obvious linguistic difference, but also because to the native German speaker each case – speaking Corneille in French and Brecht in German – presents different kinds of vocal nuances and obstacles.

Corneille-Brecht also marks Straub's return to Brecht, the original author of the film that followed *Othon*. In 1972, Straub-Huillet made *History Lessons*, a film based on Brecht's unfinished novel *Die Geschäfte des Herrn Julius Caesar* (*The Business Affairs of Mr. Julius Caesar*, 1937–39). Made during a period in which Brecht's theories on art and aesthetics dominated the discourse in both film and literary criticism, especially in Anglo-American academia, the film became a test case for a critical debate on Straub-Huillet's Brechtian tendencies, a debate that echoed and continued in some ways the earlier controversy around the couple's first short films in Germany. The critical evaluation of Brechtian techniques focused primarily on one particular concept: the so-called *Verfremdungseffekt* (alternatively translated into English as an effect of *alienation, estrangement,* or *distanciation*). In 1965, the German critic Enno Patalas had already dismissed the performances in *Not Reconciled* with the words: "Badly recited is not necessarily well alienated, as Straub, who credits Brecht […] seems to believe."[40] In the specific context of the experimental avant-garde,

40 Patalas, "Nicht versöhnt," p. 474

Cornelia Geiser in
Dialogue of Shadows (2013)
and *Corneille-Brecht* (2009)

the term came to signify formal strategies that sought to break the illusions and conventions of bourgeois storytelling (e.g. mainstream narrative cinema) while attempting, at the same time, to lay bare the material structures of larger social formations and conditions. The suggested affinity between Brechtian theory and Straub-Huillet's work practice focused in particular on their use of quotations and non-naturalistic acting. Indeed, Straub-Huillet and Brecht share, as Martin Brady has pointed out, a "fondness for quotation," which, in Brecht's case, went so far as to include plagiarism.[41]

History Lessons was mainly shot in Italy, but this time a cast of predominantly native German-speakers recited the dialogue in their native tongue. However, *History Lessons* continues the confrontation between the historical setting of ancient Rome and the contemporary location of the modern city. The narrative follows a young man collecting information on the historical figure of Julius Caesar. In Brecht's original novel the young man embarks on this research trip in order to write a biography of Caesar, an endeavor that recalls, of course, Straub's own journey through Germany on the path of the composer Johann Sebastian Bach many years earlier. Instead of consulting manuscripts, the young man in the film conducts a series of interviews with Caesar's contemporaries: a banker, a peasant, a jurist, and a poet, all of whom represent different sectors within the cultural fabric of society.

There are two aspects to the film: the interview sessions alternate with scenes that are filmed from inside a car driving through busy city streets. The young man sits in the driver's seat. These quotidian sequences (altogether there are three) are reminiscent of *Bridegroom's* extended sequence shot of the Landsberger Straße. However, the driving sequences in *History Lessons* are less obviously focused on a particular site of socio-economic relations. They open the image to the particularities and contingencies that the driver and the vehicle encounter on their way through the urban maze. These sequence shots are also profoundly different in their treatment of sound. The shot of the Landsberger Straße remains silent until Bach's *Ascension Oratorio* sets in halfway through. In contrast, direct sound recordings play a crucial role in the car sequences in *History Lessons* because they manage to open the space within an image that is visually constricted by the interior framings of the automobile. The structural-materialist filmmaker and theorist Peter Gidal took Straub-Huillet to task for these non-interpretive extended long-takes. The "interspersion with the drive through the city streets," he writes, "distanciates in a most academic fashion, questioning neither the veracity of the present-day Rome nor the faithful fiction of 194 BC."[42] Straub-Huillet's materialism, Gidal contends, is nothing but a form of non-reflexive naturalism. Similar to Gidal, Colin MacCabe criticized the film's lack of ex-

41 Martin Brady, "Brecht in Brechtian Cinema," in *"Verwisch die Spuren!" Bertolt Brecht's Work and Legacy: A Reassessment*, eds. Robert Gillett and Godela Weiss-Sussex, Amsterdam: Rodopi, 2008, p. 306
42 Peter Gidal, *Materialist Film*, London: Routledge, 1989, p. 90

position and its failure to include a political commentary or an interpretation: "to understand *History Lessons* you have to know the Brecht novel and the Roman history independently of the film."[43]

In a sense, of course, Gidal and MacCabe are correct, for Straub-Huillet are absolutely opposed to the kinds of materialist critiques that rely on exposition, illustration, and interpretation. Going back to the critical imperatives that Bazin and Truffaut, among others, had developed in the context of French New Wave criticism, Straub-Huillet's understanding of materialism, as well as their connection to Brecht, is deeply grounded in the belief that the medium of film can be entrusted with the task of recording, showing, and revealing while the filmmaker steps back to allow viewers to see for themselves. This happens especially in the car sequences, which document a contemporary environment in all its contingencies.

The dramatized sections in *History Lessons*, the interview scenes, can also be characterized as Brechtian. The young man (dressed in contemporary attire) talks to Caesar's contemporaries (who are all dressed, like the performers in *Othon*, in antique Roman robes). The narrative content is mainly in the dialogue, which is not only composed of direct quotations from Brecht's original novel, but also follows a Brechtian understanding of "narrative illusion." Whereas many Brechtian theorists in the seventies portrayed the author as an "enemy of illusion," Brecht was more specifically opposed to the conventions of *dramatic* illusion and action, as Gilberto Perez has argued: "Brecht put a curb on dramatic illusion in order to generate a kind of narrative illusion, a kind of theater that would report rather than enact characters and events, that would represent a story no longer in the form of action but of narrative."[44] In contrast to *Citizen Kane*, for instance, wherein encounters between a reporter and Kane's contemporaries merely set the stage for dramatic action which takes place in flashbacks, *History Lessons* contains no scenes that enact or illustrate dramatic action in the conventional sense. Narrative illusion occurs only in the quoted text that the young man exchanges with each respective dialogue partner.

In an article published in *Cahiers du cinéma* in 1966, Straub suggested that it was the cinema that "invented Brechtianism" through the works of Chaplin, Hawks, Mizoguchi, and above all Ford, who he calls the most Brechtian of them all.[45] Why Ford? Because "he shows things that make people think" instead of presenting them "with images that tell them what to think," which is, according to Straub, nothing but "a caricature of Brecht."[46] What Straub-Huillet oppose therefore are scenarios that merely confirm what the spectators already believe: "it doesn't make sense to show a strike or a barricade" because any dramatized

43 Colin MacCabe, "The Politics of Separation," *Screen*, vol. 16, no. 2, 1975/76, p. 51–52

44 Gilberto Perez, *The Material Ghost: Film and their Medium*, Baltimore: Johns Hopkins University Press, 1998, p. 290–291

45 Jean-Marie Straub, "Film et Roman: Problemes du récit," *Cahiers du cinéma*, no. 185, December 1966, p. 123–124

46 Engel, op. cit., p. 21

Dramatic and
quotidian scenes in
History Lessons (1972)

illustration of a struggle remains in the end without effect on the spectators. "Then they feel they don't need to do it in their lives [...] and what's more, it tends to give them a clear conscience."[47] Indeed, throughout their career, Huillet and Straub resisted integrating conventional dramatizations of social injustice or political action into their films. What interested them, more specifically, was Brecht's continued effort to highlight a connection between fascism and consumer capitalism, a topic that informed their adaptation of his Julius Caesar novel and that became equally important for their following short film *Introduction to Arnold Schoenberg's "Accompaniment to a Cinematographic Scene."*

THE "JEWISH TRILOGY:" SCHOENBERG AND FORTINI

Introduction begins at the very same location where *History Lessons* ends: the Fontana del Mascherone on Via Giulia in Rome. And yet, the production history of the two films could not have been more different. *Introduction* was Straub-Huillet's first film made for television. It was one of three shorts that the German regional network *Südwestfunk* commissioned as a response to Schoenberg's orchestral piece *Accompaniment to a Cinematographic Scene* (opus 34, 1930). The implicit tension between sound and image, music and cinema, was certainly of in-

terest to Straub and Huillet. The subtitle *Threatening Danger, Fear, Catastrophe*, Straub explains, was the only written commentary Schoenberg added to his composition. This was unusual for a composer who was known for adding detailed stage directions to his scores. However, in this case, Schoenberg seems to have been reluctant to include any visual dramatization in accompaniment to the music, which is, of course, an ironic twist to the title. Instead, the music, as Straub points out in his introduction, is meant to remain *unvorstellbar* – un-imaginable, i.e. without visual or dramatic imagery.

Theodor W. Adorno and Hanns Eisler have praised Schoenberg's composition precisely for its "expressive potentialities" of producing "a sense of fear, of looming danger and catastrophe" that surpasses the fear and horror produced "in the great sensational films, for instance in the scene of the collapsing roof in the night club (*San Francisco*), or in *King Kong* when the giant gorilla hurls a New York elevated train down into the street."[48] Adorno and Eisler were not simply critiquing popular entertainment. Their remarks must be seen in the context of Adorno's claim that "to write poetry after Auschwitz is barbaric."[49] This was less a call for the elimination of art than a pessimistic conclusion following his analysis of a modern industrial society in which commodification had taken over all sectors of life and culture. The Nazi death camps figure in Adorno's analysis as the ultimate example of this phenomenon: the industrially-planned and -executed mass murder of millions of human beings who had become dehumanized in the process.

47 Engel, op. cit., p. 22
48 Theodor W. Adorno and Hanns Eisler, *Composing for the Films* [1947], New York: Continuum, 2007, p. 24
49 Theodor W. Adorno, "Cultural Criticism and Society," in *The Adorno Reader*, ed. Brian O'Connor, Oxford: Blackwell, 2000, p. 210

Introduction is structured around two letters Schoenberg wrote in the early 1920s to his former friend, the painter Wassily Kandinsky. Often understood as the sign of an eerie foresight on Schoenberg's part regarding the changing political climate in Germany at the time, the letters address Kandinsky's latest anti-Semitic remarks and accuse him of political opportunism. Peter Nestler and Günter Peter Straschek, both sitting in a broadcast recording booth, recite from the letters at various points in the film. Straub-Huillet also include two references to Brecht. Sitting in the couple's apartment in Rome, stroking a cat on her lap, Huillet looks directly into the camera and quotes from a speech Brecht gave at the 1935 *Paris Congress of Intellectuals Against Fascism*: "those who are against Fascism without being against capitalism, who lament over the barbarism that comes out of barbarism, are like people who wish to eat their veal without slaughtering the calf. They are willing to eat the calf, but they dislike the sight of blood." In short, it is impossible to fight fascism without first fighting capitalism. *Introduction* illustrates the barbarism Brecht alludes to through a series of archival images: a photograph of civilian victims executed after the Paris Commune of 1871, newsreel footage of carpet bombings during the Vietnam War, and newspaper articles reporting the acquittal of the architects who built the gas chambers in Auschwitz. "All three images present death in the context of highly organized and standardized production processes," writes Ursula Böser. Yet, unlike in traditional documentary film and television reportage, the film keeps the visual documents and the oral commentary and exposition (provided by the letters and Brecht's speech) separate. This corresponds to Schoenberg's own aesthetic path of eliminating any form of dramatic accompaniment from his musical compositions; instead "it is left to us to see the 'Barbarei' which is visible in these documents."[50]

Schoenberg's increasing suspicion of all visual and pictorial forms of expression – especially as part of an "introduction of aesthetics into political life" as Walter Benjamin would put it in his famous essay "The Work of Art in the Age of Mechanical Reproduction" (1936) – is also the central topic of Schoenberg's unfinished opera *Moses and Aaron* which became the source text for Straub-Huillet's next film. The duo's initial interest in the material was triggered by their attendance of the opera's Berlin staging in 1959. Huillet and Straub rejected the overtly expressionist stylistic elements that had been chosen to accompany the opera on stage, a violation and complete misunderstanding, as far as they were concerned, of Schoenberg's work.

Moses and Aaron stages the conflict between representation and its taboo in respect to its two protagonists. Moses receives the word of God and functions as the guardian of the divine prohibition against idolatry. It is up to Aaron to translate the word into dramatic representa-

---

50 Ursula Böser, *The Art of Seeing, the Art of Listening: The Politics of Representation in the Work of Jean-Marie Straub and Danièle Huillet*, Frankfurt/Main: Lang, 2004, p. 92

Introduction to Arnold Schoenberg's
"Accompaniment to a Cinematographic Scene" (1972)
Peter Nestler (below left) and Danièle Huillet

tions in order to be able to communicate and appeal to the Jewish people whom he wishes to liberate from political oppression. Schoenberg establishes the dichotomy between the two not only in the libretto, but writes Moses' part in *Sprechstimme* (a declamatory mode of vocal operatic performance), while Aaron's part is assigned to the lyrical colorations of a *bel canto* tenor.

Straub-Huillet's cinematographic accompaniment to this scenario works accordingly. Set in a single location (the amphitheater of Alba Fucense in central Italy), camera angles and positions as well as the placement of the characters respect "the sense of an oscillating power struggle that is here Schoenberg's concern," as Martin Walsh has pointed out. In fact, the central characters, including the chorus (representing the people), never move. It is the camera that moves around them, either through extended pans or tracking shots, or by changing position in the transition from one shot to the next. In doing so, the compositions separate the different parties from one another, while emphasizing, at the same time, their (changing) relationships. The only scenes that depict characters in overt motion occur, not surprisingly, in the "Golden Calf" sequence which is explicitly about the violation of God's dictum against idol representation.

Moses and Aaron was not only complex in regard to its formal arrangement, it also involved an array of technological and logistic challenges.[51] Huillet, who was often in charge of logistics and usually acted as line producer for the duo's productions, had to coordinate a rela-

tively large cast and crew at the remote location, arranging for daily transportation to and from hotels in a nearby town, as well as the storage of the large number of props and film equipment. Most of the professional singers were booked years in advance, which made any extension of the schedule or reshoots virtually impossible. On several occasions, shooting was almost brought to a halt, such as when Louis Devos (Aaron) became sick and needed a few days to recover and regain his voice.

The project also posed a major challenge to the recording of the sound. If *Chronicle* was groundbreaking in its technique of capturing the musicians' live performances on screen, *Moses and Aaron* went further: the film consists of the live recording of Schoenberg's entire opera, including the unfinished third act for which the composer never wrote music. The vocal performances were recorded on location, while the orchestral part had been prerecorded "dry, without echo, and in mono," in Vienna a few months before.[52] Louis Hochet – who did sound on most Straub-Huillet films, beginning with *Chronicle* until their last Schoenberg adaptation *From Today Until Tomorrow* in 1996 – developed a highly complicated system that included the use of multiple sound recorders run-

51 These have been well documented by Gregory Woods, one of the film's assistants, whose published "Work Journal" also contains annotations by Danièle Huillet. See Gregory Woods and Danièle Huillet, "A Work Journal of the Straub/Huillet Film 'Moses and Aaron'/Notes to Gregory's Work Journal," in *Apparatus, Cinematographic Apparatus: Selected Writings* by Theresa Hak Kyung Cha, New York: Tanam Press, 1980, pp. 147–231
52 Huillet, Ibid., p. 169

The Golden Calf sequence in *Moses and Aaron* (1974)
Günter Reich (left) as Moses and Louis Devos as Aaron, chorus

Budget MOSES - AARON

I. Musiker (ORF Chor und Orchester, Gielen, Solisten, Chorleiter, Assi

1) Spesen für den Chor in Italien
   - 11 Tage x 66 Personen x 60 DM   43.560.-DM x
   - 2 Tage x 22 Bässe x 60 DM   2.640.-DM x

2) Gagen für den Chor in Italien
   - 8 Tage x 66 Personen x 140 DM   73.920.-DM
   - 1 Tag x 22 Bässe x 140 DM   3.080.-DM

3) Reisen Wien-Rom-Wien (Flug, Touristenklasse,
             weniger als 30 Tage)
   - 66 Personen x 400 DM   26.400.-DM x 149.600.-DM

4) Spesen für Dirigenten und Solisten
   a) während der Proben und Tonaufnahmen in Wien
   - Gielen (Dirigent)   45 Tage x 60 DM = 2.700
   - Rubenstein (Dir.Ass.) 45 Tage x 60 DM   2.700
   - Donat (Straub'sAss.) 45 Tage x 60 DM   2.700
   - Reich (Moses)   21 Tage x 60 DM   1.260
   - Devos (Aron)   25 Tage x 60 DM   1.500
   - Junges Mädchen   13 Tage x 60 DM   780
   - Junger Mann   14 Tage x 60 DM   840
   - Mann   15 Tage x 60 DM   900
   - Priester   17 Tage x 60 DM   1.020
   - Ephraimit   5 Tage x 60 DM   300
   - Kranke   5 Tage x 60 DM   300   x 15.000.-DM

   b) während des Drehens in Italien
   - Gielen   22 Tage x 60 DM   1.320
   - Ravenstein   22 Tage x 60 DM   1.320
   - Donat   22 Tage x 60 DM   1.320
   - Preinfalk   13 Tage x 60 DM   780
   - Reich   25 Tage x 60 DM   1.500
   - Devos   25 Tage x 60 DM   1.500
   - Junges Mädchen   8 Tage x 60 DM   480
   - Junger Mann   10 Tage x 60 DM   600
   - Mann   8 Tage x 60 DM   480
   - Priester   10 Tage x 60 DM   600
   - Ephraimit   1 Tag x 60 DM   60
   - Kranke   1 Tag x 60 DM   60   x 10.020.-DM

5) Reisen für Dirigenten und Solisten
   a) für Proben und Tonaufnahmen in Wien
   - 1 Reise à 2.000.-DM (Rubenstein)   x 2.000
   - 11 Reisen (8 Sänger, Gielen, Donat,   x 4.400
     +2?4?   Tonmeister) à 400 DM
   b) für das Drehen in Italien
   - 13 Reisen à 400 DM   x 5.200   x 11.600.-DM

6) Gagen für Dirigenten und Solisten
   für Proben, Tonaufnahmen und Drehen
   - x Gielen   30.000.-
   - x Preinfalk (Italien)   5.000.-
   - x Reich   25.000.-
   - x Devos   20.000.-
   - x Junges Mädchen   3.500.-
   - x Junger Mann   4.500.-   +1.500.-
   - x Mann   3.500.-
   - x Priester   4.500.-
   - Ephraimit, Kranke   300.-   +1.200.-
                99.000.- "
                96.300.-DM

II. F i l m

1) Technikergagen
   Tonmeister (Louis Hochet) — 7.000.—DM × ▲ 7.000 DM
   └─Kameramann (Ugo Piccone) — 7.000;—DM + 50?? 150.000X5 = G. 850.000L
   F— Tonassistent 1. (Lucien Moreau) — 4.500.—DM
   F—Tonassistent 2. — 3.500.—DM
   └─Kameraschwenker (Saverio Diamanti) — 4.500.—DM 170.000X5 = 850.000 - 7.000 DM×C 4
   └─Kameraassistent — 3.500.—DM
   Produktionsleiter 1. (D.Huillet) — ————— (500.000) + ? Dиаке Рефеłazioni
   └─Produktionsleiter 2. weniger als 3 — 8.000.—DM 3.000
   └─Aufnahmeleiter — 4.000.—DM (.
   └─Assistenten 4+1 — 6.000.—DM 100.000 X3 × Settimane = 1.5
   └─3 Bühnenleute — 12.000.—DM +Diake Viage 100.000 = 3.500 DM.
   └─Hilfe ein paarmal — 1.000.—DM
   Coiffeur)??
   └─Kostümberaterin) bis Nacht Sonntag 16.1. = 4W
   Schneiderin) bis Nacht Sonntag Montag 8.1. = 5W } 14.000.—DM
   Assistent)—bison Ende
   Regisseur (Jean-Marie Straub) — —————
   Regieassistenz + Script (D.Huillet)— ————
   Schnittmeister (J-M.S.) — —————
   Cutterin (D.H.) — ————— × 75.000.—DM
   [Autista]

2) Technikerspesen 18 Tag. a 325.50 DM (?)
   └─ 45 DM x 18 Personen x 32 Tage — 25.920.—DM × 28.920.—DM 103.920
   └─ Mittags-Körbe für die Techniker — 3.000.—DM

3) Gagen für 5-6 Tänzer, ca. 30 Statisten je — 30.000.—DM
   1 Tag, Tiere (und goldenes Kalb — × 10.000.—DM
   Spesen für die Tänzer, Statisten usw.
   Reisen für die Tänzer, [Statisten], Tonleute,
   └─Bus-Miete für die Sänger, Wagen der — ×15.000.—DM 550000
   Techniker usw. = Transporte beim Drehen

4) [PIANOFORTE] ca. 150 Kostüme, einige Perücken, Schuhe — 55.000.—DM 22-27.000×
   (Miete) +Waffen usw. [20.000 DM]
   └── Kamera Mitchell, Objektive, (Pumpstativ)usw. — 10.000.—DM 12.500+
   Tonapparatur, Wagen, Mikros, Windschutz,
   F— Lautsprecher, Funkmikros — 14.000.—DM
   └── Diverse (Wagen für die Bühnenleute mit — 6.000.—DM
   Schienen, Keile, Pratikable, Reflektoren usw.)
   └── Miete (Drehorte, Entschädigungen usw.) — 6.000.—DM 91.000.

5) Filmmaterial (30.000m Eastmancolor) und — 120.000.—DM
   Kopierwerk in Rom
   └─F—Tonbänder, Ueberspielung, Schnitt, Mischung — 12.000.—DM 132.000

5) Versicherungen und Sozialversicherungen — 8.000.—DM
   Telefongespräche während des Drehens — 700.—DM 8.700

6) Reserve — 29.380.—DM 29.380

720.000

Summe : 720.000.—DM

RAI circa 3.800.000 → 4.000.000

ning in perfect sync. Later in the editing studio, the two audio tracks – vocal performances and location sounds recorded on set and the prerecorded orchestral music – were reunited.

Straub-Huillet's decision to make *Moses and Aaron* in spite of these challenges is representative of their general approach to production. It would be wrong to assume that, in the context and spirit of other new wave or avant-garde filmmaking practices, they are indifferent to the production value of the works. It is true that many of their films qualify as small-scale or low-budget productions – their shorts and the film they would make next, the feature-length *Fortini/Cani* (which was made with a small cast and crew and shot on 16mm film). However, some others, such as *Chronicle*, *Moses and Aaron*, and the Kafka adaptation *Klassenverhältnisse* (*Class Relations*, 1983), even though they still remained well below the financial standards of the commercial film industry, required certain production values for which the filmmakers fought. Huillet seems to have been extremely industrious and efficient in preparing and keeping an estimated budget, i.e. a budget that was not stingy in regard to a project's specific needs, while saving on costs that were deemed unnecessary. This begins, of course, with personal sacrifices but also involves not paying a "star salary" for a performer like the well-known German actor Mario Adorf (the uncle in *Class Relations*). Moreover, films like *Not Reconciled*, *Chronicle*, and *Moses and Aaron* called for a style that required certain technological investments. "One should save on telephone calls but not on negative stock," Straub emphasized.[53]

Different projects call for different aesthetic approaches, budgets, and technologies, for it is "the tool that determines the film" and each tool serves different kinds of creations. Therefore, while the use of a 35mm Mitchell camera was crucial for the creation of the precise panning and tracking shots in both the Bach film and *Moses and Aaron*, Straub-Huillet filmed *Othon* on 16mm, precisely because the project called for a more mobile, hand-held approach.

In comparison to *Moses and Aaron*, Straub-Huillet's second adaptation of a Schoenberg opera more than twenty years later, *From Today Until Tomorrow*, is a case in point. Utterly different in tone – it is often described as Schoenberg's take on the comic opera – the project was not simply filmed on interior locations, but on a large sound stage located in the main public broadcasting building in Frankfurt. This meant, in some sense, that Straub-Huillet returned to the interior space of the recording studio that had been crucial in *Introduction*. But the move from exterior location to interior stage was also in many ways determined by Schoenberg's source text. Whereas *Introduction* and *Moses and Aaron* were about the radical rejection of figurative representation, *From Today Until Tomorrow* articulated a critique of representation that was more explicitly directed against the mundane platitudes and appearances of modern mass culture. The libretto was co-written by Schoenberg and his wife Gertrud, a detail that is important not only because of the obvious similarity to the collaborative rela-

53 Engel, op. cit., p. 23

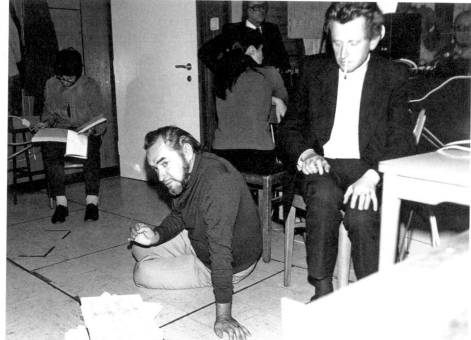

In the recording studio in Vienna for *Moses and Aaron* with conductor Michael Gielen. Photos courtesy of Bernard Rubenstein

tionship of the Straubs and the Bachs, but also because the story of *From Today Until Tomorrow* centers on the dramatic conflict between a married couple, a battle of the sexes, which reminded some critics of classical Hollywood screwball comedies such as Howard Hawks' *Bringing Up Baby* (1938), a resemblance Straub cautiously agreed to: "Let's say, there is a certain kind of political and moral affinity between the two films at the end, a certain kind."[54] The opera's setting in the modern decor of a late 1920s bourgeois household as well as the plot and tone of the libretto in many ways recall early sound comedies (Straub references Lubitsch, in particular). More precisely, the interior and stage-like set design provided the means to create a space for representing the fashion, décor, and façades of modern consumer culture. The studio setting also gives Straub-Huillet the opportunity to do what had been impossible in the case of *Moses and Aaron*: a synchronous live recording of vocalists and orchestra, for all of them fit in one room. As in the earlier film, the script was crafted on the basis of Schoenberg's original score, which was segmented into blocks corresponding to shots. While *Moses and Aaron* consists of longer segments whose beginning and end is largely determined by pauses in the music, in *From Today Until Tomorrow* the cuts rely on pauses in Schoenberg's original score and, more precisely, in the singers' vocal performances. While rehearsing, Huillet and Straub were able to determine the exact moments during which a singer would take a breath, highlighting the fact that aside from the original text it is also a performer's distinct mode of expression that shapes the film's overall form.

Othon in 1969 marks the beginning of a phase in Straub-Huillet's work that could be described as their first "Italian period" in regard to their use of locations. *Othon, History Lessons, Moses and Aaron,* and eventually *Fortini/Cani* (1976) – all of these films are set on original exterior locations in Italy and even though some of them are still within sight of either the cityscape or the archeological remains of ancient civilization, a noticeable shift occurs from the urban periphery to a rural environment to views of natural landscapes that no longer bear any discernible traces of human civilization, but which are, nevertheless, inscribed with the horrors and terrors of the past.

Fortini/Cani was their first Italian-language film and their first collaboration with a living author since Böll. Based on Franco Fortini's memoir *I cani del Sinai (The Dogs of Sinai,* 1967), it is also the first Straub-Huillet film to address a primarily Italian audience. The couple had met Fortini in the late 1960s at a screening of *Not Reconciled.* The writer was impressed and told Straub he wished someone would make a film from one of his books in the same style. Fortini himself appears in the film, reading from his own memoir. Many scenes show him sitting on the terrace of a house surrounded by the rural landscape of Cotoncello, on the island

54 Artem Demenok and Robert Bramkamp, "Eine Hexe, die eine Menge Energie verbraucht," in *Von heute auf morgen: Oper/Musik/Film,* eds. Klaus Volkmer, Klaus Kalchschmid, and Patrick Primavesi, Berlin: Vorwerk 8, 1997, p. 93

Christine Whittlesey
and Richard Salter
in *From Today Until
Tomorrow* (1996)

of Elba, reading aloud from the book. Eventually his voice-over carries on over other shots in the film, some of which are entirely black images. The text recalls his childhood as the son of a Jewish father and of a Christian mother during the period of Italian fascism and under German occupation. It is also about postwar Italy's heedless support of the Israeli side in the 1967 Six-Day War, a move resulting from Italy's inability to reflect on its own fascist past, Fortini argues.

As Fortini and the filmmakers have pointed out, the writer's reading for the camera is also a performance and as such Fortini – as he appears in the film – appears not simply as "himself" but "as a middle-aged gentleman who represents a certain central European culture from the thirties and forties."[55] The credits list him under his birth name: Franco Lattes, thus emphasizing the separation between Fortini, the historical author, and Fortini, a character in Straub-Huillet's film. During the press conference that followed the film's premiere at the Pesaro Film Festival, Straub elaborated on how the couple treated the original text. They only changed one word, three times (replacing "30 years ago" with "30 years earlier"). In addition, they took out entire passages, usually from the beginning or ending of a chapter in order to keep certain narrative segments together without alteration. Fortini considers Straub-Huillet's film adaptation a form of re-writing, a process that not only keeps the original work intact and visible but at the same time opens it up to new meanings. Straub-Huillet's "take" on Fortini's text, as it were, declares itself through

the type of scenes they choose in conjunction with the oral recital of the text. For instance, how they decide to frame the landscape shots that accompany Fortini's recital throughout the film or the kind of archival newspaper articles they choose to add at the end of the film. And yet, the specific locations as well as the additional material are prompted by Fortini who mentions them in the book.

Aside from Fortini's readings, the film consists primarily of landscape shots of different rural areas, but also includes views of the cities Florence, Rome, and Milan. Most of these shots are captured by a camera movement that has come to be known as the *plan straubien* (in English, the Straubian shot or Straubian sequence shot), a type of shot that the critic Serge Daney defined as "a tomb," because it conceals something buried underground, forgotten histories, corpses, or traces of blood spilled by acts of violence, oppression, and injustice. *Fortini/Cani* includes a series of pans that depict the natural or rural landscape in entire 360-degree circles, sometimes in multiple iterations. One of them is set in the rural region of the Apuan Alps; after the circular movement, the camera tilts down to reveal the village of Sant'Anna di Stazzema in the valley. At a later point, the camera captures, similarly, a view of the village of Marzabotto. The landscapes appear in the film because Fortini mentions them in his voice-over narration: these are places where German

55 Franco Fortini, "Pressekonferenz in Pesaro mit Danièle Huillet, Franco Fortini, und Jean-Marie Straub zu *Fortini/Cani*," *Filmkritik*, no. 241, January 1977, p. 9

Fortini/Cani (1976)
tini reading from his book
The landscape

troops massacred civilians during the Second World War. As much as the camera circles and scans the landscape, no visible traces have remained of the crimes. And yet, the Straubian shots seem to insist: something happened in those hills, something is buried underneath those stones. Only occasionally does the camera find a memorial erected in some of the villages.

Fortini/Cani exemplifies how the filmmakers approach and reconstruct the landscape as a place in which historical events remain hidden and invisible and bring these events to light without relying on the rhetoric of a conventional documentary. Like some of their previous films, *Fortini/Cani* was criticized for not being explicit enough in identifying the places and historical events depicted onscreen. The filmmaker Alexander Kluge attacked it for remaining too elusive in its representations: "I would have liked to see how Fortini washes dishes [...] or how he moves," he laments.[56] Moreover, by eliminating any historical context and explanations from the scenes, Kluge suggests, Straub-Huillet's film leaves the spectator in the dark. However, in this case, the film's lack of exposition derives precisely from the attempt to confront the viewer with the scene of a past crime that is no longer visible to the eye, that lies buried underground. Their invisibility and "cover-up" are as important as the historical events themselves.

REVOLUTION AND RESISTANCE: MALLARMÉ, PAVESE, AND ENGELS/HUSSEIN

The filmic depiction of a place that is a "tomb" because it contains and covers up an event of historical significance is a recurring operation in Straub-Huillet's work. It may involve historical sites of state-sanctioned executions (the natural landscapes in *Fortini/Cani*, the location of the electric power plant in *Europa 2005, 27 October*). But it may also involve the site of social injustice (the Landsberger Straße in *Bridegroom*) or a place of resistance (the shot that opens *Othon* by zooming toward the dark opening of a cave located at the foot of the Palatine Hill where Communist resistance fighters hid their weapons during WWII). Moreover, the use of these locations is generally connected to the filmmakers' previous encounter with the place, which often triggered the making of the film itself. Huillet and Straub discovered both the Landsberger Straße and the Palatine Hill by accident and then planned to use them in one of their future projects. Also notable in this regard is their discovery of the Egyptian landscape that plays a crucial role in the 1980/81 ethnographic film *Too Early, Too Late*. The two discovered the country when they traveled there to film views of the Nile delta for *Moses and Aaron*.

The location Straub-Huillet used for the short *Toute révolution est un coup de dés* (*Every Revolution is a Throw of the Dice*, 1977) is equally significant. The film signifies the couple's return to French soil: it was the first work they

56 Alexander Kluge, "Straub," *Filmkritik*, no. 240, December 1976, p. 576

made in France after Straub (and many others) were allowed to return to the country almost twenty years after they had refused to serve in the Algerian War. The location of the Parisian cemetery Père Lachaise is especially noteworthy in this regard. The filmmakers are less interested in the cemetery itself than in a particular gravesite.

Every Revolution opens with an extended Straubian shot that starts with a low-angle view of the sky, the clouds, and some tree tops. Panning in a circular motion the camera eventually begins to tilt down towards the ground. Filmed from a position within the cemetery, the Communards' Wall comes into view: a memorial site, located in one corner of the cemetery where the last fighters of the 1871 Paris Commune were shot and defeated. The camera continues to pan from the memorial wall to the performance site of the film: a grass area facing the wall where the film's nine performers are sitting in a semi-circle, about to deliver their lines. The ten-minute film features the recital of Stéphane Mallarmé's poem *Un coup de dés jamais n'abolira le hasard* (*A Throw of the Dice Will Never Abolish Chance*, 1897). The original free verse poem consists of a text unevenly positioned across more than 20 pages. Words and sentences are set apart from one another by changes in typeface, spacing, and alignment. Instead of merely quoting the text "word for word," Straub-Huillet's adaptation is focused on its typographical specificities. Each section,

identified in the original text by different typefaces, is assigned to a different performer. In other words, each of the nine performers recites a specific part of the poem; some of them have only single words, while others recite much longer passages, all depending on Mallarmé's typography. This becomes, above all, a matter of accentuation and pronunciation. As is often the case in Straub-Huillet's films, the cast includes both native French speakers (among them Huillet) and non-native speakers. *Every Revolution* also stages a coming-together, a reunion of sorts, because for this film, Huillet and Straub brought together a group of their friends, among them *Cahiers* critic Michel Delahaye and German critic Helmut Färber. In addition, they dedicated the film to Jacques Rivette, Jean Narboni (another writer for *Cahiers*), and the Dutch filmmaker Frans van de Staak.

It is not only the intonation and phrasing of the words themselves that count, but also the "silences" that Mallarmé builds into the structure of the written text: the alterations in typeface and the "empty" spaces between words, word groups, and entire sentences. "The 'white spaces,' in effect, assume importance, are the first that strike our eyes; versification has always required them, usually as an encompassing silence, such that a poem, lyrical or with few feet, occupies, centered, about a third of the page," Mallarmé explains in the preface to his poem.[57] "The literary advantage, if I may call it such, of this copied distance, which mentally separates groups of words or single words from each other, is that it seems to sometimes

---

57 Stéphane Mallarmé, *A Roll of the Dice*, trans. Jeff Clark and Robert Bononno, Seattle: Wave Books, 2015, p. 1

Every Revolution is a Throw of the Dice (1977)
Trees, the Communards' grave and communal gathering in Père Lachaise

accelerate and slow the movement, articulating it, even intimating it through a simultaneous vision of the Page...”[58]

Along these lines, Straub-Huillet capture each oral performance in an individual shot framing each reciter separately, by him or herself. The poem's lines determine, therefore, not only the rhythm and the duration of each single shot, but also their overall rhythm and combination into one linear montage of shots. In this regard, Mallarmé's graphic poem functions almost like a storyboard: it lays out – in writing and syntax – how the scene is to be composed by individual shots, recalling, of course, Straub-Huillet's frequent adaptations of musical scores. The film brings the poem to life with the means of cinemato*graphy* and editing. Each of the performers recite their lines while looking in the direction of the off-screen space. Thus, each individual shot separates each text-segment, each voice, each performer from one another while connecting them at the same time and bringing them into dialogue with one another. The soundtrack, beyond the spoken words, contributes as much: each transition from one shot to another registers slight differences in the soundscape depending on the specific sounds present during each take.

All of this happens in eyesight of the remainder and reminder of a communal revolutionary uprising, as the introductory shot clarifies. The filmmakers are eager to draw a connection

Danièle Huillet in *Every Revolution is a Throw of the Dice*

between Mallarmé's revolution in poetic writing, the political uprising of 1871 (and its bloody defeat), the return from exile, and the act of reassembling a community of colleagues and friends in order to read a poem and make a film together. In other words, Straub-Huillet are drawing a connection between the production of their films, their work, and a political position. Straub once suggested in an interview that what makes *Chronicle* a political film and Bach a political figure, is that he fought his entire life against a system that tried to prevent him from making his work without compromise: “the revolution,” Straub added, “is like God's grace, it has to be made anew each day, it becomes new every day, a revolution is not made once and for all.”[59] Bach's relentless struggle against creative and financial restrictions is a struggle that has to be picked up anew over and over again. What spoke to the filmmakers, Straub recalls, was how Bach “reacted against his own inertia, although he was deeply rooted in his times, and was oppressed.”[60] Revolutionary

58 Ibid.
59 Engel, op. cit., p. 20
60 Ibid.

struggle is here not defined as a sweeping societal and historical turn, but as an everyday activity, a permanent struggle against obstacles and complacency that mirrors, of course, Straub and Huillet's own uncompromising way of living their personal and professional lives, for "there is no division between politics and life, art and politics," Straub insists.[61]

The sequence shot that opens *Every Revolution* by connecting the sky with the gravesite prefigures a connection between an act of grace and everyday acts of revolutionary struggle and resistance. It also anticipates Straub-Huillet's following project *Dalla nube alla resistenza* (*From the Cloud to the Resistance*, 1978). The first half of the film is based on Cesare Pavese's *Dialoghi con Leucò* (*Dialogues with Leucò*, 1947) and features six conversations between characters from ancient Greek mythology. The segment represents Straub-Huillet's first creative engagement with a text that would also become the source for *These Encounters of Theirs* in 2005 and four short films Straub made between 2007 and 2012. The *Leucò* segment in *From the Cloud to the Resistance* establishes a particular form of mise-en-scène in which the actors recite the text in a wooded area or rural setting devoid of any specific historical or cultural markers. As the character who is furthest removed from the world of mankind, the cloud nymph Nephele sits in a tree overlooking a valley during her conversation with Ixion who is standing below, framed against the vast landscape in the distance. However, with each new sequence, the film moves further away from the Gods toward earthly matters, introducing more and more man-

made structures and artefacts into its mise-en-scène.

The third dialogue marks, for instance, the shift from the pre-historic to the pre-industrial age: the conversation between Tiresias and Oedipus takes place on an ox cart, pulled by two white bulls and led by a peasant walking in the front. The camera records the entire scene from a position in the back of the cart, mounted right behind the two main characters, looking over their shoulders, onto the animals, the peasant, and the road ahead (thus resembling a pre-modern version of *History Lessons'* car-sequences). The surface of the unpaved road and the archaic vehicle produce an unstable view, an impression that becomes even more pronounced when the image sporadically cuts to black, just for brief moments at a time. The tight framing and the visual impediment function in direct response to the narrative focus on two characters who are each identified by their blindness: first, old and blind Tiresias whose visual impairment is here a physical marker of his lifelong experiences and interactions with the Gods. Next to him sits young Oedipus, who not only awaits a similar fate, but who is also currently, as Tiresias tells him, struck by the youthful inability to see things clearly. The technique of splicing black (or white) "empty" frames in between shots was already a technique in the earlier Schoenberg films and in *Fortini/Cani* where parts of Fortini's voice-over were visually accompanied by an extended black image. *From the Cloud to*

61 Ibid.

the Resistance presents several extended pieces of dialogue over black as well. The fourth episode, for instance, features a dialogue between two hunters who recall their brutal murder of a man who reminded them of an animal, a wild beast. Shots of an actual animal, a wolf, precede and follow this image, yet the beastlike human and his brutal slaughter remain without direct representation – "covered" by the empty black frames.

Throughout the film, the line between the killing of animals and humans, between sacrificial slaughter and political execution, becomes more and more slippery. The final shot of the last dialogue ends with an act of rebellion, encapsulated in the close-up shot of the young son's open palm, a gesture that accompanies his outrage against the barbarous rituals that are practiced by the local peasants in their attempt to ask the Gods for prosperity. Thus, while the father explains to the son the inevitability of the ancient traditions, the son is no longer willing to subscribe to the violent rituals his community has engaged in as they attempt to appease either the Gods or the land.

From there the film transitions to a second part based on Pavese's *La luna e il falò* (*The Moon and the Bonfires*, 1950). The story is set in a small town near Turin where the inhabitants deal with the socio-economic changes in post-WWII Italy while still haunted by their experi-

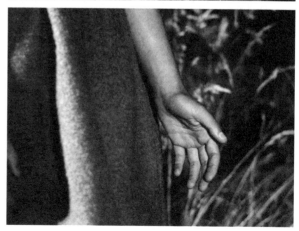

From the Cloud to the Resistance (1978)
Walter Pardini as Oedipus (left)
and Ennio Lauricella as Tiresias,
the wolf, the son's gesture of rebellion

*From the Cloud
to the Resistance*
Mauro Monni as the
Bastard (left) and
Carmelo Lacorte as Nu◼
people at the bar

ences during the war. This part echoes in many ways both *Not Reconciled* and *Fortini/Cani*, but it also recalls the later Vittorini adaptation *Sicilia!* insofar as the main narrative focuses on a character, called the Bastard, who returns to his hometown after having spent a number of years in exile in America. Like the preceding *Leucò* segment, the second part is largely structured around a series of dialogues, in this case between the Bastard and several people he encounters in his former hometown. These include a number of conversations with Nuto, an old friend and fellow comrade, who gives a bleak picture of the town's current political climate in which no one is willing to acknowledge the crimes that happened during the war, acts of murder, betrayal, and discrimination against civilians and resistance fighters, acts that had been committed by community members and sanctioned by the Fascist authorities and the church alike. In fact, the Bastard is more often shown listening attentively while Nuto is identified more strongly as the one who is telling (or reading) a story. In one case, such a story is spoken over a black image and in another we see Nuto – who appears at this point more as the actor, Carmelo Lacorte – reading from the script.

Unlike the *Leucò*-based passages of the film, whose six autonomous episodes were each set in one single location (with the exception of the ox cart sequence, perhaps), the postwar story unfolds in a more conventional narrative setting. Here, the two main characters, the Bastard and Nuto, act within or move through different modern, naturalistic locations and inter-

act with other characters. And yet, there are moments in which the mise-en-scène echoes the mythological settings of the first part and makes the Bastard and Nuto, as well as the little boy they encounter, descendants of a struggle that begins with the rebellion of the mythological heroes against the clouds and the Gods and that ends with a small Italian community in the Langhe region during the 1950s. As with the mythological conflicts between and against the Gods, Straub-Huillet's film suggests that visible traces of these struggles – the crimes, the blood – have long disappeared from the stones and the surrounding fields. They are only kept alive as part of a dialogue in which someone is willing to speak to someone else who is ready to listen.

Too Early, Too Late is one of the films that best express Danièle Huillet's early interests in ethnographic documentary filmmaking. It differs from those films within their oeuvre that are structured around staged performances of either literary or musical texts. This film, too, is based on a text, but here it is presented off screen, as voice-over narration. Divided into two sections, the film opens in Paris with a seven minute tracking shot, filmed out of a driving vehicle that circles around the Place de la Bastille, recalling the Landsberger Straße sequence in *Bridegroom* and the car rides in *History Lessons*. Both of these films similarly revolved around themes of oppression and revolt, but *Too Early, Too Late* brings them into a global, historical framework. The first part is set in a number of locations in France, most of them rural or at the outskirts of larger towns; the

longer second part was shot on various locations around the Nile Valley in Egypt. Continuing Straub-Huillet's general technique of confronting the modern-contemporary with the classical-historical, the film presents these two places in clear separation from one another. The geographical and meteorological specificities, the colors, the sounds, the composition, as well as the accompanying voice-over narration all highlight each part's distinctiveness: France and Egypt presented side by side or, rather, one after the other, without effacing their historical, cultural, and local particularities as well as the geopolitical divide between the two nations. And yet, watching *Too Early, Too Late* means, at the same time, bringing these two places into dialogue with one another, comparing and contrasting their structural and historical affinities especially when it comes to each country's futile revolutionary struggles. The second segment quotes from Mahmoud Hussein's *La Lutte de classes en Égypte de 1945 à 1968* (*Class Struggle in Egypt,* 1969), a text in which the author recollects how the revolt of Egyptian peasants against the English occupation was contained by the military revolution under Nasser in 1952.

By way of their title, Straub-Huillet suggest that what the two countries have in common is that the peasants always start the revolt too early and, then, when it comes to seizing power, they arrive too late. This assessment is taken from a letter written by Friedrich Engels

Too Early, Too Late (1980/81): French countryside, workers leaving the Egyptian factory, Egyptian landscape

to Karl Kautsky in 1889 that is quoted in the first part of the film. In addition to this letter, the first part also quotes excerpts from the so-called *Cahiers de doléances* (*Notebooks of Grievances*), official French documents that recorded the economic situation among the peasants and working-class on the eve of the French Revolution while the camera tracks or pans slowly across deserted landscapes in the French countryside. Many of these shots contain only fleeting remains of the past such as ruined building structures almost completely covered by vegetation. Thus, with the notable exception of the opening Place de la Bastille sequence, the French segment presents its revolutionary history mainly in view of a deserted landscape that lacks any presence, let alone action, of its populace. "Maybe people live there," writes Serge Daney, "but they don't inhabit the locale. The fields, roadways, fences and rows of trees are traces of human activity, but the actors are birds, a few vehicles, a faint murmur, the wind."[62] The scenes filmed in Egypt appear, in comparison, rather crowded, suggesting, perhaps, that this place – unlike the French countryside – is still inhabited by a people that bears the potential for a future uprising.

Too Early, Too Late (together with the later *Europa 2005*, *Itinerary of Jean Bricard*, and the two Cézanne films) resembles a more conventional documentary film within the specific tradition of ethnographic cinema that begins in the fifties with Jean Rouch and includes, among others, filmmakers such as Harun Farocki, Chantal Akerman, and Trinh T. Minh-ha. What these filmmakers have in common is an awareness of their own problematic position of producing, as outsiders, images of foreign cultures and foreign landscapes. These filmmakers respond, in other words, to a long precarious history in which both photography and film helped to frame larger politics of exploitation in a colonial and racist discourse. Serge Daney has commented that Straub-Huillet's position as European filmmakers within the Egyptian landscape is reflected in the film's particular way of framing. "Made up of approaches and retreats," he writes, the two filmmakers are constantly searching for "the right spot, where their camera can catch people without bothering them."[63]

This strategy occurs, for instance, in the long sequence recorded in front of an Egyptian factory. Workers and employees are walking in and out of the building or simply passing by, some on foot, some on bicycles. During the ten-minute shot the camera remains completely still. The only movement that occurs in the frame is produced by the people. In many ways, this scene evokes a canonical moment in early film history, the Lumière brothers' *La Sortie de l'usine Lumière à Lyon* (*Workers Leaving the Lumière Factory in Lyon*, 1895). The comparison arises, first of all, from the specific social scene that presumably features the documentation of everyday activities in front of an industrial production site and work place. Straub-Huillet's shot of the factory differs significantly from the

62 Serge Daney, "Cinemeteorology [Serge Daney on *Too Early, Too Late*]," *JonathanRosenbaum.com*, trans. Jonathan Rosenbaum (October 6, 1982), www.jonathanrosenbaum.com/?p=21944, np.
63 Daney, op. cit., np.

Ernesto (Olivier Straub) and his mother (Nadette Thinus) in *En rachâchant* (1982)

Lumières', however, not only because it is longer, in color, and includes direct sound, but also because the workers of the Lumière factory move according to a clearly visible choreography. In two lines, they leave the shot to the left and right while the image is tightly framed around the two factory doors. In Straub-Huillet's scene, the camera maintains a carefully chosen distance: far enough to allow the people in front of the factory to move unhindered in any direction, while staying close enough to remain visible. Thus, people walk in all directions, some fast, some slow, while some stop, clearly aware of the film crew. Some of them look toward or into the camera, while others remain either oblivious or indifferent to its presence.

Indeed, even though the Egypt segment features – in sharp contrast to the France segment – a certain amount of people in front of the camera, all of them seem to enter or exit the frame by accident. On several occasions Straub has discussed the importance of film in regard to two aspects: the "pure present" of film,[64] a direct representation of time, and its ability to capture the movement of the wind blowing in the trees – precisely the kind of movement that cannot be choreographed, rehearsed, or framed ahead of time.[65] It is the latter aspect that informs Straub-Huillet's fondness for open and often deserted landscapes, registering the visual effects of wind and weather as well as their accompanying acoustic phenomena.

CLASS RELATIONS: DURAS AND KAFKA

In 1982 Straub-Huillet made a short film that could not have been any more different from *Too Early, Too Late*. *En rachâchant* is based on the short story *Ah! Ernesto!* (1971) by Marguerite Duras, making it one of the few contemporary texts Straub-Huillet chose to adapt and, with the exception of Gertrud Schoenberg's work on the libretto of *From Today Until Tomorrow*, the only female author whose work they adapted. *En rachâchant* prefigures in significant ways their following feature-length film, the Kafka adaptation *Class Relations*.[66] Both are shot in black and white and staged in a naturalistic manner. As mentioned earlier, the two films (together with *Sicilia!*) mark Straub-Huillet's brief return to a classical film style that illustrates, much more explicitly than their other films, the couple's fondness for filmmakers like Ford, Renoir, Mizoguchi, and, above all, Bres-

64 Straub in "Question aux Cinéastes," *Cahiers du cinéma*, no. 185, December 1966, p. 123
65 "Gespräch mit Danièle Huillet und Jean-Marie Straub," *Filmkritik*, vol. 10, October 1968, p. 689–690
66 Thank you to Ted Fendt for pointing this out to me.

son. More than mere backdrops to the narrative action, the tightly framed and carefully lit interior spaces in both films function to create a precise social and spiritual milieu for any given character and narrative situation.

The Duras story is about little Ernesto who refuses to return to school "because in school they teach me things I don't know." The film's two main settings, the family kitchen and the classroom, identify two fundamental official sectors of social development, private nurturing and public education. The two meet, when Ernesto and his parents see the schoolmaster to discuss Ernesto's unruly behavior. The images in the classroom scenes clearly delineate each character's position and relationship in this dispute. In a classical shot-reverse shot pattern, the editing distinguishes between two sides: the schoolmaster on the right, behind his desk, Ernesto and his parents, sitting on the school benches to the left. More than a conflict between adolescent and grown-ups, the conflict here is between the institution and the family. Whereas Ernesto's parents are concerned with Ernesto's decisions and worry about his future prospects, they remain on his side and are similarly reprimanded by the sanctimonious slogans the schoolmaster throws at them.

However, there is also a clear hierarchy to the family, dominated by Ernesto's mother. The father remains mostly outside the frame, whereas Ernesto and his mother are more often framed together in the same shot. Social and institutional hierarchies are clearly distributed in the framing and spatial set-up as well as in the language. On one end is the schoolmas-

En rachâchant: the schoolmaster, the butterfly – "a crime!"

ter's hollow administrative rhetoric, on the other Ernesto's seemingly nonsensical responses which are, nonetheless, of utmost clarity. Asked to identify a dead butterfly pinned and framed behind glass and hanging on the wall, Ernesto responds: "a crime!" One of the shots depicts him and his parents in the reflection of the glass, pinning them down equally as objects within a frame. What Ernesto objects to is not learning itself, but a learning based on disciplining, framing, categorizing, and systematizing which is fundamental to the constitution of knowledge in modern industrial society. The neat grid of student desks in the classroom, depicted by images that attest to Straub-Huillet's fondness for diagonal graphic compositions, is another expression of this institutionalized form of exerting social control and power. Ernesto, in the end, reacts in the only possible way, that is to say, in the most utopian way: he gets up and leaves.

"The type of perfection to which commercial filmmaking aspires (the use of its technical capabilities solely to maintain the established order) [...] mirrors precisely its subservience to dominant social codes," Duras once wrote. "Commercial filmmaking can be very clever, but rarely intelligent."[67] Duras seems to be envisioning the intelligence that the child Ernesto possesses, an intelligence that begins outside of an established form and cultural convention. Straub and Huillet have a similar intelligence in mind when they declare that they are trying to make films for children or cavemen; films that do not require prior knowledge or training in order to be understood.

In 1983 Straub-Huillet made *Class Relations* based on Franz Kafka's posthumous novel-fragment *Der Verschollene* (*Amerika*, 1927). Aside from *Too Early, Too Late*, it was the only other project for which the couple worked on locations outside of Europe. A few exterior shots were filmed in the United States: in the New York harbor and on board of an Amtrak train en route from St. Louis to Jefferson City to capture the ride along the Missouri River. The scenes with the actors were filmed on mostly interior and a few exterior locations in Hamburg and Bremen.

Straub-Huillet's approach to filmic adaptation is generally structured around a series of readings and rewritings. This begins with the filmmakers' own initial encounter with a text which leads to a first transcription, already involving a certain selection and organization of the material. These selections form the first draft of the screenplay which is then used during the first part of the rehearsal process with the actors. The late German filmmaker Harun Farocki, who has a small role in *Class Relations*, documented the rehearsals for the film in a short television documentary, entitled *Jean-Marie Straub und Danièle Huillet bei der Arbeit* (*Jean-Marie Straub and Danièle Huillet at Work*, 1983).

During the first part of the rehearsal process, the actors, guided by Huillet and Straub, develop their own approach to the text. The actors read the text over and over in order to get a clear sense of how to deliver their lines. Huillet usually takes notes during these sessions and later types a new, final version of the script in which she indicates all relevant breaks, pauses, and accentuations. In a final rehearsal phase, the actors add body movements, gestures, and the use of props to their performances. Pronunciation and phrasing are to a cer-

---

67 Alan Williams, *Republic of Images: A History of French Filmmaking*, Cambridge: Harvard University Press, 1992, p. 373–374

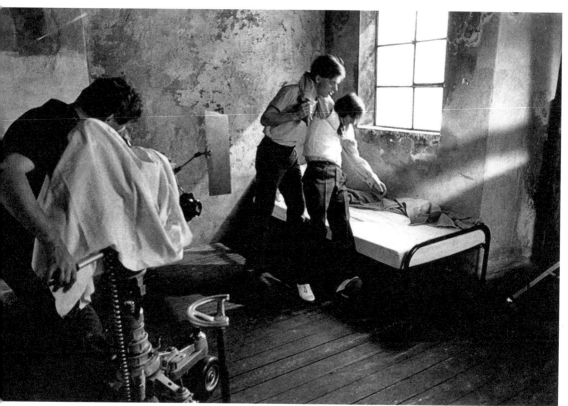

On the set of *Class Relations* (1983)

tain extent based on an actor's physicality, explains Straub: "Some of them have more breath, due to physical ability or training, but this is not the only reason. It also has something to do with the text. When Therese [in *Class Relations*] speaks of the long snowy streets in New York and her mother's death, she cannot utter the sentences in the same way in which she says, 'Good morning, Mr. Rossmann.'"[68] Moreover, how one character speaks to another in *Class Relations*, Gertrud Koch observes, is not merely "a matter of grammar," but a direct manifestation of a character's social position.[69] The film's visual composition compliments this: how a character is framed in relation to another one (or to a group of characters) reflects a scene's particular class constellations.

Class Relations was the first of Straub-Huillet's films in which each scene was broken down into individual shots that are filmed from one single camera position. Characters are rarely framed together in a shot, but address one another most often "across the frame" in alternating shot-reverse shots. Since master shots are largely absent from the film, the characters' positions and the overall spatial set-up is at first only indicated by the direction of their eye lines. Each new shot, however, introduces a variation in camera angle and distance (e.g. the shots often become wider toward the end). Thus, the scene's progression advances the viewer's understanding of its spatial parameters as well as its social coordinates.

One of the first scenes in the film stages the ship stoker's protest against wrongful dismissal in the captain's office. The film's young hero Karl Rossmann pleads on his behalf. The first shot depicts the two entering the office side by side. But then, Karl leaves the stoker's side and walks out of the frame, immediately being replaced by the head steward, who enters the frame and positions himself next to the stoker. The scene cuts to a shot that frames Karl individually, in a different position in the room. Karl begins to speak on the stoker's behalf while looking toward a part in the room that has not been revealed by the camera. Karl's spatial displacement attests to the fact that once he enters the captain's office, he is no longer able to maintain the social solidarity he had developed to the stoker in the previous scene. Furthermore, once he addresses the three superior figures in the office, his mode of speaking differs notably from the other crew members. Eventually the scene cuts to a shot depicting the three superiors: the head treasurer, the captain, and a U.S. senator who turns out to be Karl's uncle. The three figures of power are framed to the left, directly opposite the crew members which eventually include, aside from the stoker and the head steward, a third person: Schubal, the man responsible for firing the stoker. Framing and blocking follow social rather than dramatic relations, which is to say, instead of framing the stoker and Karl together and in opposi-

68 Jean-Marie Straub, "Text-Komposition," in *Stadtkino-Programm 54*, Vienna: Stadtkino, 1984. Reprinted in *Die Früchte des Zorns und der Zärtlichkeit*, op. cit., p. 143
69 Gertrud Koch, "Nur vom Sichtbaren läßt sich erzählen. Zu einigen Kafka-Verfilmungen," in *Klassenverhältnisse*, op. cit., p. 177–178

tion to Schubal, the head treasurer, and the captain, Straub-Huillet decide to position the crew members together on one side, the superiors on the other. Karl's removal from the workers' side is a direct manifestation of his changing class status. For a while he remains somewhere in the middle between the two parties, until his uncle recognizes him and the two eventually unite in one and the same frame: a visual display of Karl's (re)integration into bourgeois society. The fact that his solidarity with the stoker has been corrupted is further epitomized in one of the final shots in the scene: Karl kneels in front of the stoker while trying to convince him to speak up against the injustice; the stoker's reaction remains obscure however, for his upper body is cut out of the frame.

THE HÖLDERLIN FILMS

In 1986 Straub-Huillet produced their first adaptation of a play written by the German dramatist and poet Friedrich Hölderlin. *Der Tod des Empedokles; oder: wenn dann der Erde Grün von neuem euch erglänzt (The Death of Empedocles or When the Green of the Earth Will Glisten for You Anew)* was based on Hölderlin's unfinished play about the pre-Socratic Greek philosopher Empedocles who relinquishes his position as a political leader and chooses first exile, then death as his ultimate commitment to a free life governed only by the divine law of nature. The play ends with his suicide by throwing himself into the volcano, Mount Etna. Hölderlin wrote three different versions of the Greek tragedy.

Class Relations: the Scene in the Captain's Office

The film is based on the first version written in 1798. Two years later, the couple made *Schwarze Sünde* (*Black Sin*, 1988) based on Hölderlin's third version (1799). Both films were shot on location in Sicily. The first part of *The Death of Empedocles* takes place at a time in which the main character is still communicating with the people, is still of this world. The setting is accordingly the park Castello di Donnafugata near Linguaglossa, a place in which man has shaped nature. The second act, however, takes place after Empedocles has removed himself from most of human company; these scenes were recorded at the foot of the volcano's north slope.

As was the case in *Class Relations*, each scene is filmed from a single camera position and involves only static shots. Again, Straub-Huillet only changed the focal-lengths in individual shots, alternating between close-ups, medium, and long shots. Here, too, the direction of a performers' eyeline (to the left or right side of the frame) establishes or continues his or her relationship to other characters across the frame, a rather conventional form of continuity editing. However, the treatment of light and shadow works in direct opposition to classical concerns for continuity, for in the Empedocles films Straub-Huillet decided to rely on natural light alone; a dramatic change compared to *Class Relations'* carefully arranged artificial lighting. The natural set of *The Death of Empedocles* is surrounded by plants and trees, leading to constant changes in light and shadow either within one and the same shot or in the transition from one shot to the next.

The first conversation between Hermocrates and Critias, for instance, consists of alternating full-body shots of the two characters together and individual medium shots. Each new shot introduces changes in light, shadow, and other meteorological conditions. The first two-shot depicting the men shows them bathed in full sunlight hitting them from the front while casting deep shadows on parts of their bodies and the surroundings. The entire scene is bathed in a bright, golden light that gives the sky in the background the appearance of a deep blue and the plants and trees around them a lush green. A few moments later, the scene cuts again to an identical shot of the two, but now the light appears white and washed-out, eliminating not only all former shadows but also draining the image of the earlier color saturation. Later in the scene, the two-shot returns to its former luminosity. Similar changes also affect the shots in which each character is framed individually. Compared to the rest of the scene, one of the shots depicting Hermocrates individually registers much stronger wind conditions on the soundtrack as well as in the movements of his costume and in the branches and leaves moving in the trees behind him.

Perhaps because shooting in natural light could have created potential problems regarding the quality of the footage, an unusually large amount of exposed negative material was printed and made available for editing. Since most of it turned out to be equally usable, Straub-Huillet decided to produce more than one final version of each film, resulting in four distinct variants of both *The Death of Empedocles* and *Black Sin*. Each version's structure follows the same order of shots, but uses different takes. Depending on each take's visual and audio conditions, the cuts vary slightly, so that each version differs in length. For Straub, the shortest version of *The Death of Empedocles* (the "Hamburg edition", created as part of a seminar for film students) is also the most beautiful version, because it has the most contrast and strongest color saturation due to the specific lighting conditions of the selected takes. It is also known as the "Rooster Version," as it includes a take in which a rooster's call can be heard; while the first version, the so-called Berlin edition (it was used for the screening at the Berlin International Film Festival) is also known as the "Lizard Version," because a lizard runs through one of the shots.

Straub-Huillet establish the space in which the dramatic action takes place a long time prior to shooting. For the two Empedocles films, they created a kind of abstract map even before they began looking for locations, a map that clearly identifies each character's position in relation to one another. Moreover, the setting in which the characters perform belongs to them alone; the director and cinematographer are not allowed to step foot in it, but remain at all times behind a certain point that cannot be crossed. In the case of the first Empedocles film, the breakdown of individual shots

The Death of Empedocles (1986)
Andreas von Rauch as Empedocles; Howard Vernon as
Hermocrates (left) and William Berger as Critias;
Vladimir Baratta as Pausanias (left) with Empedocles

Claudia Pummer

follows largely the dramatic constellations established in the original play. For instance, the scene of the final confrontation between Empedocles and the society that decrees his expulsion is organized around a clear spatial divide: Empedocles (and his disciple Pausanias) stand to the right and speak frame-left to the authorities (represented by Critias, Hermocrates, and the three citizens) who stand presumably to the left and address, accordingly, Empedocles and Pausanias in the off-screen space to the right. Aside from keeping the two sides separate from one another, shots of characters within one side alternate depending on narrative context, e.g. the three citizens are sometimes framed as a group of three and sometimes together with Critias and Hermocrates. Similarly, Pausanias and Empedocles are sometimes framed together, side by side, and sometimes they appear in separate shots. *Empedocles*, finally, includes two extended shots in which the main character speaks his lines over a static wider view of the surrounding landscape. Aside from these two shots, the framing is clearly organized around the characters' recital of Hölderlin's text. Straub-Huillet resist the temptation of using the play and its adaptation as an excuse to create beautiful views of the Sicilian landscape, as some critics objected.

Most of the cast members for both films consisted of non-professional actors from various backgrounds, among them Andreas von Rauch, a teacher from Hamburg, who plays Empedocles in both films. For *The Death of Empedocles* the cast included a Dutch opera singer, an Italian philosophy professor, a Ger-

man ballet dancer, and two high-school students.[70] Aside from Rauch, only one performer appears in both films: Howard Vernon, the only professional actor, plays different roles in each film. Danièle Huillet also has a role in *Black Sin*.

Hölderlin's third draft, the source for *Black Sin*, is only loosely related to his first one, thematically and in regard to the conception of the main character. Straub has compared the first draft to a "political tragedy": "For the first time we made a film that contained something like a message, something I have called Hölderlin's communist utopia, especially in his big speech to the mountain."[71] The third draft no longer contains any message, in part because there is no longer a people, a community, to which it could be addressed. The film features a much smaller cast of only four people and a landscape that has markedly transformed from the blooming garden in the first part of *The Death of Empedocles* to the barren volcanic earth on Mount Etna, almost 2000 meters above sea level. The location, in contrast to the ones used for the first film, provided a brightly sunlit natural stage that was only darkened sporadically with the arrival of a cloud. *Black Sin* contains, for instance, an extended shot in which Andreas von Rauch recites Empedocles' lines while we see the character lying on the ground. During the four-minute shot, the lighting

70 Rembert Hüser, "Stummfilm mit Sprache: Über *Der Tod des Empedokles*," *Filmwärts: Forum für Filmkritik*, no. 12, Fall 1988, p. 20
71 "Danièle Huillet und Jean-Marie Straub im Gespräch mit Hans Hurch," op. cit., p. 110

Danièle Huillet and
Andreas von Rauch in
Black Sin (1988)

changes noticeably from exposing his body and the area around him in bright sunlight to dark shadow.

Straub and Huillet made two versions of their third Hölderlin adaptation *Die Antigone des Sophokles nach der Hölderlinschen Übertragung für die Bühne bearbeitet von Brecht 1948 (The Antigone of Sophocles after Hölderlin's Translation Adapted for the Stage by Brecht 1948*, 1991). As suggested by the title, a series of authors have left their marks on this text. There is, first, the oldest by Sophocles, which Hölderlin translated into German and Bertolt Brecht later adapted for the theater. Brecht's adaptation, as Barton Byg has pointed out, was substantial: "Brecht kept only 20 percent of Hölderlin's text without change […], adapted another 30 percent, and freely transformed the remaining half (not to mention the cutting of about one hundred verses). The insertions of lines from Pindar, not to mention from Goethe and others, are all Brecht's, not the filmmakers.'"[72]

Straub-Huillet's adaptation was filmed in the ruins of the ancient Teatro di Segesta in Sicily. Foreshadowing the stage versions of the later Pavese productions, Straub-Huillet performed the play prior to shooting both at the Schaubühne in Berlin and the Teatro di Segesta. Similar to *Moses and Aaron*, the amphitheater space provided the filmmakers with a controlled location, allowing them to develop even further the single-point camera strategy they had used in the previous productions: this time the entire film was shot from a single camera position. As in *Class Relations* and the two Empedocles films, the dramatic space is clearly divided in respect to the characters, with Creon occupying a singular position to the left, Antigone (and her sister Ismene) also to the left, but set apart from Creon, and the chorus of the elders placed on the opposite side, to the right, with the steps or seats of the amphitheater rising above behind them. However, *Antigone* differs from the former films in terms of motion. At several moments, the camera pans across the entire space (from right to left, from the elders to Creon with Antigone in the background) or from one character to another (from Creon to the guard who is about to report Antigone's transgression). Since the camera covers in some instances a substantial distance, for some shots, Straub-Huillet have to use much longer lenses, which leads, in comparison to the Empedocles films, to much greater changes in the depth of field.

Thus, there are shots in which Antigone, standing furthest from the camera, is framed in a close-up and the background with the leaves of the tree behind her is flattened and slightly out of focus. Such a shot concludes her appearance in the film, making us focus completely on her face and her words as she proclaims the city's ultimate ruination before walking toward her own demise. Fully aware of the consequences, Antigone defies King Creon's decree and buries her fallen brother Polynices, a decision leading inevitably to her own death. Her actions are certainly motivated by the wish to honor the dead brother, but they are also an open protest against a system of intolerable in-

72 Byg, op. cit., p. 216

Antigone (1991)

justice and tyranny. This places her in a long line of Straubian heroines and heroes who revolt equally uncompromisingly against a system that typically remains undefeated, from the mad Johanna in *Not Reconciled* to Camille in *Othon* to Empedocles and Ernesto to the young soldier in *The Algerian War!*. These are not individual expressions of heroism, but persistent acts of resistance within a wider history in which one system of injustice is continuously replaced with another. *Antigone*'s use of long panoramic shots attests to this; often depicting Creon, the ancient imperialistic warmonger in the foreground, the character's body is framed against the background of a contemporary, quotidian setting. The final shot pans outside the theatrical space of the amphitheater in order to reveal the agricultural and urban structures in the distance. The connection between play and reality, antique theater and contemporary life, is further highlighted by the following image: a quote by Brecht about the continuities and future reality of imperialistic warfare, over which Straub-Huillet place the sounds of helicopters.

THE CÉZANNE FILMS

With the exception of Schoenberg's portraits in *Introduction*, Straub-Huillet stayed away from incorporating paintings into their films. In fact, they were rather outspoken in their rejection of films on painting. In an interview from 1988 – only one year before they actually made *Cézanne. Conversation with Joachim Gasquet* – Straub called the task of making a film about Cézanne "senseless," based on the differences

between the two visual mediums. Here too, Straub seems to follow Bazin who, in his famous essay "On the Ontology of the Photographic Image," presents photography (and by extension cinematography) in opposition to painting, not only because the former is bound to a pictorial representation based on a direct and automatic relationship with the real world, but because it is consequently able to liberate painting from its false enslavement to pictorial representation. Straub put it similarly, when he mocked some directors' ambitions to imitate "the light of van Delft or Goya." Instead, he continued, "Film is photography. If something pictorial enters, God forbid, it should happen by coincidence, not because one aims for it. […] The greatness of film is the humility that comes from being condemned to photography."[73] In this regard, it may come as no surprise that in addition to Cézanne's paintings, quotations of filmic and photographic material also play an important role in the Cézanne film. *Cézanne* reprises Straub-Huillet's interest in the specific genre of the biographical film and in many ways recalls *Chronicle*, *Introduction*, and *Fortini/Cani*.

To a certain degree, Cézanne's paintings function like the musical compositions and their performances in the Bach film since they are the only remaining physical traces we have left of the artist and his work. However, unlike *Chronicle* and *Fortini/Cani*, where the artist or

73 Rolf Aurich, et.al. "Die Größe des Films, das ist die Bescheidenheit, daß man zur Fotografie verurteilt ist," *Filmwärts: Forum für Filmkritik*, no. 12, Fall 1988, p. 14

author is embodied by the figurative presence of a performer (the musician in the case of the Bach film, the author "himself" in *Fortini/Cani*), Cézanne's appearance in this film is split in two different registers that are deliberately not part of a moving image; they are instead auditory and photographic. The film includes a few black-and-white stills depicting the historical Cézanne at work and a series of voice-over dialogues that feature Danièle Huillet in the role of the ailing painter. The adaptation of Gasquet's memoir reanimates the original dialogue, turning it back into an oral and audible conversation performed by the filmmakers themselves.

In this respect, *Cézanne* has much more in common with *Introduction*, because here too, the voice of the artist is an oral recitation of a text, rather than a physical performance. And it is precisely the text from which Cézanne's oral discourse derives that identifies the film as a literary adaptation (rather than a filmic rendition of Cézanne's paintings). For the film is, indeed, less based on the life and work of Cézanne than on the memoir of another man, another author, the French poet Joachim Gasquet, who wrote a book about his encounter and his conversations with the famous painter, entitled *Cézanne* and originally published in 1921. This makes the film, as Sally Shafto has put it, a work about "an artistic encounter," an encounter entirely based on the unreliable mem-

ory of an obscure, conservative French poet (as some have criticized).[74] It may not be surprising, then, that the Musée d'Orsay, after having commissioned the film, rejected it on the grounds that it was neither a biographical film, nor a documentary, nor an art film about (Cézanne's) painting(s).

The film is based on the memoir's second part, about Cézanne's thoughts on painting in natural landscapes, especially in the rural countryside around Aix-en-Provence, which consists entirely of an "interview-dialogue" under the heading "What He Told Me." Straub-Huillet's second film about the artist, *Une visite au Louvre* (*A Visit to the Louvre*, 2004), is based on the book's first part in which Cézanne talks about the artists and traditions that influenced his work. The topic of each film mirrors Straub-Huillet's relationship to filmmaking. The first film deals with the relationship between the painter and the natural world around him and his struggle to capture what he sees on canvas, speaking to Straub-Huillet's own creative struggle of capturing their relationship to the world on screen. The second film deals, in contrast, with the importance of working within a classical tradition, i.e. to develop the aforementioned direct relationship to the world within the context of a cultural and creative legacy.

Visually, *Cézanne* is primarily structured around a series of shots depicting one painting or photograph at a time. These images are deliberately presented as objects since the frame around them remains visible. Moreover, they are filmed frontally by a static camera and shown for a relatively long time. The impres-

74 Sally Shafto, "Artistic Encounters: Jean-Marie Straub, Danièle Huillet and Paul Cézanne," *Senses of Cinema*, issue 52, September 2009, np.

sion of stillness is even more pronounced here because all of the paintings and photographic objects are filmed inside an interior space, which means they lack even the subtle meteorological changes of exterior shooting. These images evoke the medium of still photography with the means of the cinematographic image.

This interplay of stillness and movement reflects Cézanne's creative struggle of fixing on canvas a landscape in permanent flux. Straub-Huillet capture this struggle by integrating various drafts and sketches Cézanne produced of the same motif. As articulated in the voice-over, the painter became interested in capturing an object or a landscape that has not been contaminated by prior aesthetic conventions. In order to do so, Cézanne wishes to become a sort of photographic apparatus. A painter, he explains to Gasquet, must be a *"recording machine* [...] He must silence all the voices of prejudice within him, he must forget, forget, be silent, become a perfect echo. And then the entire landscape will engrave itself on the sensitive plate of his being."[75] These words resonate with Straub-Huillet's definition of the filmmaker's "humility in being condemned to photography." Thus, the series of motionless recordings of photographic objects and framed paintings in the film derive not only from the filmmakers' wish to make a certain type of essayist documentary or experimental biographical film, but correspond directly to Cézanne's creative process.

However, *Cézanne* also contains a number of landscape shots that work in direct relation to some of Cézanne's paintings, including several shots of Mont Sainte-Victoire, one of Cézanne's most famous motifs. Straub-Huillet's choice of framing the view of the mountain clearly mirror the two paintings that are mentioned in the accompanying voice-over: *The Great Pine with Mont Sainte-Victoire* and *Mont Sainte-Victoire With Large Pine*. Precisely because the image presents a similar view of the mountain, the historical changes that have impacted the surrounding area stand out. The few farmhouses and fields in the paintings have been replaced by a modern cityscape. A second shot makes this even more apparent, because a change in focal length produces not only a closer view of the mountain, but also draws attention to the streets and urban housing structures in the foreground.

As if to emphasize at once the specificities of and the affinities between the three different creative mediums – painting, photography, and film – Straub-Huillet include a short segment in *Cézanne* that features the work of another filmmaker (who also happens to be the son of a painter). Triggered by Cézanne's comment that a certain color reminded him of a passage in Flaubert's *Madame Bovary*, Straub-Huillet insert a sequence from Jean Renoir's *Madame Bovary* (1934). The black and white film footage replaces the issue of color that had been important to Cézanne, corresponding to the filmmakers' argument that it is impossible to translate the light and color of painting into cine-

75 Jean-Marie Straub, Danièle Huillet, *Cézanne. Dialogue avec Joachim Gasquet* (1989). Trans. Ted Fendt and Jean-Marie Straub

matography. However, what the filmmaker can learn from Cézanne, Straub-Huillet insist, is how to frame an object or a scene. Their reliance on Jean Renoir's film version follows along these lines, because according to the filmmakers, what holds true for Cézanne – "he is one of the great *cadreurs*" – holds true for Renoir as well. As mentioned before, framing is for Straub-Huillet as much an aesthetic as an ethical (if not, political) matter. Cézanne's *Old Woman with a Rosary* or the portrait of his gardener Valier (also featured in the film) are typically considered examples of the painter's non-judgmental, reverential treatment of his models (especially those that belonged to a lower social class), an approach Straub-Huillet have equally admired in Renoir's work.

The *Madame Bovary* sequence is not the only filmic quotation Straub-Huillet incorporate into the Cézanne film. Another variation on the filmmakers' technique of bringing into dialogue different texts and authors is prompted by Huillet/Cézanne's voice-over declaration in praise of the vital powers of sunlight (over a shot of Mont Sainte-Victoire): the film cuts to a sequence from their *Empedocles* film in which Andreas von Rauch recites an ode to "heavenly light." This sequence functions as a direct response to the previous quotation from Gasquet's text, adding a commentary by Hölderlin's Empedocles on a similar subject matter.

A Visit to the Louvre reanimates a critical les-

Cézanne (1989)
Photograph of the painter, Mont Sainte-Victoire,
Cézanne's *Old Woman with a Rosary*

A painting in the Louvre and the Buti forest in *A Visit to the Louvre* (2004)

were, deepens the viewer's understanding of Cézanne's own philosophy of painting. Yet this is not the only point Straub-Huillet are trying to make. Following their approach in the first film, the painter's words also generate certain propositions for their own medium to which Straub-Huillet respond by integrating a number of exterior shots depicting the Louvre's surroundings as well as the forest in the Italian landscape near Buti, where Straub-Huillet had made two films over the previous three years.

THE BARRÈS FILMS

With *Lothringen!* (1994), the first film based on works by the French novelist Maurice Barrès, the duo turned to Straub's birthplace in Alsace. The film is exclusively set in exterior locations in Metz and its surrounding landscape, a region on the French-German border that has been periodically under German rule over the past two hundred years, including during Straub's childhood: "Until 1940 I only heard, learned, and spoke French – at home and outside," he recalls. "And suddenly, I'm only allowed to hear and speak German outside, and have to learn it in school (where French is forbidden)."[76] Barrès' original novella *Colette Baudoche. Histoire d'une jeune fille de Metz* (*Colette Baudoche: The Story of a Young Girl from Metz*, 1909), which is set in the period following the German annexation of Alsace and Lorraine by the German emperor after the Franco-Prussian war in 1871,

son about the history of painting based on dialogues between Cézanne and Gasquet as they stroll through the halls of the museum. In many ways, the conversation calls to mind a lecture: Cézanne (in the voice of Julie Koltaï) comments on individual paintings and artists; an assessment that is accompanied by a corresponding shot of each painting. The lesson, as it

76 Jean-Marie Straub, *Herzog, Kluge, Straub*, eds. Wolfram Schütte and Peter W. Jansen, Munich: Hanser Verlag, 1976, p. 241

includes a similar episode. One of the central characters in the novel is a professor from Germany who teaches German in the local school and proposes to young Colette who, however, turns him down out of loyalty to her native France.

Only a small portion of the actual narrative has made it into the film. Straub-Huillet retain the most pronounced episodes about life under German occupation. Moreover, the only character who actually appears on screen, dressed in period clothing, is Colette. She appears in two shots and her dialogue is reduced to a few lines that become, therefore, all the more significant. Both emphasize her loyalty to France and the film ends with her polite yet resolute refusal of the professor's proposal. Aside from Colette, the film incorporates just two other voices from the original novel, the narrator and Colette's grandmother. Both appear only on the soundtrack as part of the accompanying voice-over, providing oral testimony to some of the events that affected the local population in the course of the annexation; even taken straight from the novel they have an almost ethnographic tone that, in connection with the visual images of depopulated landscapes and deserted streets, recalls the French segment in *Too Early, Too Late*.

As with *Cézanne*, Straub-Huillet also produced a German-language version of *Lothringen!* that differs from the original French-language version. The dialogue spoken by the two female characters (Colette onscreen, the grandmother in voice-over) remains in the original French and is accompanied by German sub-titles, while the voice-over of the male narrator – read by the native-speaker André Warynski in the original – is replaced; in the German-language version, Straub himself acts as the off-screen narrator. In other words, a native French-speaker reads a German translation of the original French text and, in doing so, deliberately addresses the presumably German audience with a French accent. Straub reminds the German viewer of his French background while appropriating and engaging with the occupier's language, a language he was coerced to learn and speak exclusively.

Lothringen! proposes a direct connection between the German empire's politics of expansion in the 1870s and contemporary German politics. Made in 1994, the film is not only tied to the historical context established in Barrès' novel but also extends it to the period following the German reunification in 1990. It begins with shots filmed underneath a massive statue of the German emperor William I in the city of Koblenz. A symbol for German unification, the statue, originally erected to celebrate the founding of the German nation in 1871 (following the Franco-Prussian war), was destroyed in WWII and resurrected in the newly unified Germany of 1990. The following shot shows a map of the area around Metz from the period of the occupation, with the German national anthem playing on the soundtrack over the sounds of gunshots.

In recent years, Straub has returned to the work of Barrès and his childhood memories with the film *Un héritier* (*An Heir*, 2010), which is based on a chapter in Barrès' novel *Au service de*

Emmanuelle Straub as Colette in *Lothringen!* (1994)

Straub, Joseph Rottne and Barbara Ulrich (le Joseph Rottner reads the Pagan Wall in *An* (2010)

Barbara Ulrich reads Maurice Barrès in *Concerning Venice* (2013)

l'Allemagne (*In the Service of Germany*, 1905). The film takes place on exterior locations in Alsace, but this time in the area around Mont Sainte-Odile near Colmar. In contrast to *Lothringen!* there is no voice-over narration, only onscreen performances. A young man tells an older man (played by Straub, again under the pseudonym Jubarite Semaran) about his experiences living and working as a physician in occupied Alsace. The first part of the film features their dialogue within naturalistic settings (walking together through the forest, sharing a drink while sitting outside a local inn). The second part, however, depicts the young man alone and this time he is reading from the script while standing with his back to the ruined remains of the Pagan Wall in the forest of Mont Sainte-Odile. His monologue is staged as part of a testimonial performance directed straight to the camera, addressing the audience directly. In comparison, the earlier dialogue in front of the inn deals more with the social structure of a conversation in which the act of listening is as important as the act of speaking. A long segment in this scene depicts Straub's character in an extended shot, looking off-frame in the direction of the young man, listening attentively to his words, which resound from off-screen.

In 2013, Straub made a third work based on a text by Barrès, *À propos de Venise* (*Geschichtsunterricht*) (*Concerning Venice [History Lessons]*). In this short film actress Barbara Ulrich sits off-screen – while two shots depict waves and water washing towards a narrow shore – and reads Barrès' text about the demise and change of Venice as a place whose autonomy and dis-

tinctiveness have been lost over the course of centuries due to the city's rise as a European tourist attraction.

COLLABORATIONS: COSTA, VITTORINI, PAVESE

Straub-Huillet's concern for the capacity of cinema to record and document a scene has had specific effects on the editing process of their films. As mentioned earlier, each cut is determined by the auditory and visual conditions during the filming of a take. This may include environmental sound phenomena, an actor's receding footsteps, the completion of a bodily gesture, as well as changes in lighting conditions caused by a passing cloud. In 2001, the Portuguese filmmaker Pedro Costa made a feature-length documentary about Straub and Huillet that provided a rare glimpse into the duo's editing process. The title, *Where Does Your Hidden Smile Lie?*, refers to a shot at the beginning of the Schoenberg film *From Today Until Tomorrow*, where this line appears in German as part of graffiti sprayed on a wall: "Wo liegt euer Lächeln begraben?!" The quote alludes to a specific moment in Costa's documentary (during the editing of *Sicilia!*), which encapsulates the creative struggle in Straub and Huillet's collaborative process. In this context, the reference to the Schoenberg adaptation gains further significance, for *From Today Until Tomorrow* is, aside from the Bach film, the only other film Straub-Huillet made about a married couple and it was co-written by two people who were aligned in a domestic and professional partnership.

Where Does Your Hidden Smile Lie? documents

The graffiti in *From Today Until Tomorrow* (1996)

the general division of labor in Straub-Huillet's editing process. Most of the film takes place in the almost pitch-black interior space of an editing studio in Le Fresnoy (where they were teaching a course in editing at the time). The only light that enters this space comes from the open door in the background and the flickering screen of a 35mm-flatbed editing table. Costa's film begins with an excerpt from *Sicilia!*, accompanied by the mechanical clatter of the flatbed. Suddenly, the moving image comes to a stop, then resumes, then freezes again. The process is repeated numerous times until Huillet, who operates the editing table, finds the precise moment to place her cut. Straub remains in the background, sometimes pacing back and forth during the process. He only comments sporadically, while Huillet silently operates the flatbed and makes final decisions. Costa emphasizes the manual aspect of her labor through a number of close-ups of her hands turning the knobs or threading a new roll of film onto the editing table. Like Harun

Farocki's documentary on the rehearsals for *Class Relations*, Costa's film also seems to suggest that Huillet's part in the collaborative process is more closely associated with the manual handling of material such as note-taking, typing, transcribing, and editing. In fact, the editing of the film resembles in certain ways the numerous stages of transcription produced by Huillet during the rehearsals. The flatbed replaces the pen or typewriter, while the raw footage inserts itself in a similar way as the voice and body of the actor had previously.

Straub and Huillet's editing philosophy specifically counters the common principles of continuity editing in commercial filmmaking. The latter works toward the production of a stream of shot fragments which nevertheless leave the viewer with the impression of a coherent space (in other words, the viewer is rarely aware of the individual shots and the cuts between them). Frequent and instantaneous insert shots or match-on-action techniques, for instance, that cut away before a gesture is completed, so that it can be picked up again and continued by a shot taken from a different angle, have become conventions in the service of creating a (paradoxically) coherent narrative space. Straub-Huillet's understanding of how a scene can be broken up into different shots and reassembled in post-production is of an entirely different nature, matching, instead, the "narrative blocks" or "movements" that form the basic segmentation of the respective source material. But since Straub-Huillet work with living, breathing landscapes and people, the elements that are recorded on film frequently intervene and, as Straub says, resist the "requirements" of the source text.

Costa's film captures this struggle. In search for the right cut, Huillet rewinds and replays the beginning of a take over and over again, sometimes frame by frame. She tries to follow the structure of the dialogue by cutting where one particular part begins, another ends. However, at times, a vocal pause is too short or a body movement lasts too long, intervening in Huillet's decision. In one scene, it is a performer's instantaneous blink of an eye that poses an unexpected point of resistance. As collaborators, Huillet and Straub frequently run into arguments about certain decisions: "This is you... And this is me," Huillet remarks and moves the material back and forth between her own preferred cutting position and Straub's: "a oneframe difference," she concludes laconically.

Sicilia! (1998) tells the story of a homecoming in which a young man, Silvestro, who after years of exile in America, returns to his birthplace in Sicily. The film mirrors in some ways Straub-Huillet's earlier *Class Relations*, not only because the narrative presents a sequel of sorts to Kafka's story of a much younger man's emigration to America, but also because the two films resemble each other in terms of their black and white cinematography and naturalistic settings.

Sicilia! begins Straub-Huillet's longstanding collaboration with members of the Teatro Francesco di Bartolo, a municipal theater in the town of Buti, near Pisa, that maintains the tradition of amateur-folk theater in central Italy. Picking up on their experience with the Bruckner play for *Bridegroom* thirty years earlier, they first performed *Sicilia!* on stage before filming it on location in Sicily. All of their Italian-language films since then, including Straub's works since Huillet passed away, have been made in collaboration with the Teatro Francesco di Bartolo and produced for the stage prior to filming.

Sicilia! is based on Elio Vittorini's novel *Conversazione in Sicilia* (*Conversations in Sicily*, 1937–38), a title that points to the filmmakers' narrative focus on direct conversations revolving around tensions or confrontations between different individuals or groups. Their following Vittorini adaptation *Operai, contadini* (*Workers, Peasants*, 2000), based on the novel *Le donne di Messina* (*The Women of Messina*, 1948–64), is guided by such dialogic encounters as well. The narrative centers on the formation and collapse of a rural community founded by migrants who fled across the country during the turmoil created by the era of post-WWII Italian reconstruction. Cut off from the urban centers, the village is forced to build and organize its own social body in order to guarantee the survival of its members. The class conflict occurs here between workers and peasants who, in light of each group's distinct needs and work practices, struggle to articulate a common ground. Perhaps in reference to this community's utopian pursuits, *Workers, Peasants* lacks any direct reference to naturalistic locations. The performers speak their lines while standing or sitting in an undifferentiated forest location. For the first time, some actors can be seen holding the actual script in their hands, at times directly

Gianni Buscarino as Silvestro (left) and Vittorio Vigneri as the Knife Sharpener in *Sicilia!* (1998, above)
Workers, Peasants (2000, left), *Humiliated* (2002)

reading from it, a practice that returns in some of Straub-Huillet's subsequent films. Moreover, the cinematography and editing clearly separates the two groups, peasants and workers, by framing each speaker and each group in individual shots. Based on a later section of *Women of Messina*, Straub-Huillet's following film, *Umiliati (Humiliated*, 2002)[77] picks up where *Workers, Peasants* ends and deals with the dissolution of the communal gathering that was imagined in the first part.

With *These Encounters of Theirs* in 2005, their last feature-length film together, Straub-Huillet returned to Pavese's *Dialogues with Leucò*. Here, too, performers recite Pavese's text in undifferentiated natural locations, somewhere in the woods and hillsides of Tuscany. The lack of specific geographical or cultural markers seems to conform to the original text which presents a series of dialogues between the Gods and heroes of Greek mythology. However, this move to the natural landscape can also be seen in the context of Straub-Huillet's collaboration with the theater in Buti.

The theater work in Buti involves a specific

type of communal theater with strong ties to the history of the Italian class struggle. Its roots lie in an ancient tradition of folk song and performance, known as *maggio* or May drama.[78] Traditionally performed in an open space (the village square, a private yard, or an open field), by the beginning of the 1800s *maggio* theaters existed in most villages in Italian mountain regions, especially in Tuscany. "As plays that were frequently written by peasant authors and acted by peasant actors for peasant audiences, the May dramas were a truly popular form of entertainment."[79] The Tuscan dialect functioned as a *lingua franca* of the plays, equipped with the potential to promote both national unity and "the rise of a new social order."[80] To this day, *maggio* performances employ mainly non-professional actors who recite dramatic texts written in verse form. Contemporary *maggio* performances remain indebted to the traditional declamatory style and reject opulent settings, psychological dialogue, and the unities of time, place, and action, all qualities that are not only equally seminal to Straub-Huillet's own filmmaking practice, but that also fit the mythological dialogues of the Pavese plays.

Although mostly set in the Italian South, Vittorini's novels share with the Tuscan *maggio* tradition a tendency to identify social politics and resistance specifically with local farming and worker communities. The theater, with its historical roots in folklore and carnivals, has a long tradition of functioning as an alternative political space. Based on local dialects and mannerisms, the language and performances used in this setting articulate expressions of resist-

77 Released in France in 2003 with a new edit of a sequence in *Workers, Peasants* called *Le Retour du fils prodigue (The Return of the Prodigal Son)*.
78 I am greatly indebted to Romano Guelfi's talk during the exhibition *Of A People Who Are Missing* (curated by Annett Busch and Florian Schneider, Antwerp, December 18, 2009) for introducing me to the importance of the *maggio*-tradition in connection to Straub-Huillet's work with the Buti theater.
79 Roland Sarti, "Folk Drama and the Secularization of Rural Culture in the Italian Apennines," *Journal of Social History*, vol. 14, no. 3, 1981, p. 466
80 Ibid., p. 466

These Encounters of Theirs (2005)

ance that counter an official and unified national Italian discourse. In 1977, Straub had already articulated these potential relations between the natural landscape, film, and "the theater" as "a space of the class struggle": "Many years ago, we had already thought about making a film about the [German] peasant wars. All characters of the peasant wars have something in common with the landscape. The same is true for the fights of the Sicilian peasants, at the beginning of the century; they have similar 'theatrical' landscapes."[81]

THE PAST DECADE

Europa 2005, 27 Octobre came out shortly before Huillet's death on October 9, 2006. The unsigned *video-tract* was initiated as part of a series commissioned by the Italian television critic and curator Enrico Ghezzi in commemoration of Roberto Rossellini's centenary. Filmmakers were asked "to imagine a moment in the life or death of Ingrid Bergman's character after the last shot" of Rossellini's *Europa '51* (1952). Aside from its title, *Europa 2005* is devoid of any ex-

plicit references to *Europa '51* and, instead, depicts in the form of two semi-circular pans, an exterior location in the migrant, working-class suburb Clichy-sous-bois, near Paris, where on October 27th, 2005 two teenagers, Zyed Benna and Bouna Traoré, were electrocuted in an electrical transformer while trying to hide from the police. Their deaths triggered the outbursts of social unrest that came to be known as the *banlieue riots* which spread in the following two months from the Parisian suburb to other socially depleted, ethnic neighborhoods in France. The French government declared a state of emergency on November 8 and two weeks later, the prime minister tightened controls on immigration. Straub-Huillet's short film is very explicit about the structure and conditions of power responsible for the two youngsters' deaths.

The 10-minute video is structured around two slow pans that are each repeated five times. The underlying principle echoes, of course, Straub-Huillet's fondness for multiple versions. However, in this case the repetitions and the variations they generate occur in one film. Each take was filmed at different times on the same day. Panning from left to right, the first shot depicts the electrical substation in which the two youngsters were electrocuted. A high barbed-wired wall, surrounded by warning signs, obscures the view of the industrial compound. The second shot pans in the oppo-

81 Jean-Marie Straub, "Pressekonferenz in Pesaro mit Danièle Huillet, Franco Fortini, und Jean-Marie Straub zu *Fortini/Cani*," op. cit., p. 5

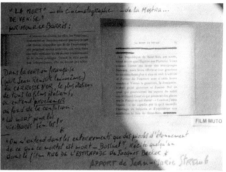

site direction and captures the close proximity between the substation and an adjacent building that belongs to a low-income, social housing complex. Both shots are completely devoid of any human presence. The soundtrack features the direct sound from the scene, which includes, in some takes, the persistent barking of a dog. Each segment ends with the superimposition of titles that bring the second shot to a conclusion and mark the transitions between the five segments. These titles read: "Gas chamber, electric chair."

What does this film have to do with Rossellini's work? The answer possibly lies in the final shot of *Europa '51*, a film about its bourgeois heroine's social awakening. After her son's suicide, she begins to recognize the world in all its structural inequalities, a kind of insight that also triggers her own social and civil decline from the interior sanctity of the bourgeois apartment to the social scarcity of the suburban slums to the confinements of an insane asylum. After she has visited a production line in a factory, she describes her vision as such: "I thought I saw convicts." As Gilles Deleuze has pointed out, this does not mean that the factory *resembles* a prison; rather, it shows *"how and in what sense"* the factory *is* a prison. As suggested by the superimposed titles at the end, *Europa 2005* depicts not a mere symbolic or metaphorical crime scene, but an everyday place that turned into a state-sanctioned execution chamber on October 27, 2006.

Straub's recent *Joachim Gatti* (2009) recalls *Europa 2005* in the sense that it explicitly addresses the issue of police brutality in France

Europa 2005, 27 October (2006, above)
The Death of Venice (2013)

but also in regard to the film's simple form, akin to a political pamphlet. In a similar style Straub made *La Mort de Venise* (*The Death of Venice*), a short commissioned by the 2013 Venice Film Festival for the *Venezia Future Reloaded* project which featured 70 shorts by 70 filmmakers in honor of the festival's 70th anniversary. Straub's response is to *not* make a film: technically, *The Death of Venice* is a still shot in the style of the letters he wrote for the 2006 festival. It is composed of handwritten notes and an excerpt from Barrès' novel *The Death of Venice*. In his own handwriting on the top of the page, Straub rearranges Barrès' title to: "La Mort *du cinématographe de la Mostra* de Venise" (which de-

Andrea Bacci and Dario Marconcini
in *Artemide's Knee* (2007)

The Witches (2008)
On location and on stage (rehearsal), right: Jean-Marie Straub

clares the death of cinema at the internationally renowned festival in reference to Robert Bresson's well-known use of the term "le cinématographe").[82] In addition, he quotes from the dialogue of Jean Renoir's *Le Carrosse d'or* (*The Golden Coach*, 1952) – "Death to the old and senile" – as well as a line from Jacques Becker's *Rue de l'Estrapade* (1953). Thus, Straub's proclamation is at once protest, act of mourning, and final tribute to a form of cinema that no longer has a place within the aesthetic, economic, and institutional framework of the festival.

Straub-Huillet's "movies appeal to people who regard 'defying Hollywood conventions' as evidence of artistic greatness," Tag Gallagher once wrote and then disagreed: "What is original in their style is authenticity, not anti-conventionality."[83] Indeed, two things have been consistent throughout their body of work (including Straub's own in recent years): first, an attentiveness to cultural traditions and, second, the production of cinematic images that are borne from the filmmakers' relationship to the material and the people they work with. In other words, their films do not attempt to use "new" rules in order to break or defy "old" ones, but on the contrary try to maintain traditional ones as far as they respond adequately to the material conditions of production. Even though Straub and Huillet are usually associated with the European new wave(s) of the fifties and sixties and the following post-'68 avant-garde movements, their specific creative methods followed the formal innovations of these "schools" and "movements" only to a certain degree. Their films are made with those

in mind who are not (yet) indoctrinated with the "right" way of making films, within and outside of the mainstream.

Danièle Huillet's death in October 2006 put a sudden halt to a lifetime of creative collaboration that had begun more than fifty years earlier in Paris when the two had started working on the Bach script together. Since then, Straub has continued to make films with more energy and fervor than ever, beginning in 2007 with the two films *Le Genou d'Artémide* (*Artemide's Knee*) and *Itinerary of Jean Bricard*. Both films epitomize aspects in Straub's solo work that continue certain traditions he established over the years together with Huillet. *Artemide's Knee* is a further adaptation of Pavese's *Dialogues with Leucò*, as are three other recent shorts, all based on individual chapters from the *Dialogues: Le Streghe, Femmes entre elles* (*The Witches, women among themselves*, 2008), *L'Inconsolable* (*The Inconsolable One*, 2010), and *La madre* (*The Mother*, 2011). With the exception of the latest, they were all filmed on exterior locations in the forests surrounding Buti.

Itinerary of Jean Bricard returns to the ethnographic-documentary aspects in Straub-Huillet's work. The black and white film is based on two interviews with Bricard, recorded by Jean-Yves Petiteau in 1994, and composed of landscape shots filmed on Coton Island and on

82 I am extremely thankful to Alexander Horwath for bringing the reference to Bresson to my attention.
83 Tag Gallagher, "Lacrimae Rerum Materialized," in *Die Früchte des Zorns und der Zärtlichkeit*, op. cit., p. 11. Republished online, *Senses of Cinema*, issue 37, October 2005, np.

the Loire. In the voice-over narration, Bricard remembers his childhood on the island, growing up during the German occupation, and then goes on to recall how the island slowly transformed and disappeared following various industrial and environmental changes in the decades after the war. Like the French segment in *Too Early, Too Late*, the landscape here attests only indirectly to any human presence. We see a few houses, cars, sheep grazing, and someone must be operating the boat driving down the Loire on which the camera sits to film the almost 15-minute long opening shot around the island. Danièle Huillet is credited as co-author of the film which had been in preparation for a while before filming was finally scheduled for the end of September 2006. However, plans changed when Huillet died in the following month and the project was postponed until December 2007.[84]

Itinerary of Jean Bricard is thus in many ways Huillet's final film. According to Straub, it belongs together with *Artemide's Knee*. Not surprisingly, both films deal with loss, solitude, and mourning. Whereas *Itinerary* grieves the destruction of a natural habitat and a place of living, *Artemide's Knee* is an ode to love, sacrifice, and death, a topic Straub highlights further through the two musical pieces he includes in the film. Mahler's "Abschied" ("Farewell" from *Das Lied von der Erde*) is heard over a few minutes of black at the very beginning, and a song of mourning by the Renaissance composer

Itinerary of Jean Bricard (2007)

Heinrich Schütz accompanies the final shot: a tomb or memorial stone on a clearing in the forest around Buti.

In recent years, Straub also circled back to Corneille and Brecht; in fact, he puts them side by side in the short film *Corneille-Brecht*. Similar to the earlier adaptations *Othon* and *History Lessons*, the two authors are aligned by their

84 Jean-Yves Petiteau and Sandrine Bridier, "Itinéraire de Jean Bricard," in *Leucothéa*, no. 1, April 2009, pp. 75–83

Barbara Ulrich and Giorgio Passerone in *Jackals and Arabs* (2011)

also establishes a kind of signature setting for Straub's recent films: the readings take place inside an apartment, often in front of a large window framed by two French doors which are sometimes open so that the street noise is included in the scene. There is often a stark contrast between the natural light outside and the relatively dark interior, since no artificial lighting is used inside. Consequently, the performer's faces and bodies often remain in the dark. The scenes are filmed in Straub's own apartment in Paris, a location he uses again in *Schakale und Araber* (*Jackals and Arabs*, 2011) and *The Algerian War!* (2014).

These interior settings form a sort of counterpoint to the forest exteriors around Buti in the Italian productions. Here too, a performer recites or reads from a text with minimal naturalistic props or costumes and within a space that is only loosely defined as a particular place. Inside and outside, domestic space and natural landscape – two poles that accomplish the same thing: to provide the filmmaker with a location where setting, lighting, and framing can be incredibly precise because the space itself is radically stripped down from any unnecessary embellishments. The filmmaker's own home as dramatic space also recalls the rehearsals for *Class Relations*, which took place in the apartment Huillet and Straub lived in while filming in Berlin and were captured by Harun Farocki in his documentary.

Jackals and Arabs marks Straub's return to Kafka. Perhaps even more than in *Class Relations*, political inequality is especially present on the level of dialogue and language. Barbara Ul-

shared interest in the politics and intrigues of ancient Rome. In the film the actress Cornelia Geiser recites first in French from Corneille's *Horace* and *Othon* and then in German from *Das Verhör des Lukullus* (*The Trial of Lucullus*, 1940). Aside from returning to two writers who had informed Straub-Huillet's career in their first years in Rome (between 1968–1972), the film

rich, as the jackal, speaks the hurtful and hateful lines with almost bureaucratic efficiency as she addresses the European traveler who remains off-screen (spoken by Straub, under his pseudonym). Giorgio Passerone, as the Arab, responds instead with great passion, addressing the camera directly, especially when he speaks to the European character off-screen. His final line, depicted in a medium close-up – "and how they hate us" – clearly situates Kafka's text, written in 1917, within a contemporary political context that is nurtured by xenophobia and discrimination in France, Europe, and beyond.

Aimé Agnel reading Malraux in *The Aquarium and the Nation* (2015)

In a relatively short amount of time, Straub has produced a remarkable number of films, averaging one to two every year. The shift from film to digital formats, first MiniDV and of late HD, may be one reason for his productivity. Turning to digital filmmaking provides not only certain economic advantages (without necessarily having to sacrifice a certain technological quality, although the Straubs in earlier times would have strongly objected to this), it also places Straub firmly within the technological context of contemporary filmmaking practices. In this light it is important to recognize that Straub (and Straub-Huillet's work by extension) remains a crucial figure in the international world of filmmaking, although the works are cornered within certain niches of the so-called "art film ghetto," as he and Huillet used to call it somewhat dismissively.

In 2011 Straub received the Jeonju Digital Project prize which funded the making of *An Heir*. The Jeonju Digital Project (JDP) is a production initiative organized by the Jeonju International Film Festival in South Korea and dedicated to the making of experimental narrative films. The recognition attested to the fact that despite Straub's continued focus on the European canon, his work remains vital to new generations of audiences, including outside of Europe and the Anglo-American hemisphere. Another case in point: the actor Aimé Agnel received the Mariko Okada Award at the Hiroshima Film Festival in 2015 for his recital of André Malraux's novel *Les Noyers de l'Altenburg* (*The Walnut Trees of Altenburg*) in Straub's most recent *L'Aquarium et la Nation* (*The Aquarium and the Nation*, 2015). An older gentleman sitting in a room at a table, reading from a manuscript: the fact that such a performance is today being considered for a film festival award indicates (at least one of) the subterranean effects that Straub-Huillet's approach to cinema may have had on international film culture over the decades.

The Aquarium also recalls a specific kind of filmic quotation Straub-Huillet had used in the

first *Cézanne* film: it ends with a long sequence from a film by Jean Renoir, two scenes from *La Marseillaise* (1938). *The Aquarium and the Nation* is not the only encounter between Straub and Malraux's texts and it is not the only film that uses excerpts from earlier films to compliment and comment on the overall thematic focus. *Kommunisten* (*Communists*, 2014), a 70-minute work, is partly based on Malraux's *Le Temps du Mépris*, which recounts a story of political imprisonment. Aside from the first three scenes with newly filmed material *Communists* features a number of quotations from earlier works by Straub-Huillet (*Workers, Peasants, Too Early, Too Late, Fortini/Cani*, and the two Empedocles projects). Lately Straub has also incorporated footage from the Bach film into his work, such as Anna Magdalena's French voice-over narration in *Dialogue of Shadows* and a musical performance from *Chronicle* in *Concerning Venice*. Among the "new" literary sources in his recent oeuvre are the writings of Michel de Montaigne for *Un conte de Michel de Montaigne* (*A Tale by Michel de Montaigne*, 2013), Georges Bernanos' novel *Dialogue d'ombres* (1928) for *Dialogue of Shadows*, and in 2009, for *O somma luce* (*Oh Supreme Light*), an excerpt from Dante Alighieri's *Divine Comedy*.

In the past few years, both Straub's new films and those he made with Huillet have experienced continued interest among audiences worldwide. Many of their works are regularly

Barbara Ulrich in
A Tale by Michel de Montaigne (2013)

part of special programming in art house cinemas and at international film festivals. Straub's new films have been shown in numerous places, not only across Europe and in New York, Chicago, and London, but also in South America (Brazil, Argentina, Chile) and Asia (South Korea, Japan, Mongolia). Larger Straub-Huillet retrospectives have taken place, for instance, in Vienna (2004), Paris (2007/08), Belgium (2009), Tokyo (2012), Brazil (2012), and Munich (2012/13) – and more and more of their films have become available on DVD, especially in France, Germany, Austria, and Japan.

In a recent comment section that accompanied an announcement of Straub's *Jackals and Arabs* in the online critical journal MUBI Notebook, the independent American filmmaker Jon Jost railed: "Illustrated literature. Very very minimalist 'cinema.' Political work done in a vacuum."[85] He went on to accuse Straub of misusing public funding to make his "pointless" and "very private films." His comment not only echoed some of the preconceptions that critics and audiences have leveled against Straub-Huillet since the time they released *Machorka-Muff* in 1962, but by placing the word "cinema" in quotation marks, Jost also identified himself as someone who is able to envision the cinema in only *one* way, a concept, precisely, that Straub and Huillet attempted to depart from. Instead, they tried to create films that captured their own encounter with other texts, works of art, authors, and collaborators. This is more than a mere private endeavor. Combining, in a sense, the intellectual rigor of a literary salon with the popular appeal of a *ciné-club* screening, Straub-Huillet's films give us not only a glimpse of their vast collection of literary and political writings, music, paintings, and, not to forget, films; but with each distinct cinematographic presentation of these works, the filmmakers open a space that invites and encourages us to discover (and rediscover) parts of their "private" collection for ourselves and alongside them.

Perhaps the writer Andy Rector said it best in his response to Jost. After highlighting a number of factual errors in Jost's account, he concluded: "The only true statement that Jost writes about Straub is that he continues to do 'Political work.' I agree. Whether it is done in 'a vacuum' is always up to us."

---

85 "Video of the day. Jean-Marie Straub's 'Schakale und Araber' (2011)," MUBI Notebook, https://mubi.com/notebook/posts/video-of-the-day-jean-marie-straubs-schakale-und-araber-2011

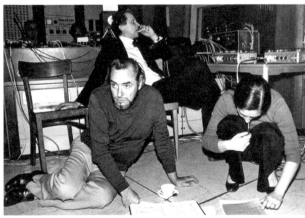

Moses and Aaron: in the Vienna recording studio
Photos courtesy of Bernard Rubenstein

Moses and Aaron: on location in Alba Fucense, Italy
Photos courtesy of Bernard Rubenstein

*Von heute auf
morgen:* on set
in Frankfurt
Photos courtesy
Karl Thumm

Sickle and Hammer, Cannons, Cannons, Dynamite!

Danièle Huillet and Jean-Marie Straub in Conversation with François Albera

JEAN-MARIE STRAUB: First of all, I have to say that using the "and" conjunction is always bullshit: cinema *and* history, cinema *and* literature, cinema *and* music. All this stuff is like the end of the world, an intellectual failure…[1]

Now, as for political cinema: I don't really know what it is, I know it less and less and I hope I never will. That's the first thing.

Secondly – leaving cinema aside – there is no political film without morality, there is no political film without theology, there is no political film without mysticism.

What does that mean? Well, for instance, it means that Anton Webern's music is more political than Alban Berg's, that Arnold Schoen-berg's music is more political than Alban Berg's, that Hanns Eisler's music is more political than Kurt Weill's. And to mention our most recent experiences, it means that a film such as Fritz Lang's *Fury* is much more political than *M*, contrary to what much of the left said about the rise of Nazism in *M* and *Dr. Mabuse*.[2] That may have been interesting for people like Sadoul[3] at a certain point in time but it's no use repeating it like parrots…

Which means that a film like *A King in New York*[4] is a great political film.

No political film without morality, no political film without theology, no political film without mysticism.

---

1 This interview was conducted on March 19, 2001 in Paris at the request of the Pompidou Center. It was to appear in a publication devoted to the theme of "Cinema and Politics" scheduled for June-July 2001. The person in charge of the event was Sylvie Astrik. However, the programmer of the series and the management of the Pompidou Center's Library of Public Information (BPI) demanded various cuts in the interview, specifically the parts involving the criticism of Jean-Louis Comolli and Dario Fo and the comparison between the industrial extermination of animals and the Holocaust. Jean-Marie Straub and Danièle Huillet refused any censorship for the statements they had made, reviewed, and assumed. The text was rejected by the very institution that had requested it. Jacques Rancière withdrew his contribution to the publication. The interview found a home in the August 2001 issue of the journal *Hors-Champ* that was sold during the Locarno Film Festival. It caused a series of rumors regarding the Straubs' "anti-Semitism" which briefly surfaced in an article by Olivier Séguret published in *Libération*. The newspaper denied the filmmakers any right of reply. Letters (signed by Louis Séguin, Anne-Marie Faux, and François Albera) were published in *Hors-Champ* no. 7, Fall–Winter 2001–2002.

2 Fritz Lang, *Dr. Mabuse, der Spieler* (*Dr. Mabuse, the Gambler*, 1922), *M* (1931), *Fury* (1936)

3 Georges Sadoul (1904–1967), influential French film critic and historian. Author of numerous books on filmmakers and film history including *Histoire générale du cinéma* (1945–1975), *Dictionnaire des films* (1965), *Dictionnaire des cinéastes* (1965) and studies on Lumière and Méliès.

4 Charles Chaplin, *A King in New York* (1957)

It also means – if you want to uphold that paradox, more of a provocation than a paradox in fact – that our own three most political films are *The Bridegroom, the Actress, and the Pimp, Chronicle of Anna Magdalena Bach* and *Moses and Aaron*.[5]

In *Moses and Aaron*, for the first time – since until then, aside from a subtitle in *Not Reconciled*[6] which was "Only violence helps where violence rules," we had always refused to let any message whatsoever slip into our films, we destroyed them as we went since we didn't want to inflict or impose a message onto the viewer: we didn't feel we had a right to do so. It so happens that thanks to *Moses and Aaron*, thanks to Schoenberg, suddenly at the end of the film there is a political message which sounds more and more relevant today: "Whensoever… your gifts had led you to the highest summit, then as a result of that misuse you were ever hurled back into the wasteland."

One day, at least fifteen years ago, by chance, we saw an open air screening of two films in Rome, Renoir's *La Marseillaise*, which is a magnificent film I know very well since I've seen it many times, and Griffith's *Orphans of the Storm*, a film I didn't know well at all, for I had seen it only once.[7] Well, that night, we suddenly thought that maybe the Griffith was politically stronger than the Renoir. So the strength of a political film has nothing to do with its ideology. Since then, we've had the opportunity to see *Orphans of the Storm* again at the French Cinémathèque – the screening was more or less annoying because it was the tinted print from MoMA (it could be that it contained things we

had never seen before…) – but we didn't have the same feeling again, we saw the film's Sadeian aspect instead, in short, its cinematic aspects. But I don't think we were mistaken when we'd seen it fifteen years before, after Renoir's film. Of course, one of the two films was devastating and the other one optimistic. You'd have to start from there and see where it gets you.

I now want to add one thing to my three earlier points and say that there can be no political film without memory.

By memory I mean that you have to take a firm stand against social democracy, reformism and all that junk, because the only truth these people refuse is the fact that there ever was a past, that things were different. They are completely anti-Marxian: the Marxian method *par excellence* consisted of searching all the way back to the Assyrians to find out how things were different, what had changed. And Marx was going further and further as he grew older. On the other hand social democracy keeps taking flight into the future; people don't even have the right to experience the present time anymore. They're being told that progress must go on, that there is no alternative but to rush down into the abyss of progress until disaster takes place. Growth is infinite, it can't be stopped. As

5 Danièle Huillet and Jean-Marie Straub, *Der Bräutigam, die Komödiantin und der Zuhälter* (1968), *Chronik der Anna Magdalena Bach* (1967), *Moses und Aron* (1975)
6 Danièle Huillet and Jean-Marie Straub, *Nicht versöhnt oder Es hilft nur Gewalt, wo Gewalt herrscht* (1965)
7 Jean Renoir, *La Marseillaise* (1938), D.W. Griffith, *Orphans of the Storm* (1921)

soon as a glitch occurs, the solution is for growth to resume, to multiply. Therefore we live in "the best of all possible worlds" and all that preceded us was necessarily not as good. This is exactly what Walter Benjamin rebelled against when he said that revolution is "a tiger's leap into the past."[8]

So a political film must remind people that we don't live in "the best of all possible worlds," far from it – something Buñuel already said – and that the present time, stolen from us in the name of progress, is going by and is irreplaceable… That they are ransacking human feelings like they ransack the planet… That the price people must pay, whether for progress or well-being, is far too high, unjustifiable. Not to mention that this system multiplies poverty – and let's not only talk about the Third World, but of the unbelievable things we've learned recently about England, the very cradle of capitalism! We should make people feel that the price is too high, that the only thing worth defending is precisely the passing moment, that they should under no circumstances take flight into the future.

So we must come back to what Benjamin said: revolution "is also reinstating very ancient

but forgotten things" (Péguy). Films that make you feel this way are political films. The others are *truffe*, scams.

What people call political cinema comes and goes with fads… When Comolli came to our place, in Rome, to prepare *La Cecilia*,[9] he had only one thing on his mind, an obsession. He wanted to convert us to the religion of aesthetics, the religious aesthetics of Monsignor Dario Fo. Which gave us *La Cecilia, Durruti*…[10] We must understand once and for all that Hölderlin is a hundred times more political than Jacques Prévert. That's it! Even if you haven't discovered yet that Hölderlin was the only European mind, at least the only poet, who, before the threat posed by industrialization and the materialization of that threat, had been able to invent the only thing that might save "Earth's children," as he called them, and "their cradle, the Earth" from catastrophe. He invented what I've called a communist utopia, while at the same time the finest minds of the era were rooting for progress and development.

FRANÇOIS ALBERA: What part may circumstances play in making political films and is it possible to escape them?

JEAN-MARIE STRAUB: *A King in New York* was truly made under the threat of McCarthyism, which was personally targeted at Chaplin among others.

Nothing is more difficult than making militant's films or militant films.

DANIÈLE HUILLET: When Eisenstein was shooting tractor commercials, it was forced upon him by the times he lived in.[11] But it's also extremely dangerous because if you're going to say that

8 Walter Benjamin, "Theses on the Philosophy of History," XIV [1940], in *Illuminations*, trans. Harry Zohn, New York: Schocken, 1968, p. 261
9 Jean-Louis Comolli, *La Cecilia* (1975)
10 Jean-Louis Comolli, *Buenaventura Durruti, anarquista* (2000)
11 Sergei Eisenstein, *General'naia liniia* (*The General Line*, 1926–1929), eventually released as *Staroye i novoye* (*Old and New*) with an industrialist epilogue dictated by the new Soviet policy

tractors are very useful you should also mention the damage they cause. When you see these commercials today, you can't help thinking that he didn't follow his work to its conclusions.

ALBERA: The tractor breaks down, don't forget. It takes Marfa's political will to start it up again... And in the original version of the film, before they changed the ending as well as the title, the tractor driver chooses to stay in his village. We find him in an ox cart filled with hay!

STRAUB: At least this is a Marxist position.

HUILLET: Eisenstein wasn't that dumb. There must, however, be a better way to urge people to rebel and take action besides falsifying reality in order to make them believe that they absolutely must rush down a certain path.

STRAUB: Militant films trap people into emergency again. And we are in an emergency situation: it's the outcome of the system that invented the gas chambers. The current emergency comes from British and French social democracies: the point is not to slaughter Jews anymore but hundreds of thousands of animals as a preventive measure to maintain market values. Some Jewish people may resent what I'm saying but I see no difference between this slaughter and the Holocaust; it's the same spirit, the same industrial system. "Der gleiche Geist," as Hölderlin would say, invented both the gas chambers and the system. After all there is no need to be a Hindu to figure out that a living being is a living being, whether it's a Jew or a sheep. In fact the Jews know this very well since they're the ones who invented the Easter Lamb.

To me Dovzhenko's *Arsenal* is a great political film – for I see a peasant named Ivan who, alone in an empty field, starts hitting his horse; he's too exhausted to stop, and suddenly you hear a voice telling him: "Ivan, Ivan, you got the wrong enemy!"[12]

There is a foreword to Webern's *Bagatelles for String Quartet* by Schoenberg in which he says: "Every gaze can extend to a poem, every sigh to a novel; but to express a novel with a single gesture, happiness with a single breath, such concentration only exists when sentimentality is equally absent."[13]

We could use this as a way to define political cinema: totally avoiding what keeps capitalism alive, such as inflation. If, at the aesthetic level, you practice the same inflation which fuels capitalist society as well as the world we live in, then there's no point; you're just grist for their mill.

Elio Vittorini said this in *Les Lettres Françaises* of June 27, 1947: "This is how I first became politically aware, looking at the spectacle of the society I lived in. This gigantic lie, I knew it well enough. They were all talking about some pre-Fascistic morality – the very morality from which Fascism itself had sprung. They were all leading back to Fascism – or, at best, to moral stagnation and sterility. They were trying to heal the wounds, again and again. They never attacked the disease itself. This is something you could see even if you hadn't read Marx. In

---

12 Aleksandr Dovzhenko, *Arsenal* (1929)
13 Arnold Schoenberg, Preface to Webern's *Bagatelles for String Quartet, Op. 9*, Universal Edition, Vienna

each historical era there is a given sum of possible means, a given reserve of means if you'd like. Now in every period of history, every available means have been used, no matter what the avowed morality of the era. Machiavelli already denounced such hypocrisy when he tried to awaken the Prince's consciousness to what he was doing. Today we have just discovered new means, those of atomic energy. Did we refrain from using them? No. Let us therefore postulate that an era will use every available means at its disposal. But such is the capitalist world that these means are used in total absurdity and hypocrisy. They are endless means, a chaos of means. We live in an era defined by a phantom morality."[14]

And this is from 1947, imagine what he would say today! Today there are not even phantoms left, nothing but a cynicism that won't even say its name…

My God! Great political music is not agitational or cabaret music, even if one may hear some very sarcastic and funny stuff in cabaret – even then, the only great cabaret songs are Schoenberg's, after all: there are three of them, they last barely ten minutes.

Where do you find great political music? Well, in Beethoven. In the same line of thought, Renoir's *This Land is Mine* is a great political film.[15] It's also a kind of agitational film, by the way. Or, on the other hand, *A King in New York* is a great political film in the same class as Beethoven's music.

What Comolli and Monsignor Dario Fo are doing is enormous in that it is already what Brecht was fighting against. Their aesthetic religion exactly mirrors our banker's mental attitude in *History Lessons*.

Brecht's banker in *The Business Affairs of Mr. Julius Caesar* is the guy who says: "Zum Volk muss man volkstümlich sprechen…" (To the common folk, one must speak folk-lorically). And Brecht later said: "Ich bin nicht tümlich, sagt das Volk" (I am not "lorical," say the "folk").[16] On the contrary, you must treat people as adults and help them to see and hear, since only when their senses are attuned will their conscience start developing. Contemporary society does the opposite by promoting restrictions, Malthusianism, the ransacking of feelings. The history of peasantry is the same. What did the burgeoning bourgeoisie do? Wage war on the peasants. The latest one of these wars ended thanks to the House of Lorraine, then one of the greatest French provinces. People on the other side of the Rhine needed its help to slaughter Alsatian peasants. Later they invented industrialization, intensive agriculture, fertilizers and everything else. What was it all about? Getting rid of the peasantry. In the meantime the bourgeoisie seized power in 1789 and now they're still trying to eliminate the remaining farmers with regulations and European standards.

So a great political film would not give statistics – we must not fall for that trend from the

14 "Une interview d'Elio Vittorini," interview with Jean Gratien and Edgar Morin, *Les Lettres Françaises*, no. 162, June 27, 1947

15 Jean Renoir, *This Land is Mine* (1943)

16 Bertolt Brecht, *Die Geschäfte des Herrn Julius Caesar*, Berlin: Gebrüder Weiss, 1957

other side of the Atlantic – but figures instead. In *Fury* there are figures: how many people have been lynched per week for such and such a length of time. In *Too Early, Too Late* we have included figures: a third of the population of such and such village is unable to survive... We found these figures in the *Cahiers de doléance* quoted by Engels.

ALBERA: In the controversy between Eisler and Schoenberg, however, the former raises the question of the addressee, the recipient as opposed to laboratory music. He chooses to conduct workers' choirs, to write stage and film music, songs...

STRAUB: Eisler didn't wonder about these things, he knew very well that on the other side of the wall his music was kept in the dark ("under the bushel"), as he puts it in his interviews with Bunge. He was lucky enough to live in another society, but what happened to him because of ideological reasons also happened to Schoenberg, for less overtly ideological reasons.

ALBERA: I was talking about the twenties, not the German Democratic Republic.

STRAUB: The quarrels of the twenties were not serious, they were friendly quarrels. Eisler rejected his master's "academic music" and Schoenberg advised him to focus less on politics and more on music. There were more biting comments – in a letter to Kandinsky for instance – which we removed from our film. But Schoenberg was also cozying up to a number of socialists in Vienna, such as Kafka. By the way, Benjamin told Brecht one day that Kafka was the Great Socialist Writer, whereas he himself was a Catholic writer. Which is not silly

at all provided you don't use the expression "Catholic writer" with scorn.

ALBERA: Is this related to what you called Rossellini's "Catholicism" in an old article?[17]

STRAUB: We all make youthful mistakes. In any case even that was censored since you couldn't use the word "Catholic" in *Radio Cinéma Télévision*, it became "Christian filmmaker." Above all you couldn't mention that he was a Catholic because it would put Catholicism in question. I only said this because of the fact that he'd made *Joan of Arc at the Stake*, that's it.[18] But fundamentally Rossellini was not a catholic filmmaker at all; he was a Voltairian filmmaker flirting with the Christian Democratic Party's ideology and he made propaganda work for De Gasperi. Therefore I was wrong in writing this and they may have been right to censor me...

Let's say that Brecht was interested in the idea of moral edification...

HUILLET: Whereas Kafka was not!

STRAUB: ...It's very clear in one of his strongest plays, *Saint Joan of the Stockyards*.[19] It's the practice of every Christian virtue, including resignation, charity and the others, before the discovery, as Johanna says, that "Es hilft nur Gewalt, wo Gewalt herrscht" ("Only violence helps where violence rules"). She's had it...

17 Jean-Marie Straub, "Does Rossellini's Work Have Christian Meaning?," *Writings*, New York: Sequence Press, 2016. First published in *Radio Cinéma Télévision: hebdomadaire catholique des auditeurs et des spectateurs* [Paris], no. 265, February 13, 1955

18 Roberto Rossellini, *Giovanna d'Arco al rogo (Joan of Arc at the Stake*, 1954)

19 Bertolt Brecht, *Die Heilige Johanna der Schlachthöfe* (1929–1931)

At the risk of being a bit pompous, political cinema is the one that ends with saying: "Sickle and hammer, cannons, cannons, dynamite!"

This is where we're at, there are no alternatives, we shouldn't be afraid of saying this. But when it happens, it will be very costly.

The world we live in and the humanity we're part of are ill, terminally ill even, because of this system and this spirit! Therefore if there's still a possibility for a political film to be made, we'll need a period of convalescence. So the people who make this film, with that ending, will not stop there. They will add more; by asking Beethoven for a gift, they will add the idea of convalescence.

And if one of these two aspects were to be missing, it would not be a political film.

You must never fear contradictions, otherwise you end up doing what the society we live in does: working at manufacturing robots or legless cripples. Robots on the moral and intellectual level and cripples on the emotional level. So you have to go against the grain.

I don't mean to turn my nose at agitational films – which by the way I have no right to do – but I think it would be even harder to make them, and if you're going to do it by following the fads, it's really not worth it.

HUILLET: It's not worth making such films out of anger, either. Rage. Fury.

STRAUB: Because as Brecht said, rage makes your voice hoarse. "We had no choice, but you must know that we have hoarsened our own

voice." But if we can afford to hoarsen our own voice, you have no right to do it to people whose voice is already hoarse for other reasons... And above all we have no right to make them believe that by applying such and such a miracle formula upon leaving the theater, everything will improve, etc... "How simple! Why didn't we think of that..." In the words of Delahaye the good guys are always behind the camera and the bad guys in front of it.

ALBERA: There is, however, something in your films that has to do with internal necessity. They are anchored in a sense of place, of time. Can we still call it an emergency?

STRAUB: It is different every single time.

In The *Bridegroom, the Actress, and the Pimp*, the emergency came from the fact that we were leaving Germany at a time when the police were axing the doors of universities, that we had been treated like dogs for ten years trying to make films, particularly *Chronicle*, which was the first project, and the other two: *Machorka-Muff*[20] and *Not Reconciled*. We were leaving, that was it, and at that time what was later called "May 68" happened, and there was a slight lag. We were away, and I had no intention, like Cohn-Bendit and others, of coming back to France to end up in jail for a year. So we were away, experiencing a certain nostalgia, even if the May events were after all partly a "chienlit," [damn mess] as this joker [De Gaulle] put it... By the way, he had to leave office after the failure of his last referendum a couple of years later, this much is clear, because he had requested crumbs: participation. This was enough to get de Gaulle liquidated! You could laugh

20 Danièle Huillet and Jean-Marie Straub, *Machorka-Muff* (1962)

at "participation" back then, now it's back in vogue: workers and employees becoming share-holders... However that was enough to send him back to his home in Colombey, back to "milking his cows" to quote Anna Magnani in *The Golden Coach*.[21] So much for circumstances...

HUILLET: Of course we react to circumstances as individuals. But that's not a good enough reason to insert these individual reactions into a film, it would bring us back to sentimentality.

Look: when Cézanne painted card players, God knows nobody would have called it political. And suddenly you go to a bistro in Froidcul, above Moyeuvre-Grande in Lorraine, and in this café you see a reproduction of Cézanne's *Card Players*.[22] It's a strange feeling. So you ask the guy behind the counter and he goes: "Yeah, I just liked it..."

STRAUB: It may not be directly political, but I'm fascinated by the fact that Cézanne is entirely a realist. I've seen people playing cards for twenty years down by my place. Socially, they are miles apart: they wear jeans, there are a few punks, some are former metal workers, but when I take a good look at how they stand, sit, or move, it's amazing to realize what a realist Cézanne is. Well, political films start with realism. The kind of realism which, Brecht says, starts with the particular, and only once well rooted in it rises to the general. He said: "Let's start with the unique item, buttoned up / linked with the general."

Furthermore in our personal little biography – our "career" which has been progressing tremendously since we can't even get funding

from the CNC any longer! – we've had a switch-back career. Our film chronology doesn't match the chronology of the projects: *Chronicle* should have been the first and *Moses and Aaron* the second, but that's not the way it happened. *Machorka-Muff* was never supposed to be the first.

Making films politically also means doing what Cocteau said: "You must cultivate whatever it is you're being criticized for: it is what you are."[23] We made *Chronicle* the way we wanted and not the way we were advised during the ten years we waited to be able to shoot. First with Curd Jürgens, secondly by giving us twice the budget provided we hire Herbert von Karajan... And we told everyone to get lost because we wanted Gustav Leonhardt who wasn't a star in the cultural industry, at a time when everybody, including musicians and musicologists, would say "What? Who?" and we had to write his name on a small slip of paper. Same thing with Nikolaus Harnoncourt. As for poor [August] Wenzinger, Paul Sacher's assistant in Basel, he wasn't any better known. They are in the film, together with Leonhardt, and since this had no box office appeal in the cultural industry, no one would give us a dime. But if you make a film politically, which is to say by organizing what you do, that means ignoring casting agents or the box office that tell you what to do and not to do if you want to get funded: without Depardieu, no film, without the latest

21 Jean Renoir, *Le Carrosse d'or* (*The Golden Coach*, 1952)
22 A series of five paintings depicting card players which Cézanne painted in the 1890s
23 Jean Cocteau, *Cock and Harlequin*, trans. Rollo H. Myers, London: The Egoist Press, 1921

starlet, no CNC money, you can't go to Cannes, etc… Otherwise, on top of not making films politically, you don't get to do what you want. Brecht himself already said so in his foreword to *Kuhle Wampe*: "Organization cost us much more than *die künstlerische Arbeit*… the artistic work itself."[24] According to him it was because the film was a political one.

That's another answer to the original question: if you want to make political films, you have to organize them yourself instead of relying on institutions, even friendly ones, even dear friends who help a little…

HUILLET: There always comes a time when you have to say: "Hell no! That's the way it's going to be and if you don't want it we'll take care of it ourselves." Even writing on a flyer: "This film was turned down by the Selection Committee of the Cannes Festival," which is the absolute truth, can start a deluge of recriminations from friends: "What are you trying to do? Rock the boat?" And we say: "Listen, if you don't want any trouble with your milieu – since after all, it's your milieu, not *ours* – we'll take care of it ourselves."

And finally, since "Straub" has become something of a brand name, since they like us, they give in. But it's still a struggle.

STRAUB: Making a film politically means using the lenses you need, the amount of film stock you need, shooting in the order you need, with the equipment you need. It means paying the

crew at least union wage, at the beginning of each week rather than at the end, and not accepting ridiculous budget restrictions at a time when commercial production as a whole is wasting money in incidental expenses and useless stuff while they force filmmakers, even prestigious ones like Bertolucci, to use black and white for dailies or to limit themselves to two lenses. It happened to us with *Lothringen!* When we asked for a Primo zoom lens they told us it was way too expensive for a short. But we know what and where we want to shoot and what it means technically and if you don't want to fund it then we'll pay for it ourselves.

HUILLET: The meaning of the word political is also that of freedom. If I feel I must say this about the Cannes festival, it's not out of revenge or to rock the boat in any way because it won't rock anything at all. I do it because some of the younger people must know…

STRAUB: … that there is no artistic freedom in a capitalist system! That even the so-called cultural institutions only serve the cultural industry of French cinema, and when they chance upon a film that doesn't cast the latest starlet or Depardieu or God knows who else, they're not interested.

HUILLET: When we designed the posters for *Not Reconciled* and we brought them to the person in charge at the theater where the film was released she told us: "Ach! Das ist nicht unser Geschmack" ["It doesn't suit our taste"]. We said: "Very well, we'll pay for them ourselves." And at the time we were completely broke and we had to find a thousand marks. Of course you could say it's still a privilege: a working stiff cer-

---

24 Slatan Dudow (director), Bertolt Brecht and Ernst Ottwald (writers), *Kuhle Wampe, oder: Wem gehört die Welt? (Kuhle Wampe or Who Owns the World?*, 1932)

tainly can't do that. But strangely enough, when you listened to the longshoremen in Saint-Nazaire, at the time of the great strikes, what they talked about was freedom, being able to not go to work if they want to, being able to change location, "just being able to change wharves whenever we feel like it!" This was the longshoreman status they were fighting for. It's quite extraordinary that they should be the ones talking about freedom…

STRAUB: Toscan du Plantier is proof of it![25] I will only mention two colleagues of ours, both held in high esteem, as they say. One is Syberberg, and the other Benoît Jacquot. Here are two young fellows – they're not granddaddies, so they should still be able to resist – who both got scammed twenty years apart by the same system: Toscan du Plantier's. Syberberg wanted to record Wagner's opera live, in sync sound, and had to give in because Toscan unloaded a recording made in Monte Carlo onto him: he had it in his sound archives and so it was less expensive. So he made a film that has nothing to do with what he wanted![26] This is not a political way to proceed.

The same thing just happened to Benoît Jacquot, who I believe is shooting *La traviata*.[27] He worked with a sound engineer for a few weeks or months since he had sworn to use sync sound and suddenly he had to switch to playback.

ALBERA: Did the morality alluded to earlier define an individual stance?

STRAUB: No, I quite simply meant that we live in a world where morality is replaced by cynicism. Cynicism on the walls, in slogans, com-

mercials… You could even go further and call it the liquidation of public morality.

Morality also means knowing how horrible informing is. Now the Italian government passed a law to encourage informers. The result was that [Bettino] Craxi and [Giulio] Andreotti went to the committing magistrate several times a month to tell him: "Wait! I'll inform on another pal of mine from the Party…" It was supposedly meant to fight the Red Brigades and even some of the Red Brigades informed on people because the law provided they would benefit from mitigating circumstances if they did. They were led to believe they would be treated more leniently. They did the same thing with the Mafia and all the mobsters started informing like crazy. The only one who didn't is the old guy, the oldest of the mobsters, who's been in a New York jail for almost forty years. They went to him and said "So? What have you got for us, any names?" And he went: "Names? I won't give you a single one. I'm here, doing my time, and you won't get a single name from me…"

Here is a guy who still had a sense of morality.

The government that passes such a law is a training ground for cynicism: it demoralizes the nation. When D'Alema[28] – by the way when

25 Daniel Toscan du Plantier (1941–2003) was a French film producer. He was the director-general of Gaumont from 1975 to 1985 and the president of Unifrance from 1988 to 2003.

26 Hans Jürgen Syberberg, *Parsifal* (1982)

27 Benoît Jacquot, *Tosca* (2001). The film is based on Giacomo Puccini's *Tosca*, not Giuseppe Verdi's *La traviata*.

28 Massimo D'Alema (b. 1949), Italian politician who served as Prime Minister from 1998–2000

our Angela [Nugara] from the Pisa branch of the Communist Party was selling *L'Unità* on Sunday mornings, "Please, ladies and gentlemen," when she brought the money back, the secretary was D'Alema – so, when D'Alema, not so long ago, after a few weeks of the war on Milošević, made a statement published on the full front page of the *Messaggero di Roma*: "Usciremo più forte di questa guerra!" ("This war will make us stronger!"), that's what I call public demoralizing.

It's a statement full of dizzying cynicism and unfathomable stupidity… Furthermore he should have known that no victor ever came out stronger from his victory! Just look at the Vietnamese. To say a thing like this after you went to the Gulf War like a bunch of lackeys, and when you participate in the war against Milošević, that's a lack of morality.

As for financial morality, it's even worse. The morality of the "New Economy" is quite simply that of the supermarket.

It's striking when you look at workers restoring a courtyard, they bring down the falling stucco, then paint over with four layers of cement, then another kind of cement, two layers of paint, etc… for six months. You're struck by the professionalism involved. When they see this, the bourgeoisie, who are not capable of such professionalism in their work any longer, should either laugh in the face of such naïveté or confess to their priests and ask for forgiveness.

There is only one irredeemable crime in the Gospel, the crime against the Spirit. Well, it's been a long time since our society has not only committed this crime but practices and cultivates it day in and day out.

ALBERA: What is the role of theology as you mentioned it earlier in the definition of political cinema?

STRAUB: What I call theology has to do with God or the gods. One must realize that with civilization, the peasants invented gods. One must realize what the invention of monotheism means, that it is very difficult to do without gods. That it will still take us centuries to get there and that doing without gods like the Voltairian bourgeoisie did is certainly no solution. It's only cynicism. And you must add that theology – going back to Péguy once again who said: "I am not pious, says God" – means helping people shun phony feelings, the practice of sentimentality and piety. Which is exactly the *ersatz* in use; in this respect you could again acknowledge that Goebbels won the war. We live in an *ersatz* society, on every level: water, air, feelings, morality, God, everything. Which is why we invented sociology and shrinks to replace confession.

ALBERA: Are cinematic representation and mimicry part of the same simulacrum, *ersatz* ideology? And is your insistence on direct sound and the materiality of objects and locations connected to theology?

STRAUB: You could say it another way: "Back to reality! Back to reality! Back to reality!"

ALBERA: In your relationship to texts there are several approaches: some are used in their entirety, others in fragments… Is this part of a "political reading"?

STRAUB: Corneille: it's the play, I only changed

one word. Pavese: these are six dialogues out of many more. Then the second part is only one layer of the novel. The latest film, it's thirty-nine pages out of four hundred, or *History Lessons*: thirty pages out of three hundred, etc...

It's different every time, but the idea is always to avoid descriptive texts. I guess I've always hated literature! The guy who starts trying to illustrate Balzac's or even Kafka's descriptions in his film has failed from the start. What interests us is not what the writer sees: you can't illustrate what he sees, that would only hinder the viewer's imagination, and you can't know what he sees. What he saw in the words can't be translated into images. Cinema is not descriptive – which is what Orson Welles did, by the way... What interests us is how the text is embodied in human beings, dialogues, not the plot. What interests commercial productions is to buy a plot. Then you won't find a single one of the author's words in the film but you've bought yourself a very expensive plot! We take the words and keep them as they are. In the Kafka we kept almost all of the dialogues, ninety percent or more of the first chapter, the only one he published. For all the following chapters, sometimes there are only three or four dialogues, since his friend Max Brod, who had promised him to destroy everything, had betrayed him. Apart form the first chapter – "The Stoker" – Kafka considered the work unfinished and in fact it isn't finished, you can feel it. It's no accident if I kept almost everything in the first chapter whereas in the others I kept very little, and tried cautiously and very slowly to figure out which parts resisted and which

parts Kafka would certainly have left in. One makes mistakes; it's the "Stalinist censor" in me, but I'm fairly sure. In all humility...

In the letter to Kandinsky, we censored a few of Schoenberg's paragraphs or entire sentences, every time there's black. But, what interests us is the writer's words. From Hölderlin's *Empedocles* we kept almost everything other than the last scene since it's barely a draft. These texts do not interest us as literature, otherwise we would have read everything. I'm very far from having read all of Corneille however, or all of Kafka, Hölderlin, Böll...

It's a bit different with Böll and also with Brecht: we built something completely different from Brecht's novel, but every word is his own and we kept what we felt were the most solid parts of the economic analysis and the strongest literary parts.

We're not interested in competing with literature, but in pushing it to the other side – in going back from Gutenberg to the times before the printing press, when there was no TV, when people gathered around the fire at night to tell stories. Let's call it going from a writer-based civilization to an oral tradition that has been totally repressed.

ALBERA: Walter Benjamin devoted a text entitled "Der Erzähler" (The Narrator) – which he translated into French himself – to the contrast between oral narratives and novels at the level of the exchange of experiences, of community and solitude.

STRAUB: Really? You know him better than I do. There's no doubt, however, that writers are condemned to individuality in our capitalist society, and in others too. In the alternative social experiment, on the other side of the wall, in the so-called popular democracies, artists were still condemned to individuality even when they dreamed otherwise. If they weren't individuals, they couldn't be artists. It is the same society that doomed Lenin to becoming more and more of an individual – this is what he meant when he said his political work didn't allow him to listen to music. In the world we live in, since human beings are limited and the world is what it is, you can't do three things at the same time, not even two. We're doomed. This is what Schoenberg meant, or close enough, when he told Eisler, "Instead of getting involved in politics so much you'd better concentrate on your work." It's a provocative statement, a bit... à la Poujade,[29] but it's a fact, you can't simultaneously be involved in politics and make so-called aesthetic objects or works of art or films.

HUILLET: You can let things mature, however. You were talking about circumstances earlier. When you're obsessed with massacres and peasants as we were and still are, when you finally make *Too Early, Too Late*, it's precisely because all of this resurfaces in a certain way once it's found the appropriate form.

STRAUB: This is the form we chanced upon through a triple encounter: a first trip to Egypt for *Moses and Aaron*, followed by a second trip, and then the return to Italy and the discovery

of a book written by two people who had spent a year in one of Nasser's concentration camps...
HUILLET: Plus the *Cahiers de doléance* from which Engels takes his figures. All of this, the French part of the film, ends with the inscription "The peasants will revolt," partly masked by a pole. When the film was completed in 1981, they told us peasant revolts were all but impossible. Now you can see what's happening.

It's the opposite of films that follow fads...
STRAUB: Even in good faith! At the moment I like *A Film Like the Others*[30] better than some films that were made by the group calling itself Dziga Vertov. Dear Jeannot would certainly not agree since he'd rather conceal this film, but that's my opinion. Here's a guy who tried to be humble at a very precise moment in time and just tried to monitor something without imposing his grid of interpretation. He was really within the moment and within the fashion of the time, but he functioned without being grist for the mill of fashion.

ALBERA: I believe I discovered *Chronicle of Anna Magdalena Bach* in Locarno in August 1968, when Buache picked it up along with other militant films from the May 68 movement, which brought out some contrasts. I remember Jean-Luc [Godard] telling us he had issues with the film in relation to Germany, what came after Bach, Nazism, etc...
STRAUB: That's because he had trouble looking at a Marxian object. I don't say Marxist, but Marxian, since, as we discovered much later, the intellectual process of the film is really the same as young Marx's. So the film is Marxian by chance. Still, that's not what he told us. He told

29 Pierre Poujade (1920–2003) was a French book seller and politician who instigated an anti-tax movement that came to be known as Poujadism in the early 1950s.
30 Jean-Luc Godard, *Un film comme les autres* (1968)

me: "I should really talk to you about your film." And then he said…

HUILLET: "Well here we go: during the first part I thought 'No! This won't do at all…' During the second part I thought: 'Yes! This is what we should do,' and during the third part once again 'This won't do'…"

STRAUB: What he meant was: you should add a voice-over, either less or more content plus a voice-over providing political comments on the situation. At first he thought: "You should have done it," then during the second part: "No, no, he's right not to do what I would have done" and during the last part: "No! No! I was right all along…"

I wasn't saying anything, I was a bit shy and I didn't feel like joking. I looked at him and asked with a faint smile: "So what would you want me to do, put 'Everything is political' at the end?" And he said: "You see, maybe that would have been enough."

Now, there already is a film that ends with the words "Everything is grace." And since I would have never made *Chronicle* if it hadn't been for *Diary of a Country Priest*, for different reasons, I wasn't going to end a film with "Everything is political" just to please Jeannot!

Furthermore everyone knows that everything is political. So it's just crap.

I believe political films are made by people who don't try to be too clever…

HUILLET: "Don't be clever for the sake of being clever," that's the title of a small Glenn Gould piece we heard this morning…[31]

STRAUB: When Lang, who was half Jewish, from Vienna, after years of silence, after ending up on the other side of the Atlantic, tried to assimilate American speech and reality as he was capable of doing, with daily patience, through dictionaries and research, finally made *Fury*, there you have it: the film does not convey the impression of a gentleman trying to be clever, but rather the crystallization of x years of experience, work and discoveries. When Chaplin made *A King in New York*, he wasn't trying to be clever. When the author of *Durruti* makes *Durruti* you can see the result for yourself. It becomes mental vacuity, *deficienza*… So what's the point?

There is so much bullshit in the world that making a political film should at least not add more to it. There are times even when you could say that one should work hard enough to be able to make a film that isn't harmful to people – since everything they buy, everything they're told is harmful to them.

First, you should work on yourself, to avoid self-complacency, and, ultimately, so-called originality.

ALBERA: Isn't the prospect of reinstating an oral culture one of the political projects of your films?

STRAUB: It sounds very flattering the way you just put it, but you shouldn't believe it's done systematically or consciously, it came about slowly. It's meant to help people dream of something that's been stifled, eliminated by industry in general and the cultural industry in particular… To hear something that not only relates to

31 Huillet is likely referring to Glenn Gould's *So You Want to Write a Fugue?* (1963), which features the lyric "But never be clever for the sake of being clever."

the sense of community, but also which they knew nothing about. When people sent letters to a German TV station after seeing *History Lessons* without knowing it came from a novel by Brecht, asking, "What is this text? What's the title?" we were rather pleased. For the same reason I said the Bach film was dedicated to farmers in the Bavarian forest who never had a chance to hear Bach in their catholic churches, who never went to a concert. Or – which is when all the Bonitzers and all the others accused me of militant voluntarism – that Corneille was made for the workers of Renault.[32]

HUILLET: Take almost illiterate people such as Angela [Nugara], or tilers, bricklayers or even construction engineers and give them a text like the one in our latest film…

STRAUB: Whether or not they know Vittorini, it's not a factor at that point!

HUILLET: … and they start claiming this text for themselves – because quite frankly all the stuff about the alienation effect and so on is pretty silly! There can be no film in which the text is more a part of the people than our films! Of course, since there are months of work, the film enters their nervous system. It's a kind of popular culture, the kind everybody was talking about during the infamous "Pop" years, the one nobody achieved because it's too difficult, too lengthy.

STRAUB: Since the French film industry, even at

an artisanal level, will not allow it because "Time is Money".

HUILLET: It's the caste system; you're up against a wall. When Cannes turned *Workers, Peasants* down, it wasn't only because we didn't have Depardieu or the latest starlet. It was because they knew immediately – they have an infallible sixth sense for these things – that our protagonists are not among the "beautiful people," that they don't belong to their world. Aumont said this much, what they talk about "is not interesting."[33] They're not interesting people. These are the people we make popular culture with, which is difficult since they're working people, they have a day job. Therefore if things work out it's because they really want them to, they want to discover something else. On the other hand they show up at 6 p.m. for rehearsal exhausted and it's hard. But they still bring solutions that none of the "beautiful people" would have imagined since they're not trapped in a preset mentality.

ALBERA: It sounds like young Marx's version of communism, when people hunt in the morning and write poetry in the afternoon…

STRAUB: It would be great!

HUILLET: Hunting!!!

STRAUB: The "bastard" only said that because he would never have been caught hunting….

ALBERA: He was thinking of the Neolithic age, gathering, hunting, pottery…

STRAUB: Beyond the Assyrians again!

HUILLET: What makes cinema great is the collective work, something it shares with theater, except that theater is made by an elite. They don't try to work with people from the street,

32 Pascal Bonitzer (b. 1947), French film critic, screenwriter, director and actor
33 Jacques Aumont (b. 1942), French academic and film theorist

it's even worse than in film! Collective work is what makes it fascinating. That's where the relationship with politics lies.

STRAUB: But you don't suddenly get the urge one fine morning, you don't go: "Why don't we go back to oral culture?" It's the same for anybody in any similar line of work. It comes perhaps from *Farrebique, Diary of a Country Priest* or *The River* or even, why not, from Gance's *Captain Fracasse*, since it makes you feel that something's happening…[34] Or from a couple of Michel Simon's lines in *Boudu Saved from Drowning*: "What do you care, you old fart!"[35]

ALBERA: What was your evolution since your first films regarding the question of professional versus non-professional actors?

STRAUB: In *Not Reconciled* we really had one actor who couldn't spell his name and two or three more who couldn't read the newspaper. In the Kafka film it was a bit different but there's still one: the doorman with his lantern. But it's really a mix since on the other hand you have Mario Adorf, Alfred Edel, Laura Betti and Libgart Schwarz.

Some of the films have a mix of actors and non-actors, others don't, but it wasn't designed this way, it depends on the characters. Obviously for the part of the Uncle in the Kafka, it was better to have an actor rather than a hick, it would not have worked out. The actor is an *ersatz* bourgeois in a way, but a bourgeois wouldn't have been right either in this particular case. And in *Not Reconciled*, the mother after all is not an actress; she's an old lady we met in our elevator, she's not an intellectual. We found Ferdi on a street in Cologne; he was throwing his bicycle on a truck that his father was loading with barrels of Dortmund beer.

ALBERA: Did you pick him because of his looks?

STRAUB: When you choose actors, it's always because you fall in love with them for one reason or another.

The old lady we met in the elevator was always grumbling when it broke down; two hours later we offered her the part, but we had previously made a little trip to the Berliner Ensemble. We were set on casting an actress for the part of the old lady so she could "recite" the past, a bit like the lines uttered in *Pierrot le fou*: "Forty centuries marveling at us!" or "The parade of centuries…"[36] In her case it wasn't the centuries but the economic crisis and the arrival… of the people called upon to solve it. We had seen [Helene] Weigel a few times on stage at the Berliner Ensemble, in three or four of Brecht's plays, we liked her as a woman and as an actress so we went to see her, a year before the shoot. She read it and suddenly told us: "Why do you insist on having a professional actress play the part? Actors are always bad in films! Why don't you try a non-professional?" So we said: "Thank you very much."

So you see, we had to meet someone that legendary to begin with so we could be told that all actors are bad, we really didn't expect it from her. Someone like Libgart Schwarz or Peter Stein would never have told us something like

34 Georges Rouquier, *Farrebique* (1946); Robert Bresson, *Journal d'un curé de campagne* (1951); Jean Renoir, *The River* (1951); Abel Gance, *Le Capitaine Fracasse* (1943)
35 Jean Renoir, *Boudu sauvé des eaux* (1932)
36 Jean-Luc Godard, *Pierrot le fou* (1965)

this. That proves that Weigel had certain meaningful personal experiences and had learned something from living and working with Brecht. It's the last thing we expected from her. Incidentally after ten minutes we thought she was too young for the part...

What people see isn't the film, the reality of the matter of the film; they always project themselves onto it, at least these people. It's very hard to perceive only what's on the screen, what you hear and what you see. It took me twenty years and sometimes even now when I see a film I hadn't seen for twenty years I still realize I hadn't really "seen" it the first time. So when people see Angela Nugara in *Sicilia!*, they like her, "Oh, she's breathing with her stomach... and since she's a mother.... She's great, great!" But the same woman in the other film [*Workers, Peasants*], they don't like her at all, even though technically she's made a nice little step forward. She had been thinking on her own, for two years between the films... She thought a lot about it without us making speeches, she'd reflected for two years between the two films. We didn't have to argue, it just happened and she had made progress, instinctive progress you could say.

But no one notices it: they're not interested. Even Vittorio [Vigneri], since he doesn't have a bicycle anymore and isn't pedaling anymore, it's the same thing, they're not interested.

I was struck when I saw my first films after my amnesty in France, after eleven years in exile, for instance *La Bête humaine*, at the French Cinémathèque.[37] It was already a time when only students would attend screenings, our colleagues didn't come anymore or very seldom, nor would the educated bourgeoisie. So there were these more or less tardy students, and when Renoir came up on the screen, with his acting style, they started sneering at him. And I thought: "My God! Not much has changed!" since after *La Chambre noire*, my film club in Metz, I started a small 16mm film club at the university in Nancy, with two screenings per month. When we showed *Les Dames du Bois de Boulogne*, guys were constantly sneering until someone would shut them up.[38] Even during Hitchcock's *Suspicion* or Dmytryk's *Give Us This Day*.[39]

Translated from the French by
Jean-Pierre Bedoyan and George W. Antheil,
with revisions by Ted Fendt

The translation was first published in
Die Früchte des Zorns und der Zärtlichkeit.
Werkschau Danièle Huillet / Jean-Marie
Straub und ausgewählte Filme von John Ford,
ed. Astrid Johanna Ofner, Vienna: Viennale and
Austrian Film Museum, 2004

37 Jean Renoir, *La Bête humaine* (*The Human Beast*, 1938)
38 Robert Bresson, *Les Dames du Bois de Boulogne* (1945)
39 Alfred Hitchcock, *Suspicion* (1941); Edward Dmytryk, *Give Us This Day* (US release title: *Christ in Concrete*, 1950), script and dialogue by Ben Barzman. Made in England after Dmytryk's involvement with the "Hollywood Ten" forced him to leave the country. Jacques Doniol-Valcroze and Claude Roy wrote separate long reviews of the film in the first issue of *Cahiers du cinéma* (April 1951).

Danièle Huillet, Jean-Marie Straub, and
William Lubtchansky on the set of *Class Relations*

At Work with Straub and Huillet

Thoughts and reflections from their collaborators

Danièle Huillet and Jean-Marie Straub's collaborators have been asked far too rarely to comment on their work. What follows are remarks, arranged thematically, from a number of the actors, actresses, and technicians who have worked with the filmmakers over the years.

These collaborators are, in the order of appearance: **JEAN-PIERRE DURET**, sound engineer on, among others, *Sicilia!, Workers, Peasants, These Encounters of Theirs, Artemide's Knee, Oh Supreme Light*. **WILLIAM LUBTCHANSKY**, director of photography on, among others, *Every Revolution is a Throw of the Dice, Class Relations, Black Sin, Antigone, Sicilia!, Itinerary of Jean Bricard*. **ASTRID JOHANNA OFNER**, actress, *Antigone*. **CORNELIA GEISER**, actress, *Corneille–Brecht, Dialogue of Shadows*. **DARIO MARCONCINI**, actor, *These Encounters of Theirs, Artemide's Knee, The Mother*. **ANDREAS VON RAUCH**, actor, *The Death of Empedocles, Black Sin*. **GIANNI BUSCARINO**, actor, *Sicilia!* **ANGELA NUGARA**, actress, *Sicilia!, Workers, Peasants*. **GIOVANNA GIULIANI**, actress, *The Witches*. **LIBGART SCHWARZ**, actress, *Class Relations, Antigone*. **URSULA SCRIBANO**, actress, *Antigone* (as Ursula Ofner). **GIOVANNA DADDI**, actress, *These Encounters of Theirs, The Witches, The Inconsolable One, The Mother*. **ANDREA BACCI**, actor, *From the Cloud to the Resistance, These Encounters of Theirs, Artemide's Knee, The Inconsolable One*. **ADRIANO APRÀ**, actor, *Othon, Fortini/Cani*. **RENATO BERTA**, assistant cameraman, *Othon, Moses and Aaron*, and director of photography on, among others, *History Lessons, Fortini/Cani, The Death of Empedocles, Workers, Peasants, Oh Supreme Light, Dialogue of Shadows*. **CHRISTOPHE CLAVERT**, assistant, director of photography, and editor on, among others, *Europa 2005, 27 October, Corneille–Brecht, An Heir, The Inconsolable One, Communists, The Aquarium and the Nation*. **BARTON BYG**, actor, *Class Relations*, and subtitles for *Class Relations, The Death of Empedocles, From Today Until Tomorrow, Sicilia!*

If not noted otherwise, these remarks are excerpted from telephone and e-mail conversations conducted between September 2015 and January 2016.

T. F.

TRUST

JEAN-PIERRE DURET: Jean-Marie and Danièle are not people who really say what they want. They trust you. [...] We have a lot of room for interpretation. It's artisanal work. Everyone brings what they have. There was never any direction about how to work or what to do, except one single thing that Jean-Marie told me through the intermediary of Danièle: the off-screen voices were more important for him and had to be just as present as the on-screen voices. That's the only direction they gave me. After that, they trusted me. It was my work, it was my interpretation, it was my way of belonging to their cinema.

WILLIAM LUBTCHANSKY: The first time I worked with the Straubs in black and white was on *Class Relations* (1983). I asked Jean-Marie, What kind of black and white? He responded, "Do what you did with Rivette in *Duelle* but in black in white." That was enough of an indication since *Duelle* (1976) was a film with a lot of contrast – in color, but it could have been black and white. After that, we didn't say anything else about the lighting.[1]

ASTRID OFNER: The entire school was gathered in a light-flooded room, there was a wide open view through the windows up to Grunewald. Everyone was around a big table listening to Jean-Marie Straub who was talking about Antigone. I came very late, when everything was almost over. But Jean-Marie looked at me and asked if I lived in Berlin. And then very simply, if I wanted to be Antigone. In the Schaubühne production and later in the film they were planning to shoot in Sicily. Danièle had gone out of the room and as she came back, she saw me talking to Jean-Marie. I noticed her joy and later I learned that she had thought independently of Jean-Marie that I could be their Antigone.[2]

REHEARSALS

CORNELIA GEISER: Each time we try a bunch of things. We set a length of silence at the end of the verse or the line and we look. Often we keep it. We decide something, then we do exactly the opposite, then we do a third or a fourth thing until we've found the right rhythm. He makes suggestions or the actors make suggestions. It's extremely free. I think that's the fundamental idea of the rehearsals that's stayed with me. It's extremely free and nothing is taboo. We can always, always question what we're doing. He can be pretty radical in his questioning.

DARIO MARCONCINI: Their way of working was simple and rigorous. There was neither psychology nor identification with the characters. [...] Rehearsals lasted 3 to 4 months in their room for 3 to 4 hours almost every day.

ASTRID OFNER: Danièle always sat on the floor with the text in her hands or on the floor in front of her. I stood before her, reciting nervously and uncertain, while Jean-Marie paced back and forth behind us, a cigar in his mouth.[3]

ANDREAS VON RAUCH: I tried not to leave any long intervals between practices, so I repeated the text wherever I was, in the bus or taking a walk. That certainly must have amazed some people who thought I was crazy... I tried in this way to internalize the mental process of the text. But there are sections in Hölderlin's text that are hymnic. There, thoughts are repeated, and it is not easy to separate them from each other. There was no plot structure to hold on

---

1 Lubtchansky in *Positif*, no. 475, September 2000, p. 80

2 Ofner in *Recherche Film und Fernsehen* no. 1, 2007. "The entire school" refers to Berlin's *DFFB (Deutsche Film- und Fernsehakademie)*, with Ofner among the students, at its old location in the building of the TV station SFB (Sender Freies Berlin).

3 Op. cit.

Jean-Pierre Duret (with Danièle Huillet), Cornelia Geiser in *Corneille–Brecht*,
Dario Marconcini in *The Mother,* Astrid Ofner in *Antigone*
(clockwise from top left)

to, and yet I had to differentiate between the smallest nuances.

The Straubs helped me with that a lot. They gave me suggestions for amplifications and variations in a given segment of text. Our procedure was that I would learn the text in advance in Hamburg, then travel to Rome to the Straubs and we deepened what I had learned.[4]

GIANNI BUSCARINO: During the rehearsals, which lasted months, the directors were very demanding: you couldn't make a mistake twice and at the end of each rehearsal, Huillet would give each actor a list of the mistakes they'd made. They could be related to movement, breathing, etc. It was incredible, she didn't forget anything.

ANGELA NUGARA: During a rehearsal in the theater, I made a mistake and didn't look down. Danièle said to me: "Angela you didn't look down" and I asked, "But you were turned away facing the room and couldn't see me, how did you know?" She replied: "Angela, that's my job." She was a genius.

INDIVIDUALITY

JEAN-PIERRE DURET: It is up to each of the actors to interpret it with their own voice, their own history, all while following a metric that Jean-Marie has worked out. That's what's required. Once this rhythm is respected, that's it. That's why it isn't important to them if it is whispered or not, if it is strong or loud. The particularity of each person is invented based on his own life experience.

ANDREAS VON RAUCH: That is in the pronunciation, for one thing. I say König [King] with ik on the end, a hard g, while the handbook for stage pronunciation says it has to be Könich with a soft ending. I lived in Vienna for two years and perhaps it comes from there. Critias speaks in a slightly American-flavored Viennese, and the Barattas have a Rhenish melody in their speech. That could be investigated using criminology: the mother, who is from Bremen, studied with a girlfriend who was from the Rhineland, and she must have passed this intonation on to her children, who grew up in Rome.[5]

GIOVANNA GIULIANI: The clothing, which Danièle would usually take care of, became our proposal or we would simply wear our normal clothes. For example, since I came down to the rehearsals from Mount Serra, where I was living, on a road that ran along a stream, I would wear galoshes. The character of Leucò whom I quote onstage and in the film is therefore wearing galoshes.

LIBGART SCHWARZ: The accentuation of the text was principally pre-determined by them or changed by them during rehearsals. Nevertheless, I always thought that it didn't need to sound artificial. I was interested in making the accents seem quite normal and organic. And since they never questioned this, I did it that way. But I would not have considered discussing it with them.

4 "Andreas von Rauch in conversation with Harun Farocki," in *Die Früchte des Zorns und der Zärtlichkeit*, Vienna: Viennale and Austrian Film Museum, 2004, p. 107–108
5 Op. cit.

Gianni Buscarino and Angela Nugara, both in *Sicilia!*,
Andreas von Rauch in *The Death of Empedocles*, Libgart Schwarz in *Class Relations*
(clockwise from top left)

SPEECH

JEAN-PIERRE DURET: The vowels, the consonants, the *e*'s, all of it – very, very important. It's a total respect for language. Not manipulated language but language where every word has its own weight. That's the work on the sound. There's nothing spectacular to it. It's about respecting the weight of things, voices, what is said; respecting the weight of language.

RHYTHM

GIOVANNA DADDI: The pauses – my agony – were already marked on the text we were given. Only, for *The Witches* Straub and I worked together for one week sitting under a big tree with the noise of a stream in the background. The diction was essential. I was amazed that two non-native speakers could hear when accents and conjunctions were not precise.

URSULA SCRIBANO: The breathing, the little movements of head and eyes, the pauses – none of this was written in the text. It was Danièle who really seemed to be kind of obsessed by finding the very right combination of word and gesture, of where to put the pause and how long the pause has to be.

ANDREA BACCI: Once you learned the text by heart, the work began of integrating the pauses and the correct diction, which were also based on the characteristics of the person playing the role. In other words, the rehearsals – beyond learning the text as best as possible – were also necessary for setting the pauses which the directors kept, varying the lengths for short pauses that corresponded to one slash and long pauses that normally corresponded to five slashes.

CORNELIA GEISER: When it's written in verse, the end of a verse is already a strong indication that you can pause, breathe or not breathe, hold a silence or a longer or shorter interior tension before moving on to the following verse. The text is already cut up. In *Corneille-Brecht*, twice, we were dealing with a text written in verse. But the kind of verse wasn't at all the same. And in *Dialogue of Shadows*, he had cut up the sentences himself so that there were longer or shorter lines that were treated like verses, but it wasn't verse.

ANDREAS VON RAUCH: In Hölderlin's text there is much that is musical. One should perform Hölderlin and hear him. I found it extraordinary, almost strange, how much Hölderlin uses metrics, the order of stressed and unstressed, to add to the so-called meaning of his verses. Let's take the line, "Und Schönes stirbt in traurig stummer Brust nicht mehr" [And beauty dies in the sorrowful silent breast no more]. At first I was tempted to work out the psychological aspect and said, "in *traurig* stummer Brust," – I emphasized "sorrowful" and I remember that Danièle Huillet immediately insisted on following the rhythm exactly and thus giving the two words equal weight: sorrowful and silent. Only then does the actual meaning become apparent, namely that sorrow is silent, that it cannot be spoken.

The Straubs always pushed for following the rhythm, and I noticed how, dictated by the rhythm, the special meaning of the verse construction was unearthed.[6]

6 Op. cit.

Giovanna Giuliani in *The Witches*, Ursula Ofner (Scribano) in *Antigone*,
Giovanna Daddi in *The Mother* (clockwise from top)

Andrea Bacci in *The Inconsolable One* (left), Adriano Aprà in *Othon*

GIOVANNA GIULIANI: Behind the pronunciation of each word, the rhythm, the weight of the front, middle or back of a syllable, there was a logic of historical meaning that Straub knew how to explain to us. He gave us the courage to pronounce words without being rushed or hurried or casual, but to finish pronouncing a word through to the last letter, to stop and listen to the effect, the echo. He taught me to give myself permission to breathe without hiding it, that it was my right to breathe simply and without shame, without needing to show off my ability to hold my breath and be indifferent to the air…like in certain virtuoso performances; to create emphasis by bursting out with my voice, to exclaim without fear of being vulgar or indiscreet, to ask with the intonation of a question that isn't hidden, but explicit and eager; not to make a question mark elegant but to use it with a clarity that demands an answer. Sometimes, on the contrary, he would have us slip quickly through a sentence, almost with rage, as if by closing it we would never again have to open our mouths. At other times, he would instead suggest sweetness. We would obtain a tone, however, without ever describing it with an adjective, without anticipating the color of the result, only following the thrust of a musical *tempo*. It was the courage to hold a position without unnecessary casual or embarrassed gestures; courage to stare, allowing heard and spoken words to pass through oneself, without changing the direction of one's gaze or letting it be distracted; courage to pronounce the awkward or ridiculous sense of a word.

SCORES

ANDREA BACCI: Straub and Huillet's way of working was very precise and meticulous. Phrasing and grammatical mistakes were not accepted and the original punctuation in the text was not considered, only the pauses that they indicated.

JEAN-PIERRET DURET: It's wonderful to see the scores at their apartment. We call them scores. They're no longer texts, they are musical scores. They don't talk about character psychology at all or that a scene must be performed one way or another. What they have in mind, first, is the language, respect for the language to an infinite degree. The vowels, the consonants, everything has to be heard, the language has to be respected in an extraordinary manner. It has to be respected as rhythm too. Jean-Marie draws on the text with periods, commas, all of the timing.

ADRIANO APRÀ: Talking fast was how I recited the text naturally. The Straubs marked the pauses, the emphases, etc. on the script, as they would continue to do. For them, the annotated script was like a musical score. Each actor had a different rhythm and they were the conductors.

ANDREAS VON RAUCH: They always had me read first, then there was a conversation about the divisions, in which I was only tangentially involved. Then I would mark the text on the page: arcs to indicate which lines of verse belonged together, slashes at the end of the line – one slash for a short pause and four slashes for the longest – then I would read the piece of text aloud again, and that would perhaps produce yet another change. There were changes until just before the shooting. For example, those that arose from problems with breathing or because segments of the same length should be avoided: not to have groups of four occur three times in a row. But even in that case there are exceptions.

CORNELIA GEISER: We concentrate solely on the text, which is very, very intense work. It's a little like when one learns to perform a piece of music, working on the rhythms, on the intonations, on the pitch, on the volumes, on what could be called 'inner tension,' on consciousness and the meaning of words, on clarity of diction.

GIOVANNA DADDI: I became aware of the importance of precision – the gaze, the clarity of the words and giving up character psychology in favor of the pleasure of the pure words and the truth.

POSES

DARIO MARCONCINI: You have to keep your body still in an uncomfortable position, which demands physical control to hold during the performance. Special attention is given to the eyes and their direction, which must turn to precise points in space. The head also makes small, occasional movements to follow the eyes. The body is not always still.

GIOVANNA GIUILIANI: For the positions, he let us choose the starting one and then he might interpret and clarify it. He would have us choose the step to the next position. It was important that we were comfortable, feeling like roots in the ground, without making any muscular effort to hold the position, arriving at it comfortably.

PRESENCE

JEAN-PIERRE DURET: Often, when I saw the films recorded by [Louis] Hochet and the shots with an 18mm lens, a 16mm lens, very wide shots, I'd ask myself how he did the sound. And the truth is that it was with the three meters of space above the actors. It's not very complicated because the voices have a presence. The voices exist. The voices are not documentary voices and the actors don't whisper. That's not part of Jean-Marie and Danièle's cinema. Jean-Marie and Danièle's cinema is based on rhythm.

The voice is what is closest to us. It's what best represents us. The voice is the memory of our entire life, of where we're from. When you hear someone, you can understand a lot of things if you are really hearing them. I really believe the voice is the naked soul.

In *A Visit to the Louvre*, there was a considerable amount of work. I think they worked with this girl for three months. Again, on the rhythm, on the musicality of the text. This girl who has a voice that is so personal to her, took charge of it in such a particular manner. I think it brings to life the images of the paintings and the memory of this conversation the two painters had together. The voice itself was easy to record. The appropriation of the text by the person is so personal that you don't really need to do a lot.

GIOVANNA GIULIANI: I met Giovanna Daddi at the rehearsals for *These Encounters of Theirs*. What amazed me about her, like the other actors, was that they looked more themselves onstage, in those steady, stable positions that helped them pay attention to their breathing, as opposed to making them the authoritarian and ungrateful bosses of it. They seemed to me, therefore, more themselves in that way, in that suspension from the frenetic and rushed everyday present (Dario Marconcini, for example, in his farmer outfit) as opposed to after the rehearsal, when they would leave the theater with their jackets and their elusive, everyday expressions. As if Straub and Huillet's work was a big act of love that gave back to the people on stage some lost dignity like that belonging to animals, stones, tree trunks, wind and streams. Through the artifice of the text, the scenic space, outfits made for working and not performing, the final result was more natural than nature and you could see how, for example, Andrea Bacci would be in those conditions. And, I'll stress, the Andrea whom Straub and Huillet bet on seemed more like Andrea and more absolute an Andrea than the one in everyday life. You could see him as he really was. All this amazed me and I never tired of studying it, of trying to understand it.

CORNELIA GEISER: We rehearsed for an extremely long time before the shoot. As a result, I think that Bertrand [Brouder] and I attained an enormous amount of freedom that allowed us to integrate the elements outside. There are birds singing, the wind, farm machines passing by, planes, and so on. There are a bunch of variables outdoors that make it so that when you've rehearsed inside – since we never spoke the text outside before the shoot – you really have to be extremely well prepared to be able to film.

URSULA SCRIBANO: I loved performing the play out in nature in the theater in Segesta. I had the feeling that this play was finally where it really belonged. No feelings of claustrophobia, only wind, sky and birds singing, mixing with the wonderful words.

FRAMING

RENATO BERTA: Then there's the work of framing the shot. That was always very interesting. We'd spend hours discussing how to frame a shot. It was very exciting. Jean-Marie would look through a viewfinder. Then we'd verify with the camera. We'd choose the focal length based on the point of view. As soon as we'd say, "this is where the point of view is," we'd put the camera there.

For *Empedocles*, there were days where we had five characters speaking and we'd find a single camera position and the shots based on the lenses we had. We didn't want to move the camera while filming the five characters. There were wide shots, then closer shots. I remember that we spent an entire day framing them. But it was always very practical. It wasn't something that went off in every direction, it was very reflected.

Straub, contrary to what one might imagine, is a person inside something very thought through. What are you doing the moment you're framing something? You have to ask yourself what you'll leave out and what you'll keep in. Sometimes what was kept out of the frame was almost more important. But the method was connected to a praxis. We worked in a rather pragmatic manner. It wasn't theoretical.

LIGHT

WILLIAM LUBTCHANSKY: With the Straubs, on *Too Early, Too Late*, we were shooting exteriors all over France. We had about two shots a day and we would film the same thing from morning to night. The light evolved throughout the day and then they'd choose during the editing. It was a fifteen day shoot that could have been done in three if someone else was doing the

scheduling. We had wonderful moments, black skies in Brittany...[7]

RENATO BERTA: Over the course of the day, the light would move. There was an evolution. We let the natural side of the light come in. I tried to follow all the changes of the light with the exposure. Sometimes we'd put a little something on the faces, if necessary.

DIRECT SOUND

JEAN-PIERRE DURET: I knew that Hochet always used one microphone, or most of the time, in any case. The first time, I was trembling, but on the following films, when I understood more and was more confident, I put the microphone very, very far from the voices in order to be able to mix the sounds of the birds at the location with the voices of the characters. I could amplify them enormously since I put the microphones so far away that I didn't hear the voices anymore.

RENATO BERTA: And Danièle would listen to the sound right away and then decide if we'd do another take or not.

JEAN-PIERRE DURET: Danièle listened to absolutely every take. With a lot of concentration. Everyone kept quiet. We'd shoot and then she'd listen, Jean-Marie pacing back and forth in front of her, waiting. It was a very religious ritual. And when she finished, she'd say, 'It's good,' and we moved on.

They work with the truth of the moment. The reality of the locations, the accidental eruptions of sounds act on the recorded material, act on the way the actors or non-actors speak. They are directly related and become one

7 Interview with Patrick Blossier and William Lubtchansky, www.afcinema.com/Entretien-avec-Patrick-Blossier.html?lang=fr

unique and indissoluble whole, a piece of time. Direct sound is a block of time. The moment when one adds things, it's no longer exactly the same. The intentions are different.

FLEXIBILITY

RENATO BERTA: At one point in *Fortini/Cani* there's the same pan twice. We'd agreed on the movement, and then I said to Jean-Marie: "Listen, I start with a static shot and then I do the pan and I stop on the same shot. If you want to cut on the movement, it might be interesting to start with the static shot, I'll do the pan, I won't stop, and I'll do another so that you can cut right on the first frame where it starts. I'll do the pan twice and you can choose the best one." And when they saw this, they decided it was good like that and they kept it twice. That was not planned at all! That's why they are very attentive people and very close to their work. You just have to suggest things that go in the direction they're looking and not make big speeches about light.

CONTINUITY

JEAN-PIERRE DURET: The principle of the Straubs' films is that there is no continuity. Continuity is considered in larger terms. That's to say, it's not the illusory continuity of someone who's going to make it seem like the sequence is happening on one train on one day and that there's the same time continuity. There's no cheating. That forces the viewer to be much more inventive, to participate more, I find.

CHRISTOPHE CLAVERT: Jean-Marie chooses the takes he likes best, then we do an assembly and

then we work on the transitions from one shot to another. That work is purely rhythmic. It's done in two stages: first, what is being said in the text, do we need to cut immediately, does time need to be left in relation to what is said in the text in the shot before and after? And then, in relation to the material that is in the dailies, meaning if there's a noise, if there's something that happens in the background of a shot, an actor's gesture. Each shot is an autonomous block in his films. It's the relationship of one block to the next and not the continuity of one shot to another as it would be in other films.

JEAN-PIERRE DURET: In a train if you move the microphone, the noise of the train changes too. So I had two microphones [for *Sicilia!*]. It was rather complicated because the background noise was imposed. What's complicated is that in the editing, the noise of the train is constantly changing. But, in the end, I'd say that takes part in the editing. The sound itself creates a rhythm to the image and the cutting.

RE-MEMORIZATION

JEAN-PIERRE DURET: All three of us got together for four days and we transferred the sound to 35mm mag stock in a lab. We listened to every take again. This took a long time. Based on this, we could see if there were problems or not. But above all, before attacking the editing of the picture, it was a form of reorientation through the film's sound. It was a form of editing in a way. Or, not of editing but of re-memorizing the material. It was the material they were going to edit. And the sound already said a certain number of things about the film.

Barton Byg (right; in the background: Thom Andersen) in *Class Relations*,
Renato Berta and Jean-Marie Straub on the set of *Joachim Gatti*,
Jean-Marie Straub and Christophe Clavert on the set of *Concerning Venice*
(clockwise from top)

SUBTITLES

BARTON BYG: In keeping with the aesthetic of the films, Danièle's key word for the subtitling was 'simplicity.' She wanted to convey only the materiality of the words. In English, more than in French, it is possible to find linguistic correspondences with the origin, sound, and form of the German words, even if the meaning would be somewhat strained. She encouraged me to go in this direction, as long as it did not become too 'Shakespearean.'

The quest to return to an author's original words applied to the smallest detail. For instance, the *Class Relations* screenplay had Delamarche remark of Brunelda, "She is sitting on the sofa, but perhaps she is asleep," but Danièle corrected the subtitle: "no 'but', that was Max Brod!" Also, whenever I suggested an English 'equivalent' for a saying or phrase unique to German, Danièle would emphatically reject it. One of her parenthetical notes, typed with the red half of the typewriter ribbon: "no equivalents, please; awkward is better." Danièle's concern was always with the material specificity of the words: "It's better to be awkward than inexact." But once she had made her comments on my drafts, she never questioned my choices or made changes after the fact.[8]

DIGITAL

CHRISTOPHE CLAVERT: I think Jean-Marie wanted to shoot a lot faster, without having to figure out whether or not there was money. To have a certain amount of production freedom. I had my camera, which I think he liked especially, even in spite of the rather abominable quality of

DV. It was about being able to do something freely, economically speaking. Then I bought a 5D and we moved on to that. I know that on *Oh Supreme Light* where Berta worked with a RED and in 16:9, he found it to be all the inconveniences of shooting on film, in terms of the cumbersomeness, without the quality of film.

I don't think he's fundamentally changed how he works. With miniDV, there was a zoom lens, so he did the framing directly with the camera. With the 5D, I have three lenses, so depending on what he wants in terms of the shot and the place where we are, he has a choice between a 35, a 50 and an 85. In general, he rather likes the 35. There are films with all three, there are films where there's only one. There's only the 35, for example, in *Dialogue of Shadows*.

LUXURY

RENATO BERTA: Danièle was always saying, "film stock is our only luxury," meaning the fact that we really shot a lot. We'd have at least four takes that were really good.

JEAN-PIERRE DURET: If we do a lot of takes, it's not in order to forget the thing we're doing. If we do a lot of takes, it is because we're waiting for something from the moment. Plenty of things happen and at a certain moment, a miracle comes. Something happens that won't happen again. In any case, not in the same way.

ADRIANO APRÀ: I remember a very long shot that needed, over the entire day, something like

8 Byg, in the DVD booklet of *Class Relations*, Edition Filmmuseum no. 11, Vienna–Munich, 2006

36 takes. It's me and Anthony Pensabene (who kept forgetting his lines) and Plautine at the end. It's the most difficult shot in the film. There were only two good takes. One time I said "cut," thinking that I'd made a mistake. It wasn't true but we were nervous and Straub forgave me.

PRINCIPLES

GIANNI BUSCARINO: I'll remember how they loved each other, their love for animals, the cigarettes and papers Jean-Marie would pick up from a piazza or a street. I'll remember a quiet assistant going to buy milk for their dinner and the herring roasted during the filming and then saved for dinner. I'll remember their economic efforts to realize 'pure art' without compromise, their bitterness and resignation towards an often deaf, blind, and mute society. I think that Danièle and Jean-Marie found in some way an island in Buti where they 'cultivated' art and gathered friendship and love.

BARTON BYG: Looking at the world on a walk with Danièle was to see it with new eyes, to become aware of its concreteness and history and beauty in a very attentive and pleasurable way. She was fascinated with the signs of human activity down the alleys of South St. Louis – the garden walls, the plantings, the animals. She did not dispute my protests that things were quite run-down, as in much of the U.S., and simply ugly. "But not only ugly," was her subtle corrective.[9]

GIOVANNA GIULIANI: From the work that came before our meeting, Straub was already familiar with the real main characters, the natural subjects: the clearing near the river, the two stones we sit on. And he studied them to understand how to treat them better, how to watch them and stare at them in the way that would most respect them. Because as Danièle would say, there is only one way to shoot each object and it is useless, after the Lumière brothers, for example, to invent other ways to shoot the arrival of a train in the station… And we would place ourselves as supporting actors without disturbing, without controlling or interfering through useless actions, gestures or noises, but learning to 'stay' or 'remain' among them and at their side: a stone, a tree trunk, a fly, a mosquito would enter our score and we would enter theirs.

JEAN-PIERRE DURET: One day we were all eating at noon… And Jean-Marie always ate very little. We were eating and then at one point, I see Danièle looking out a window with a big smile. I looked and Jean-Marie had been talking to a homeless guy outside for an hour. Sitting on the sidewalk with him. That's an image that has left a mark on me because usually when we're talking to a homeless person or someone who's asking for something, we look down at them. He had sat down. He'd been talking to him for an hour and he was looking at him with such a smile, saying "Voilà, mon homme." And at the end of the conversation, Jean-Marie gave him a bill. Not coins, it was a bill! I don't know how much money it was, but it was a bill in any case. A lot of money. That's the Straubs for me.

9 Op. cit.

John Gianvito

Tough Love

Reflections on Some Ideas and Practices of Danièle Huillet & Jean-Marie Straub

My first screen encounter with the work of Danièle Huillet and Jean-Marie Straub was in May 1976 at the now long-vanished Theater Vanguard in Los Angeles. The screening was *Moses and Aaron*. I still have the flyer as a memento. Not owning a car at the time I somehow managed to persuade a few fellow students at the college I was attending (CalArts) that this was something worth checking out. I don't quite recall their reactions but one thing was clear – I wasn't disappointed. Despite having spent way too much of my youth in the dark watching movies (albeit of a fairly wide breadth of expression), I can still conjure up how strikingly different this experience was. While I was sure I wasn't *getting it* all, from the first shot of Moses on I was intrigued, if puzzled, by the unusual framing and atypical pace, intuitively appreciative of the film's near lapidarian edits, and – having had some advance awareness of what lay ahead – pleased that I was more or less able to follow the libretto. Certainly I hadn't yet come to understand the ways in which the film both respects and radicalizes Schoenberg's opera, but the richness of the struggle between ideas and their messaging, between mysticism and persuasion, and the very contemporary image of a public caught between two dueling would-be leaders, was co-

herent. Reflecting back, the impression that lingers most is the degree of concentration the whole experience demanded (although *commanded* is likely the more appropriate word).

This many years later, I have seen the majority of the films of Straub/Huillet, quite a number of them multiple times. I remain neither a scholar of their work nor a disciple. My own cinematic journey leads where it will and, much like dear Chantal Akerman used to say, "I have no theory. It's whatever I need." I've little doubt that were the 'Straubs' to have seen my films they'd have things to critique. It matters not (besides, I do too). What does matter, a great deal actually, regardless if they ever thought that it might mean something to anyone else, is the example they set.

I've no wish to be hyperbolic, and others will have their own way of measuring such things, but in my experience it's been relatively rare to find two individuals as resolutely loyal to the courage of their convictions (and to each other!) as Jean-Marie Straub and Danièle Huillet. What I've often found and continue to find interesting is not just how these convictions are revealed in the films themselves but how they inform virtually every aspect of the way these films are made. And this is already enough. This is useful. While one can only surmise the sacrifices and

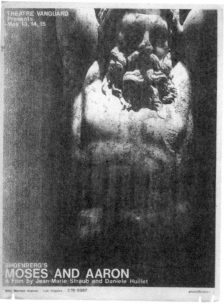

Water into blood: *Moses and Aaron*
Theater Vanguard flyer

toll paid for so doggedly standing by their beliefs, the fact that for some 43 years Jean-Marie
Straub and Danièle Huillet succeeded in doing
it *their way* (as remains the case for Straub solo)
is for me nothing short of exhilarating. Whenever I have the opportunity to see one of their
works or read one of their texts or interviews, I
am reminded again and again that one can always work harder, always reflect more deeply,
continually demand more of oneself and of
those around one (and not just as a filmmaker).
It's been, at varying times, both tonic and
provocation. Thus, in the spirit of trying to be a
bit useful myself, here is a short compendium of
some of what I've taken away, and some of
what I continue to ruminate about.

GENEROSITY
Among pronouncements that Jean-Marie Straub
has made through the years that have had resonance for me in my own practice is the remark
that, "We make our films so that audiences can
walk out of them." No doubt detractors can
gleefully seize upon such words to say, "Well, if
that's your goal, you're pretty good at it!"

"Films that pretend to be made for the
masses," Straub argues, "are really made to
keep them in their place, to violate them, or to
fascinate them. Consequently, these films are
made in such a way that they don't give people
the liberty to get up and leave. Our films are
made so people can leave if they want." Huillet
goes on to clarify that it is not that they are
happy when people walk out of their films, "but
it is clearly a risk, for those who leave might
have been moved if they had seen more." The

strength of such an approach is the refusal to
partake in a certain fascism of conventional cinematic narrative which is all about keeping you
in your seat, about controlling your eye, about
orchestrating your emotions, about not afford-
ing space to think. For Straub and Huillet there
is intrinsic generosity in denying the employment of traditional dramatic devices designed
to 'hook' viewers and hold them captive.
Come, look, listen…or not.

*"I don't think a film should impose at all the ideas
of a director. He should propose ideas that people
can accept or refuse. He shouldn't impose them, no
matter what they are. Even if he wants people to participate in his ideas, he must present them in radically different ways than in commercial films. If he
used the same selling methods to sell his so-called
beautiful and good ideas, it's an absurd contradiction, because these methods only hit you on the head,
and even if you are hit on the head with the best of
intentions, it still hurts.*

*If I show you an audio-visual object which deaf-
ens you or blinds you under the pretext of convincing
you of a beautiful and good idea, I can't even convey
the idea to you because it must be perceived by the
senses I have just diminished. So, I will succeed only
in making you more unconscious."* [JMS]

~

Paying it forward. Recently I happened on the
anecdote that at the very beginning of his career,
Jim Jarmusch met Straub and Huillet on the fes-

1 *Film Forum: Thirty-Five Top Filmmakers Discuss Their
Craft*, edited by Ellen Oumano, New York: St. Martin's
Press, 1985

tival circuit and they donated some black and white negative film stock from *Class Relations* to help him complete *Stranger than Paradise* (1984). This again reminded me of Glauber Rocha generously giving prize money he'd just received for *Terra em transe* (*Entranced Earth*, 1967) to help the completion of *Chronicle of Anna Magdalena Bach*. It also conjures up memories of the screening I attended of the U.S. premiere of *Too Early, Too Late* at the old Collective for Living Cinema in New York. Unannounced in advance, Straub and Huillet decided that they would first show the audience a short Super-8 film from a young filmmaker they'd met earlier in the day (based in New Jersey, though I've never been able to ascertain his name), which they proceeded to project twice and discuss before going on to their own projection. And while Straub and Huillet regularly and emphatically extolled the values of a very classical pantheon of directors including Renoir, Dreyer, Ford, Mizoguchi, Stroheim, Lang, Godard and others, they also made it a point to draw attention to the work of past and contemporary filmmakers far less championed including Jean Grémillon, Luc Moullet, Frans van de Staak, Peter Nestler, Jean-Claude Rousseau and Yann Tröller.

WORK/ETHICS (ON MAKING FILMS POLITICALLY)
"...if you make a film politically, which is to say by organizing what you do, that means ignoring casting agents or the box office that tell you what to do and not to do if you want to get funded: without Depardieu, no film, without the latest starlet, no CNC money, you can't go to Cannes, etc... Otherwise, on top of not making films politically, you don't get to do what you want. Brecht himself already said so in his foreword to Kuhle Wampe: 'Organization cost us much more than die künstlerische Arbeit... the artistic work itself.'"[2] [JMS]

As they don't tend to expound on the difficulties of their labors, I have but a glimpse of the travails that Straub and Huillet went through in order to make the films they made in the ways they wanted to make them. Glimpses of years of planning and preparation, of exhaustive driving, walking, hitch-hiking in search of the proper location, of countless, pain-staking rehearsals with their casts for months on end, sometimes a year or more in advance of the proposed project. There is the example of *Chronicle of Anna Magdalena Bach*, a film they waited ten years to make and not entirely due to lack of funding. In fact, at one point they were offered twice the requested budget provided they cast the more renowned Herbert von Karajan as Bach instead of insisting on Gustav Leonhardt. But they insisted, and waited, until they could make their film. One comes away with the distinct impression that across their entire body of work there isn't a frame out of place, or a decision in pre-production, production, or post-production that wasn't thoroughly considered or that they now regret. How many of us, if any, can say that about our work?

~

2 "Sickle and Hammer, Cannons, Cannons, Dynamite! Danièle Huillet and Jean-Marie Straub in Conversation with François Albera," see p. 117–118 in this book.

On each of their productions, it was customary to always pay the crew at the start of the week, not demanding as in classical capitalist fashion to repeatedly prove one's worth throughout the week in order to receive recompense. At the end of each long day of shooting, it is more often than not the Straubs who would drive the film to the lab, not out of over-anxiety about its safe delivery, but out of the desire to allow their assistants to get some extra sleep. Similarly, it is recounted that it is always Straub and Huillet who would do the last sweeping up and cleaning, never too self-important to leave such unglamorous necessities to others.

~

Long before Clint Eastwood dropped the habit of shouting "Action!" or "Cut!" on his directorial sets in order to eliminate unnecessary tension, this was also the practice on the sets of Straub / Huillet – Jean-Marie simply saying something such as, "If you please" and concluding with "Thank you, good, that's all." One can feel how such a simple detail – the elimination of this routine protocol and its subtle sense of a whip being cracked – could contribute to the actors feeling more respected.

No detail too small. *"The sentence we heard most often, even before* Machorka-Muff, *when we insisted on a certain detail...because we thought, there are no details...they always said, 'Nobody will notice, nobody will see it,' also when it comes to sound: 'Nobody will notice it, nobody will get it.' This is based on contempt for the audience, or on cheating, which comes to the same thing. But when somebody really knows something about costumes,*

and hasn't just picked up a thing or two, he knows that in a certain period many more possibilities are open than one really thinks; it isn't so limited. The same is true about furniture. We have had this experience ourselves, we were also uneducated and naïve, usually you only know the typical things and not the untypical; people believe that in the baroque period they hung certain pictures on the wall and that there were tapestries and drapes everywhere, and then one reads in a book written by someone who is a specialist in these things: 'In the baroque period, people – except, of course, those who lived in a palace – had very little furniture, at most one cupboard in a room, usually nothing on the wall and no curtains either', and when someone sees it made like that he says, 'That is a caricature, that is not historical enough.'"[3] [JMS]

The above said, the fact that the films of Straub / Huillet have frequently been characterized as minimalist might suggest that this perceived austerity is the result of some self-conscious stylistic hallmark or is dictated purely by having to work within their means. Rather, it is the consequence of working within their ethics. *"If, at the aesthetic level, you practice the same inflation which fuels capitalist society as well as the world we live in, then there's no point; you're just grist for their mill."*[4] [DH]

What might still come across as luxuriant is the aforementioned amount of film typically expended on every shot (which of course has also enabled the editing of multiple versions of a

3 Andi Engel, "Andi Engel talks to Jean-Marie Straub, and Danièle Huillet is there too," *Enthusiasm*, no. 1, December 1975
4 "Sickle and Hammer...," op. cit.

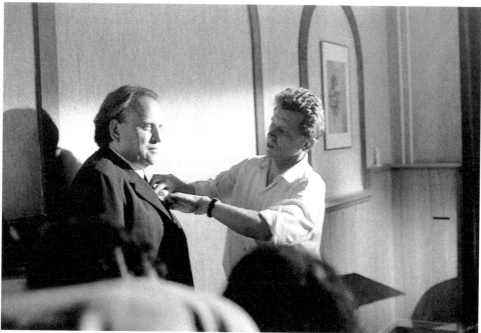

Danièle Huillet and Jean-Marie Straub at work
on the set of *Class Relations*

number of the later films). Straub defends this as being integral to obtaining the results they are after – pointing out that Chaplin would sometimes shoot up to 100 takes to achieve the perfection we all admire.

As instructively and often humorously documented in Pedro Costa's *Where Does Your Hidden Smile Lie?*, the demands of the editing room for Straub and Huillet are no less intense and rigorous as every other stage of their process, wherein debates can rest on the difference between a single frame.

Even after the editing was done, the Straubs would not just blindly outsource the subtitling of their films into various languages, Huillet often undertaking the laborious translations herself or over-seeing the choice of translators (advising but never dictatorially controlling them). Additionally within the subtitling work, it was periodically decided to omit subtitles in order that audiences, at times, be able to experience the images unobstructed and to listen more fully to the sound, including the cadence and musicality of the words spoken.

INTELLIGENCE

Like anyone who holds in admiration the work of Straub/Huillet, I've often witnessed, read, and debated those for whom such works appear unduly, even excruciatingly, challenging; perceived as being overly intellectual – elitist – opaque… Nor am I myself immune from the experience of feeling tested or confused by the challenges the works can pose. Thus it was reassuring when I first learned that Straub and Huillet's own avowed interest was in exploring

texts that "resist" them, that they too had undertaken a wrestling with each literary text chosen, a wrestling that extends throughout each stage of the production. While I am not always convinced of the value of embracing such difficult, sometimes unyielding, texts, I remain intrigued and respectful of the rationale of Straub's defense that "…you can never make your films intelligent enough because people have enough stupidity to put up with in their work and daily lives."[5]

BEAUTY (COMING TO ONE'S SENSES)

In Barton Byg's superb book on the German films of Straub/Huillet, *Landscapes of Resistance*, he recounts that, to the suggestion someone posed that their films "seem to be built on a strict system, based on renunciation," Danièle Huillet replied, "I hope not *only* that. I hope that one can feel sensuality and pleasure [*Lust*] at the same time. Can sense the fragrance of things." It puzzles me still that films so spatially alive and pulsing with intense emotion can be regarded by some as so dry, cold, and detached. Perhaps

5 An equally useful retort to such a critique is that of Glauber Rocha who, in a round-table conversation with Miklós Jancsó, Pierre Clémenti, and Straub stated that, "On this question of minority audiences, there's one thing I'd like to say. There exists a very paternal attitude towards the public. You find for example leftist intellectuals who are writers, not filmmakers, claiming that we are making films which are difficult for the public. And that is a very paternal point of view. Because you can't decide without research…What it amounts to is that only the bourgeois are sensitive or intelligent enough to understand a film. There is a mechanism of distribution, imposing a certain type of film product on the public, which has completely corrupted the public."

they walked out before giving the films their chance. Or perhaps, in their wholesale rejection of such works, other things are made clear. In another comment by Straub that would seem to stand somewhat in contradiction to the earlier remark about the openness and generosity of the formal structures of their work, he states: "I think these films find their audiences in dividing. One divides the audiences... It is the dividing lines that make one's public. And the dividing lines end up in one way or another being lines which correspond to the lines of class, and class struggle. I believe that, or, I hope that."[6]

~

"...you must treat people as adults and help them to see and hear, since only when their senses are attuned will their conscience start developing."[7] [DH]

"There are those who poison the planet and those who poison souls. Our films are addressed to dulled senses. There are certain senses and certain sentiments that are in danger of disappearing from the earth, of becoming extinct like the dinosaurs. It's the fault of the social structures in which we live."[8] [JMS]

"I believe that a film cannot be too beautiful. It's only a question of what kind of beauty. Even Brecht

said, towards the end of his life, 'We won't do it, without a concept of beauty.'"[9] [JMS]

~

On set, while Straub and Huillet may spend hours deciding on the precise compositional framing or insuring that the sound is just so, they do not subscribe to any notion of "waiting for the light." Instead, says Straub, "We work, we work, we work, and we wait only for the light to bring us some presents... Because one is always surprised. Nature has a lot more imagination than you do yourself."[10]

In the editing room, again as observed in Costa's portrait, the final determination on where to make an edit splice at the end a lengthy panning shot in Sicilia! is decided by Huillet not based on the image alone but based on going a frame or two beyond the chirp of a distant bird on the audio track. No need to "assassinate" the bird, Huillet declares.

~

"Most American films are humanist, whereas we are trying to make films where the men in the frame are no more important than a small stone, rock, or blade of grass, a breath of wind, a cicada, or a bird that passes."[11] [JMS]

ANTI-STYLE

It seems that whenever I've finished a film someone or other will comment on how different it seems from my previous work. This bothers me for two reasons. First off, because usually I can't see it, the films seem so recognizably my way of doing things. The other reason being

6 Joel Rogers, "Moses and Aaron as an object of Marxist reflection," Jump Cut, no. 12/13, 1976
7 "Sickle and Hammer...," op. cit.
8 Jean-Marie Straub, la resistenza del cinema, a film by Armando Ceste, 1991
9 Susan Dermody, "Jean-Marie Straub and Danièle Huillet: The Politics of Film Practice," Cinema Papers (Australia), September 1976
10 Maintenant dites-moi quelque chose, ed. Philippe Lafosse, Hoenheim: Scribest, 2011 [trans. John Gianvito]
11 Film Forum: Thirty-Five Top Filmmakers Discuss Their Craft, op. cit.

On the set of *Class Relations*

– so what? why should this matter? Thus it was a pleasure to read in Philippe Lafosse's book, *Maintenant dites-moi quelque chose*, Straub declaring that, "No, there's no style, there's no style! I hate style! Style is the man himself, that's all! It doesn't exist. Style…is shit!"[12]

POWDER BURNS (ON MAKING POLITICAL FILMS)
Where I agree:

"There is no division between politics and life, art and politics."[13]

"Everything is political, everything you do in your life is political."[14]

"If a film doesn't open the eyes and ears of people, of what good is it? It's better to give it up… The only thing one can do with film is give information and open ears. That's a lot; but if one does the opposite, it's better to change your profession, and go fishing, or learn grammar…"[15] [JMS]

Where I question:

"At the risk of being a bit pompous, political cinema is the one that ends with saying: 'Sickle and hammer, cannons, cannons, dynamite!' This is where we're at, there are no alternatives, we shouldn't be afraid of saying this. But when it happens, it will be very costly."[16] [JMS]

I am, with some regrets, not a pacifist. That said I have not yet been convinced of the argument that "only violence helps where violence rules." I spoke about this a while back with another of the most militant of filmmakers, Bolivian director Jorge Sanjines, and he too felt, from what I surmise is fundamentally a tactical decision, that the dream of an armed revolution is no longer a workable strategy (though I would myself say this depends on which part of the world one is talking about and which battles). Dislodging and destroying concentrated power's unrelentingly cruel and blood-soaked clasp upon this planet remains the task before us, a task that feels most days beyond-Herculean (though perhaps it is not strength that's required). Sharing the rage, the frustration, the scars, I am nevertheless unwilling to be a signatory to Straub's infamous Venice Film Festival statement that "So long as there's American imperialistic capitalism, there'll never be enough terrorists in the world."[17] Even good provocateurs can go too far.

Such a remark, typically side-stepped by admirers, cannot simply be shrugged off as the consequence of some sudden if regrettable outburst, seeing as how Straub has made related comments in support of "terrorism" throughout the years. As recently as 2008, Straub told an audience at the Reflet Médicis cinema in Paris that, "I really believe that if I had not had the chance to make films at the beginning, I would have become a terrorist."[18] One wonders if he would still

---

12 *Maintenant dites-moi quelque chose*, op. cit. [trans. Ted Fendt]

13 *"Moses and Aaron* as an object of Marxist reflection," op. cit.

14 "There's Nothing More International Than a Pack of Pimps: A Conversation between Pierre Clémenti, Miklós Jancsó, Glauber Rocha and Jean-Marie Straub convened by Simon Hartog in Rome, February 1970," trans. John Mathews, *Rouge*, no. 3, 2004 [www.rouge.com.au/3/international.html]

15 Jean-Marie Straub, cited in Susan Dermody, op. cit.

16 "Sickle and Hammer…," op. cit.

17 Jean-Marie Straub, "Three Messages," trans. Tag Gallagher [http://kinoslang.blogspot.com/2006/09/three-messages.html]

18 *Maintenant dites-moi quelque chose*, op. cit. [trans. John Gianvito]

make this claim (at least publicly) after the events of Paris in 2015. It's not that I am unaware of the blatant hypocrisy and doublespeak that attends officialdom's usage of the words "terrorist" and "terrorism." As Howard Zinn repeatedly sought to point out, "How can you have a war on terrorism when war itself is terrorism?"[19] State terrorism perennially disguising itself as self-defense. Still, as Zinn further observes, "if you respond to terrorism with more terrorism…you multiply the amount of terrorism in the world."[20]

I do not want to shrug Straub's comment away, especially from someone who has given me so much to think about (and to experience) through the years. But what I think he fails to recognize or take full ownership of is the fact that it was his *choice* not *chance* to make films instead of bombs. And this has made all the difference. While wishing I could pin Straub down further on the terms of his language, in the interim my memory led me recently to go digging out an old VHS tape I had of one of the earliest works of the late documentarian Peter Wintonick, *The New Cinema* (1984). Late in the film, for all of 5 minutes, Jean-Marie Straub and Danièle Huillet appear and deliver what is for me one of the most lucid defenses for "militancy" in filmmaking I know. In response to a question about whether they think it is necessary for filmmakers to be enraged at the world, Straub begins:

JMS: Yes…I don't know. No, it's not necessary. It would be much better if one did not have to be angry but we find that, in this society in which we are living, if one is not angry, if one does not resist, than one is nothing at all. It is essential to realize that we don't know what is happening in so-called 'popular democracies' or in countries that are called socialist states. It is not there that we live. But in the countries where we are living, that are capitalist countries, what one learns by buying an illustrated newspaper or tabloid in France or the USA, or in Germany or Italy for that matter, when one reads a newspaper in these countries, it appears they contain 95% advertising. And what one reads in these advertisements are things that are enough to make you vomit.

We are living in a society that really makes one vomit. Therefore I do not see how you can be anything but angry with this society, unless you are some kind of masochist, or unless you kept forgetting, forgetting that life could be much more beautiful. These days life is not beautiful at all. And what's more, it's a society where – we could enjoy life – but, as Jean-Luc Godard says, we are living in "a desperate society."

DH: And, in any case, we are living in a society of assassins and murderers. You…you can hardly take a step without…

JMS: Without tripping over a corpse…

DH: But that doesn't prevent flowers from existing or children from being born… Well, in fact, it does prevent these things in certain cases, and in certain places.

JMS: When people walk on the pavement, do they think of the hands that laid the cobblestones there? Do they think of the hands that buried them there? I do not know. But there is blood there also, and sweat. Sweat is also blood.

19 Howard Zinn, *Howard Zinn On War*, New York: Seven Stories, 2011
20 Ibid.

Jean-Marie Straub on the set of *Class Relations*

That is not to say that it is necessary to live as the bourgeois do these days. The bourgeois see, as rats do, when they see that the ship is in the process of burning. The bourgeois begin to create the apocalypse.

DH: No, rats desert the ship.

JMS: Rats desert the ship and the bourgeois say, "Look, it's the end of the world." They feel that the ship will perhaps sink one day in any case.

DH: It's already beginning to sink.

JMS: It is sinking. It's taking on water. Therefore one speaks to us of death all the time. But it is whose death? It's the death of a social caste system. It's the death of a social class. I wish to state that to be angry, to be revolted, to be passionately outraged, is not to practice a certain nostalgia and desire for the apocalypse, or the great catastrophe, or the mystique of death. It is exactly the opposite!

~

It is in the spirit of such words that I retain conviction in the work of Danièle Huillet and Jean-Marie Straub. It is, as well, a spirit that I find flowing through Glauber Rocha in such works as *Terra em transe*, *História do Brasil* (*History of Brazil*, 1974), *A idade da terra* (*The Age of the Earth*, 1980), in the Pasolini of *Uccellacci e uccellini* (*The Hawks and the Sparrows*, 1966), *12 Dicembre* (1972), and *Salò* (1975), coursing through the works of Tsuchimoto, Hondo, Maldoror, Ogawa, Vautier, De Antonio, and so many countless other combatants. It is in this spirit, and this sense, that one can properly define effective political filmmaking as that which illuminates through the brightness of its ideas and the glow of its incendiary power.

For such light as Straub/Huillet have shed I remain forever grateful.

Harun Farocki

Stop Coughing!

In 1982/1983, the Straubs were living at my place in Berlin for a couple of weeks while they were preparing their film *Class Relations*. I asked whether I could not join in too and was granted the role of Delamarche. The film was initially supposed to be shot in Berlin and I looked at a few locations with them. Later the shoot was relocated to Hamburg and the surrounding areas, but the scenes were rehearsed in Berlin. A lot of it took place in my apartment, and I gained insight into the Straubs' way of working. At the rehearsals, Danièle almost always sat on the floor. She looked and listened very attentively and made notes for herself in her script. She remembered and noted pauses and emphases in the speech, gestures and facial expressions. In the evening, on a portable typewriter, she would copy and add to the pages of the script what had been decided and written down during the rehearsals.

Danièle ran the entire production. She was as responsible for the planning of the shoot as she was for the costumes and props. The film cost around one million marks but there was no office. Everything was kept in Danièle's papers. She would later write to me not to forget the bobble cap; we had decided I would wear it in a certain scene. She wrote to me twice about this cap.

It was obvious that both of them did not much care about making choices. The actors were not chosen in an elaborate manner, nor were the locations or costumes.

It wasn't about finding the most suitable actors, but rather conforming to the actors' specific skills, as well as the suitability of a location or an object. The long and meticulous rehearsals probably served to ascertain this suitability.

In this work it became clear to me once again that the Straubs always determine some things exactly and other things not at all. Some things they leave entirely up to chance. But what is decided must be performed precisely.

While it is already hard enough to write about the Straubs, it is made even harder because they both loved precision so much. They could quote a line from a film or even a thirty-year-old newspaper article by heart. Straub recounted a trip in the beginning of the 1960s that he had to make without Danièle because there was not enough money. This misfortune had happened twenty years before but he still knew the exact dates and destinations.

I've witnessed Danièle correct Jean-Marie but almost never the reverse. Once she said "auch" (also) instead of "Hauch" (breeze) and Jean-Marie pointed it out to her.

When we listened to music in the evening, Danièle often sat down as well, but always had something to do. She did hand work, darning a sock or a shirt. A few years earlier in Rome, I had noticed that the Straubs never went out to eat and also walked long distances in order to save on travel fare. Now, we often had dinner in a pizzeria and Danièle paid.

She allowed Jean-Marie ten cigarettes a day. She said that she had nothing against him dying from smoking but his coughing in movie theaters bothered her.

We saw Godard's *Passion* together, in which Michel Piccoli, a lollipop in his mouth, is constantly coughing. I guess he had just given up smoking. In the film, "Poland" is a new Jerusalem. Danièle objected to a lot of things in the film, but said that it was maybe Godard's best. Later, when we were back at the apartment, Jean-Marie coughed and Danièle shouted, "Stop coughing." She'd already said that a number of times. Now she added, "If not, I'll go to Poland."

Class Relations set: Jean-Marie Straub, in the background Harun Farocki (with bobble cap) Danièle Huillet taking notes

Translated from the German by Ted Fendt
First published in German: "Hör auf zu
husten!", in Der Standard *(Vienna),*
October 17, 2006

Jean-Pierre Gorin

Nine Notes on
Where Does Your Hidden Smile Lie?

1

Something superbly irritating. All the articles I read on *Où gît votre sourire enfoui?*[1] manage somehow to erase Pedro Costa's name out of the equation. The simple mention of the genre this film is supposed to locate itself in suffices to do that trick, as if to tag it as a "documentary" was enough to dispense with the need to analyze the choices made and the strategy elaborated by the filmmaker. It is as if Danièle Huillet and Jean-Marie Straub were somehow miraculously present and not *presented*. In short, to really talk about *Où gît...* would be to talk about Costa (more accurately about Costa's work) even before talking about the Straubs (more accurately about the Straubs' work). What did he do to give us the Straubs with such vitality?

2

During one of the epic tussles that punctuate this film, the one in fact that gives it its title and that is prompted by the difficulty to excavate out of the footage the stirring of a smile in the eyes of an actor, Jean-Marie Straub, *sotto voce*, throws a question Danièle Huillet's way: "You are a bit afraid, aren't you?" To type it on the page betrays the gentleness and the love that tempers the irony. I can't help feeling that fear must have been part of the equation for Costa

right from the start. How to give just weight to filmmakers who are staking their lives on the excavation of such essential minutiae? How to deal with the requirement of the exercise (a portrait for the *Cinéastes de notre temps* series) without betraying or flattening? And I suspect that when he captured Danièle Huillet's exasperated and fierce bark of a response – "I am not afraid, I am looking" – he must have known he was on the right path.

3

Film sprockets running through the gears of the editing table; rewind of picture motion and soundtracks; stops on frame; overlaps of shots and contrast of scales at the junction of two shots; dance of grease pencil marks; explosion of white light on the screen of the editing table or, in contrast, absolute absorbing blackness; the sound of editing tape being stretched; the insistent thud of film splicers; the whirr of rewinds; the penumbra of the editing room; its moments of absolute darkness; the intermittent burst of light from the lamp clamped to the editing table; the assistant editors on the side silently doing trims or cleaning the print, their

1 *Where Does Your Hidden Smile Lie?* (2009), a film by Pedro Costa

Jean-Marie Straub, Pedro Costa, Danièle Huillet

faces framed by a light that seems straight out of a Georges de la Tour, etc. Before we even start to go the way of the Straubs, as Proust would say, to discover editing as they practice it, the film anchors itself in the materiality of the editing process. It makes of it its drama. Costa insists on keeping you there for most of the hundred and four minutes of the duration. The stop and go rhythm, the stutter that gives birth to form out of the relentless attention to the material gathered according to the idea, the intention that presided over its collection.

4

This comes with a rigorous staging of the space. The camera height determined by the scale of the editor (Danièle Huillet) seated at the editing table; the distance mostly an invariant determined by the need to give her space. Editing as a deep-seated patience made palpable by the way in which Costa quietly sustains his gaze and respects the mental space Danièle Huillet constantly claims or tries to reclaim. But to say that is not to nail down yet the intelligence of the visual set-up that Costa constructs for us. There is his insistence on de-centering the space, the monumentality of the editing table both acknowledged and yet tempered by the fact that it is almost never pre-

sented frontally, that the viewer has it in the periphery of his/her vision on the left side of a line that parts the space and draws our attention toward a door that opens the editing room to the drabness of an institutional corridor. The space of the editing room seen in diagonal with the eyes of the Straubs' favorite filmmaker, John Ford. How reassured these cantankerously demanding filmmakers must have been when they glanced at this dramatic hinging of inside and outside that sets the proper stage for the drama at hand, everything at a proper scale, the machine anchoring the space but yet delivered without the usual fetishisms, the seat of the editors, the bins and the enforced intimacy of the editing room delivered to the nth power by the very fact of that rectangle opened on the right hand side of the frame.

Stills from *Where Does Your Hidden Smile Lie?*

5

And as a consequence of this rigorous staging of the space, the "actors," perfect. But even before I speak to that perfection, let me insist on the fact that the stage is not simply occupied by Danièle Huillet and Jean-Marie Straub and the occasional assistants in their role as studious elves of the editing process. Let me insist on the fact that there is a third (or fourth, if you count the assistants) party whose presence allows the articulation of the drama. It is Costa himself, constantly interpellated and obdurately silent. He is our stand-in, the one that allows this extraordinary live footnoting of their work that Straub and to a lesser degree Huillet find themselves coaxed to do. He is this silent presence that prompts in Straub an extraordinary comedic number couched in the intonations and rhythms of a Vigo or early Renoir actor; this silent presence against whom Jean-Marie Straub thinks he has to run interference to leave Danièle Huillet the time and the space to think; this silent presence that allows for the romantic rant against the forces that keep cin-

ema from realizing its definition according to Huillet and Straub.

6

But what makes the "actors" perfect? Perfect first and foremost because like a lot of things in that movie, Costa gives us a tangential view of them. This is a portrait that avoids the full frontal, that openly pornographic stance lesser filmmakers than Costa reserve for the subjects of such "portraits." It is a tangentiality that is achieved by camera position as much as by the artifice of light (or the refusal to create it, which is ultimately the same thing). We see profiles, the eyes locked in a stare that goes beyond the frame, solicited by the intonations of a Sicilian dialog, by the whirr of sprockets or by the rewind of a track. And when we do not see profiles, we see backs of heads or shoulders. They are not sculpted by the source of light; they are abstracted by it. This is a film haunted by the power of the silhouette. The faces presented and which we are allowed to glance at always tend to gravitate toward that state: an abstracted two-dimensionality that makes both Danièle Huillet and Jean-Marie Straub exist at the periphery of their own work in some patient acknowledgement, pondering, and shaping of its physical properties. There is a rigor in this abstracting of the human form, in this willingness to be in such close proximity to a figure and yet to never openly play the game of tracking the revelatory explicitness of an expression. The rhetoric of Costa's portrait goes against all the conventions of film portraiture. We are not invited to witness the blossoming of a memorized anecdote on a face; we are not invited to decipher even the force of conviction in the articulation of an expression: we are just seeing bodies or parts of bodies silhouetted by the tenuous yet potent light that comes from the film material they relentlessly try to shape. Silhouettes by the glow of their work.

7

By the glow of their work. Allow me to spend some more time on these words. This silhouetting of Danièle Huillet and Jean-Marie Straub against the glow on the editing table shoots more holes in the rhetoric of the film portrait that even series as replete with wonderful moments as *Cinéastes de notre temps* live and die by. These moments of *Sicilia!*, endlessly wound and rewound on the flatbed, punctuate Costa's film and give it its creative stutter. But they are not quotes or illustrations of a reified discourse that would exist after the fact. The moments of *Sicilia!* that take over the entire screen are revocable and presented as such. They are the

matter being molded and shaped. This is the miracle that the silhouetting delivers us to: not the discourse about the work but the work itself, or more accurately: the drama of any consequent work, its rhythm, its inherent obsessiveness, its cumulative sketchiness, its slow accretion. This is a film that is relentlessly interested in the sweat of it, the embattlement of it, and that sets for itself the task of making it perceptible. There is in that process a materialist stance which mirrors that of the Straubs', an attention to the details of the circumstances at hand (Danièle Huillet, Jean-Marie Straub, a room that opens on a corridor, the disjointed elements of a film idea in the process of finding its form, words thrown at the screen and at each other). It pours on the makers of *Sicilia!* the attention that Danièle Huillet and Jean-Marie Straub pour onto their own material. At one point, Costa chooses to spend time with one of the characters of *Sicilia!* It is a long monologue in a train, when a character pits the profoundly felt emptiness of his soul against the worldly reasons he has to be satisfied. The way it is performed, it is a quintessential Straub/Huillet monologue, delivered with an attention to the beats and respirations that they impart upon all the non-professionals they manage to coax into working for them. But it is one of the few pieces in Costa's film that is not molded in front of our eyes. I wondered why, until I heard the voice of Straub mouthing the very words that the actor intones on the screen and until I heard Danièle Huillet underscore the homage Straub had given his actor at the end of the take: "Giovanni, I'll never forget you!" It dawned on me then that this was the kind of gratitude that Costa wished to express toward the generosity of the Straubs and their willingness to take him into the work of their work. There is all across *Oú gît...* the intense emotion of a "Danièle, Jean-Marie, I'll never forget you!" With the Straubs, the generosity for which they thank their actor is the result of the clarity of their own intention. This applies to Costa, too: it is the clarity of his intention, his attention to the work of the work, his staging of it that gives us this exemplary distillation of the Straub, Huillet ethos at the core of *Oú gît...*

8

To talk about this ethos is first and foremost to talk about a miracle that holds to a comma. Danièle Huillet comma Jean-Marie Straub. I might be wrong, but Costa is to my knowledge the only one who doesn't use an "and" or a/to link these two names. He joins them by the breath of a comma. It is not one of the smallest of the miracles of this film to give its viewers such a tactile sense of how this exemplary collaboration played itself out. It is not a small miracle to take us so effectively and elegantly out of the pathetic assignation of relative authorship that remains the rule for most of those who tackle what they insist on seeing as a mysterious beast, collaboration. Once again Costa delivers a surprise to us: in the darkness of the editing room, under the reflected glow of their own material, a comedy takes place. There is the hilarious passage from the formal "vous" to the informal "tu" that punctuates some of the most volatile moments created by the need to

properly excavate the material. There is the push and the shove, their crescendo, the hilarious coarseness of the banter. What serves the comedy is the fact that everything emerges out of silhouettes, bounces in the penumbra of the editing room, or skids briefly across the surface of a few photograms. Anything else, any effort to capture the tussles on the faces of the "actors" would have been vulgarity; anything else would betray its innocence, its childlike quality. The sure hand of Costa is all across this film. He uses his silent presence to get the "little music" of it all. The door that opens up the space of the editing room on the corridor of Le Fresnoy becomes a prop. This frame around Jean-Marie Straub's silhouette provides the perfect illustration of a phrase which he attributes to an old Neapolitan; at one point he uses it to talk about the actors of *Sicilia!* – "The body is the shape of the soul. It's Thomas Aquinas who said that. He was Neapolitan, he knew what he was talking about." In a comedic twist, this validation of a fundamental principle of Straub, Huillet's aesthetic falls upon Jean-Marie Straub himself and delivers us the shape of his body and the shape of his Puckish soul. He dances through this film; he sing-songs through this film; he mumbles through this film or raves and rants with the accent of a confederate from *Zero For Conduct* who, despite the years, despite the films, has maintained his capacity for rebellion and mirth. But this attention paid to the comedic volubility of Jean-Marie Straub is also a way to establish Danièle Huillet. The attention to the body and thus to the soul is ultimately as intense, though more anchored. She embodies all the gestures of editing. It is through her that we feel the weight of its long patience. We see her seated for so long that to see her standing and moving editing bins around really feels like the end of the day. We hear the tension and the exhaustion of maintaining attention. We hear the impatience that cuts across Jean-Marie Straub's irrepressible volubility and reclaims some space and silence for herself as she tackles the material. There is something stern, exasperated, amused, loving and tender that passes in turn through it all. It flows in the confined space of the editing room from Danièle to Jean-Marie; it gives sense to that comma by which Costa linked their names. At the end this film manages to give us something momentous. From Godard on down, the words "love and work" have often been pronounced. In most cases they end up having the hollow sound of slogans for a couples utopia. Costa's attention to gestures and enunciations makes a reality of these two words. Early in the film, at the end of an editing battle, we hear off-screen Jean-Marie Straub ask the difference between the choices they each proposed. We hear Danièle Huillet say "Half a frame." A comma, half a frame, love and work.

the material mediation of an idea, which are at the core of Danièle Huillet and Jean-Marie Straub. In short, nobody has ever given us a clearer view of the classicism they claimed for themselves, and nobody has made clearer the legitimacy of that claim. Nobody has put in sharper relief the politics of such an affirmation: the insistence on preservation (of nature and culture) as the essential component of revolution. The hidden smile that the title of this film claims is buried (a better translation for "enfoui") and in need of being unearthed is only anecdotally a glint in the eye of an actor. It is the smile of the world that Danièle Huillet and Jean-Marie Straub want to excavate from the debris. The last shot of this superb film gives that quixotic quest all its poignancy. The filmmakers, their backs to us, are peering into the darkened theater where *Der Tod des Empedokles* is playing. The strains of "Heiliger Dankgesang" from Beethoven's Op. 132 are heard, muffled. Danièle Huillet exits left, up the stairs toward the projection booth. Jean-Marie Straub sits on the stairs and his hand gently flutters to the music. Alone.

San Diego, July 2007

9

Où gît...reinvents the idea and the practice of portraiture, or more generally of the homage. Through intelligence and attention it avoids maudlin hagiography. Nobody has put in sharper relief, made more tangible the dedication to clarity, the conviction that the image is appearance and the conviction that the form is

First published in Portuguese: "Nove Notas sobre Onde Jaz o Teu Sorriso?" in Cem mil cigarros: Os filmes de Pedro Costa, *edited by Ricardo Matos Cabo, Lisbon: Orfeu Negro, 2009*

11 décembre 68 *

8 München-15
Schwanthaler Str. 7

Enormous Daniel,

Coming back from Cologne,
I find your letter...

Okay, my decision
is made, you can have
DER BRÄUTIGAM, DIE KOMÖDIANTIN
UND DER ZUHÄLTER
for U.S.A. and Canada. But please,
you send the contract: I have none,
and you have printed ones —

The print may be in Paris
at the end of december, but I'm
not sure you can have it already
by january 15. They have much
work by CINÉTITRES. If Bunch
wishes, he can make the titles:
I'll send him the french ones,
so that it'll be easier for the "Repérage"
too,

write all!

and perhaps he can translate the
synopsis (CAHIERS) in english,
my english inexistent (these words
are from my wife!). - Will you
write him (Bunch) two words about it
and about the titles, and send
me his address and your assistant
address in Paris.

Je vous embrasse,
Jean-Marie Straub

P.S. My God,
Man. what a price (for a short
- and what a man, who is plann
a war against the whole America
system, alone!

Letters from Huillet and Straub to Dan Talbot
and other documents from the archives
of New Yorker Films. Most documents relate to
the 1975 traveling retrospective of their films
in the United States and Canada, their 1982
U.S. trip and the 1983 shoot for *Class Relations*,
including a letter by Manny Farber (p. 169),
the filmmakers' entry in Gregory Woods'
private guest book (p. 173), and a letter to
Fred Camper (p. 180/181)

cher ami,
          merci pour votre lettre, et le chèque/Bridegroom.

The lavoratory (Bavaria) will send to you, on March 6 or 7, a 35mm
print from MACHORKA-MUFF (in 2 reels, for the undertitling) - against
payment 1)this M-M.print, but also for 2)the new 35mm print from
NOT RECONCILED - which they will send not to you, but directly to the
titling-lavoratory in Genève - und also for 3)the expedition. I am sorry,
but they know that we are going away and they do not know you, they
say, so that's the reason... You must also know that nobody pays
anything in West-Germany, unless they have no other choice. We hope,
it will mean to you no complication ?!
You will receive the new undertitled print from NOT RECONCILED, sent
from Genève, around March 20 (copy from my letter to Mr. Hirschi
hereby) - and against -again- payment for titling and expedition...
I hope, everything will be all right.

I have told Roud in London a week ago, about the "old" CHRONICLE print,
which you want to have, and I have written to him again this morning,
saying that I want to know very quickly if you agree together,
to order the reel 5 a, which must be replaced, before we leave
Munich... I hope, it will work. They had to send this print back to the
USA (Lincoln Center) -because of customs in England- one week ago.

The new 35mm print from CHRONICLE should be undertitled already. Mlle
Herbout should phone Cinétitres (I have told her), because they have
received the print from Hamburg at least 3 weeks ago!
At the end of March an english print (i.e. english commentary, undertitled dialogues) will exist... We had to do this because of an idiot,
the english distributor (CONnoisseur) - and we had to do it, because he
would have done it in any case and changed the film by changing the
text and the edition... We had to fight 2 weeksfor the translation, the
voice, the registration - but finally we have done what we wanted with
a german girl who speaks english (like the french version - only the
german accent is not as strong - because the english people are more
sensitive about their language - and because they had no Renoir to
educate them; the american pictures have not educated them, because
"American is not English" !)

Next week we shall send to you some more stills from M-M. and
BRIDEGROOM; when you come, you can learn from Aprà (new address: viccolo
del governo vecchio 8, Roma) if we are already in Rome or still in
Munich...
          A bientôt, nos amitiés, good luck,

                                        Danièle

26 . 2 . 69

27.2.: PS. Last minute: Undertitled print from CHRONICLE is leaving Paris
            to-day for New-York... Saluts!

9 mars 69 ✱

Bien cher ami,

Stills from M-M. and BRIDEGROOM were sent to you yesterday, you should have received/from Paris the/print from CHRONICLE, the new print from M-M. will be sent to you from Munich on next Tuesday 11;

as for the reel 5 a to be replaced for the print CHRONICLE/Lincoln Center, we̶Ihad ordered it already as I became your precedent letter from GEYER-Hamburg, so that it should be travelling now to Paris for the english titles. Fortunately, it is the reel where there ar̶ the least undertitles!! We had screened the film in London at the Festival: the print is not bad,that's true, but something had happe̶ to this reel 5 a (what? where: New-York or San Francisco; but Leonhardt has seen the film in San Francisco and X̶X̶X̶X̶X̶X̶X̶X̶X̶X̶X̶X̶ did not notice anything; so that it should have happened in San Francisco, after the screening, by rolling up !): it was teared thrice as Leonhardt plays on the harpsichord the 25th variation, sticked together with scotch-paper (to loose no frames!); teared again at least twice when the bassist sings "I X̶X̶X̶X̶X̶X̶X̶ rejoice upon my death, oh, would that it had already arrived", sticked together once with scotch-paper, the second time without, because it was too bad, so that frames are missing, and there is a hole in the music.. The scotch-stickings won't hold̶ very long, so that it is also your interest –and not only the one of the film and the public!- that this reel is replaced: you can show this letter to the Lincoln Cent̶ which is responsible for it: they should have an insurance to pay for it, when something like that happens.
I am glad that the finegrains worked out well, I wish to you some good luck and hope to see you soon, in Rom! *Jean-Marie S.*

You did well in sending me the N.Y.T.review: I have seen german reviews which we̶r̶e much more stupid and vulgar (and not funny at al̶ and the critics had not pay anything to see the films... Alors?

---

*8 München-15
Schwanthaler.
Str.7*

Dear Daniel,
From J-M.: thank you for your letter – and your question! But "everything is cricket", so you can give (contre-remboursement!) Andi Engel the prints he wants (from M-M., N.V., and DER BRäUTIGAM)...
Thank you very much for doing so – it is the only way to show these films in England, for it seems to be, concerning Straub, the most "refractaire" country of the world !
LES YEUX NE VEULENT PAS EN TOUT TEMPS SE FERMER ou PEUT-ETRE QU'UN JOUR ROME SE PERMETTRA DE CHOISIR A SON TOUR will begin (with God's help!) on August 27....
Hoping to see you soon –with your wife- in Rom,
salutissimi, *Danièle Straub-Huillet*

20 juillet 69

OCT 23 1973

october 16
1973

Dear Dan,

1) How was it with G. and Introduction to...at the N.Y.Festival - very bad??!!? We only saw VARIETY - which we found very amusing!

2) 16.000 old francs are 160 new francs!

3) I'm sending you hereby a budget from MOSES AND AARON - not in english, but I think, it is understandable;

so we need 720.000.-DM to make the film (without anything for our work, Jean-Marie's and mine, so we are co-producers) and the participation of the austrian radio-television, which brings us the orchester and the choir (4 mOnths for the preparation, 7 weeks in sound-studio for recording - which was not to be paid otherwise, it would have made 1.000.000.-DM !!)

For this they have the RECORDS - rights and the Right to show the film at the Austrian Television →

and we have : 400.000.-DM from the 3rd German Television Programms all together ;
70.000.-DM from the Italian Television;
70.000.-DM from the French Television;
100.000.-DM from Janus;
we need 80.000.- DM. still.

$40.-

Thank you for the informations about the negatives you have, for Sharits' address, and for giving Richard the Italian reviews.

With much love from us both,

Danièle

Marty Segal
Max Raab
Bob Montgomery

Schuyler
Chapin

$300,000 - total budget
30,000 - needed

Atlas - 16mm

(script)

MAY 8 1975

Dear Dan,

Here the extension agreement on CHRONIK.

Did you get my postcard about writing to Hellwig upon
M&A ? Let me know how it's going on. Something you should know:
in the contract between Janus and Taurus is written / "Ausgeschlos-
sen von der Rechtseinräumung sind die Rechte des Komponisten an
der Oper (Autorenrechte). Soweit durch die Auswertung des Film-
werks in diese Rechte eingegriffen wird, müssen die Rechte an der
Oper vom Lizenznehmer bzw. von den jeweiligen Lizenznehmern des
Lizenznehmers zusätzlich erworben werden. Die Weltrechte an der
Oper liegen beim Musikverlag Schott & Söhne in Mainz."

One reason more for you to get the film from Taurus/Beta without
paying or paying ver little! And you should know it, so that they
cannot play you...

Have you any possibility of showing the film - if - in
some cinema? For this film, it is important, and the 16mm prints
for universities are only a solution of emergency, but not a very
good one; and we think, this film could even make some money in
a cinema... But don't tell Kloiber! And think it over.

The negative will remain in our name, don't worry.
The print is going with us to den Haag (english undertitling)
next week - we are paying for it now and will get the money back
later on from beta through Hellwig. But we think it's better
now to own this print till you find an agreement with these
gangsters. M&A will be shown first on Edinburg (but don't tell it
now, wait : only Richard knows it), and they want to show also
History Lessons, and to invite us. Maybe we'll go, because J-M.
does not know Scotland at all.

As for New York: Richard cannot pay any ticket, he told
us already at Eastern, because of the economical crisis his
budget has been shorted! But don't worry: we are not longing so
much for going to the States, and in some way, if we cannot go
because nobody can afford to pay for it, we'll be happy: M&A
does not need us, it speaks for itself alone. And we are very
tired, and want to think about our next film next year. So,
patience. And you will surely come some day to Europe, won't you?

We are glad, you finally got the right of showing
GESCHICHTSUNTERRICHT... It is so idiotic, losing so much time
and so much energy for things which should be normal; the same
with the "Widmung" to Holger. But one has to.

Nuria (Schoenberg's daughter, Nono's wife, Lawrence
Schoenberg's sister) saw the film 4 days ago: she said, she
finds the dedication ok. (right) and no effence at Arnold Sch. -
and she will write to her brother. But please don't speak about it
yet. If we need help, we will tell you.

Much love,

29th april 75

Saturday 30th August 75

Dear Dan,

thanks for your letter from august 18th, that we found
today, coming back from Edinburgh-Festival: we are very happy with
M&A in a cinema immediately after the Festival showing and you
finding an agreement with Lawrence Schoenberg; as far as i know,
he should be fair, and hold what he said....

But: we do not agree, absolutely not, with the idea of
making 16mm prints from the 35 one; we think that it could work
if it were not a musical film, but with such a one, it is not
possible. It is not only because of us and "our" work, but too
much people did their best for getting a good sound (the
musicians, the recordists, every one), that we could accept of
getting in such a compromission. We saw a piece of an OTHON 16mm
made like that, and it was already bad for OTHON; what would it
be with music, and with this music. No, definitively.

If the Universities do not want us without the last
work "à la mode", well, there will not be universities and we
won't see North-America. It is a pity, and I would regret it
even more than Jean-Marie, but it is still not worth destroying
the work of so much people - and, first, of Schoenberg!

If (some) Universities want us without M&A, but with
other films, you can choose what you think best to show, but we
want every time to have History Lessons and Introduction being
shown; the other films are up to you - and them, eventually!

As for your 16mm prints, later on, to show in the
Universities, we made already a 35mm reversal from the original
negative for you : but we want to speak with you before sending
it to you, and, anyway, we have to make in Paris (coming back
from New York eventually), where they made the orginal mix and
sound negative which are very good, a second 35 and 16 mm
sound neagtives; so you can print your own prints in New York,
and have them subtitled there too - I can give you the list of
the english subtitles, you only tell them to follow that exactly.
But we can speak about that when we are in New York.

"Your" print was sent today from Edinburgh to New York,
so you can see the film very soon; the print is very fine,
please do not make any showing of the film before the festival,
because we want the print to be still new when it will be shown
on the festival... Only one screening for you and your friends,
and then no more till the press-screening for Richard, and then
no more till we are in New York... We don't want to suffer
when the film will be screened in our presence, and we don't
want Schoenberg's sons, if they come, to see a bad print! OK ?

From 13th september we will be in Paris, and fly to
New York from there, because M&A is to open in Paris (in 3 cinemas
- we think, it is too much!) on september 17th!

To-morrow we are going to Venice, Mostra del Cinema,
where they make a Straub's retrospective from 1st till 7th sept.
I'll send the stills to you from there...

You can put your N.Y.Films release logo at the very
beginning, before the bible text on Moses. Tell them to take care
in doing that, because the bible text is very white, and you see
every scratch on it!

We are very happy to see you soon, we hope you will
like the film; our address in Paris (don't write, if you do, any
where else, we won't become it!) is: c/ Foussarigues
                                        6 rue Cavallotti
                        F 75018 Paris

                                        Phone; 5223617

Love, D

Write to us if you liked M&A; and if you received
the stills... we are interested
If some universities still want us,
particularly in such towns: Chicago; Washington;
Boston; Philadelphia (Philadelfia??) Try to get the
University of Missouri because of the Mississippi River.
I would like, evidently, to see the Grand Canyon, but
there is no university there!!!

STRAUB TOUR

	Date	Venue			Amount	Paid	
1	10/8-9	Univ. of Calif., Berkeley			400 —	11/14	
2	10/10	San Francisco Museum of Art			300 —	4/17	
3	10/11-12	Univ. of Calif., Santa Barbara			500 —	10/20	
4	10/16-17	Univ. of Calif., San Diego			300 —	11/17	
5	10/19-20	Univ. of Missouri			200 —	10/22	
6	10/21	Goethe House N.Y.			200 —	10/15	
7	10/22	Harvard Univ., Cambridge, Mass.			500 —	10/20	
8	10/24-6	Northwestern Univ., Chicago, Ill.			500 —	300 - 10/14 200 11/17	
9	10/23	S.U.N.Y. - Buffalo			500 —		
10	10/27-9	Toronto, Canada			450 —	250 - 10/29 210.28 -12/1	+ 218 fare
11	11/3	Lafayette C., Pa.			500 —	11/26	
12	11/5	Hartford, Conn.			350 —	11/7	

Total $4700.00
Less: (Expenses)   2027.14
                     $2672.86

Pd   1300 —   ck. #3565   11/10/75
Pd   1372.86 ck. #3566   12/3/75

Expenses

Airplane ticket - N.Y. - S.F. - N.Y.	800.20	
Airplane ticket - Boston-Buffalo-NY	426.94	
Cash - expenses	700 —	
Cash - U. of Missouri	100 —	
	$2027.14	

Straub tour

Sept. 13, '75

Manny Farber
file

Dear Amanda

Dan Talbot,
New Yorker Films,

This is to verify the Straub visit. We'll show a selection of his films, according to you: Not Reconciled, History Lessons, Machorka Muff, and the new film. We are announcing their presence on campus for the date: October 17th. We invariably announce these things, but the director and/or films never arrives. I'm pretty sure we can scrape $300 for their visit. I wish it was more. You have no idea how many asses have to be licked. Only for Straub would I do this again.

Manny.

We'll show their films on the 16th and talk with them on the 17th. See you soon.

UNIVERSITY OF CALIFORNIA, BERKELEY

BERKELEY · DAVIS · IRVINE · LOS ANGELES · RIVERSIDE · SAN DIEGO · SAN FRANCISCO   SANTA BARBARA · SANTA CRUZ

Pacific Film Archive
University Art Museum
Berkeley California 94720
Telephone (415) 642-3035

Sept. 17

Dr. Patricio Rossi
Film Studies Program
South Hall, Room 4501
University of California
at Santa Barbara
Santa Barbara
Calfiornia

Dear Dr. Rossi:

Just to let you know that Jean-Marie Straub and his wife
and co-director Danielle Huilett will be here Oct. 8-10
in SF and will be Oct. 15-16 at Fresno.

This means that they would be available to appear at UCSD
Oct. 11-14 if you would be interested to have them there.

If so, contact Dan Talbot of New Yorker Films. 212 CI 7 6110.
He will tell you what it costs and he will be very cooperative
in making all the Straub films available for the occasion.

Also, Jean Eustache is in LA til Oct. 1 and until then would
be able to show some of his films for a small fee. Call him in LA
at 474 9867 if you want to discuss it with him. He has LA ROSIERE
DE PESSAC (1968, 50 mins) , LE COCHON (1970, 40 mins), and
his new film MES PETITES AMOREUSES (1975, 122 mins, 35mm, color,
subtitles) with him.

Keep in touch and best regards,

TOM LUDDY

cc: Dan Talbot

Tel. (212) CI 7-6110

INVOICE

OCT - 2 1975

NEW YORKER FILMS 43 W. 61 St. · New York, N.Y. 10023

№ 11104

CONFIRMATION
No. 2

SOLD TO
Mr. Tom Luddy
Pacific Film Archive
UNIVERSITY OF CALIFORNIA-BERKELEY
University Art Museum
Berkley, Calif.   94720

SHIPPED TO

SAME

CUSTOMER'S ORDER NO.	DATE ENTERED	SHIPPING DATE	DUE BACK DATE IMMEDIATELY AFTER	VIA			TERMS
				EXPRESS	MAIL	WILL CALL	NET PAYABLE UPON RECEIPT
	9-22-75						

PRINT NO.	DESCRIPTION	AMOUNT
	JEAN-MARIE STRAUB APPEARANCE	$400.00
	☐ P.	SALES TAX
	☐ O.R.	DELIVERY CHARGES AND INSURANCE
	☐	AMOUNT DUE $400.00

PLEASE READ THE TERMS ON THE BACK OF THIS FORM AND RETURN SIGNED BY AN
AUTHORIZED PERSON

Tel. (212) CI 7-6110

INVOICE

№ 11449

NEW YORKER FILMS 43 W. 61 St. · New York, N.Y. 10023

PRODUCER
REPORT

SOLD TO
Ms. Linda Beath
NEW CINEMA ENTERPRISEZ
35 Britain Street
Toronto M5A 1R7
Canada

SHIPPED TO

SAME

CUSTOMER'S ORDER NO.	DATE ENTERED	SHIPPING DATE	DUE BACK DATE IMMEDIATELY AFTER	VIA			TERMS
				EXPRESS	MAIL	WILL CALL	NET PAYABLE UPON RECEIPT
	10/21/75						

PRINT NO.	DESCRIPTION		AMOUNT
	AIRFARE-JEAN-MARIE STRAUB & DANIELLE HUILLET		
	CHICAGO to TORONTO	$57	$114.00
	TORONTO to NEW YORK	$52	$104.00
	☐ P. Pd 12/9/75 (NCE)	SALES TAX	
	☐ O.R.	DELIVERY CHARGES AND INSURANCE	
	☐ # 418	AMOUNT DUE	A$218.00¢

$210.78¢

1999 sheridan rd/evanston,illinois 60201

CINÉ CLUB

October 8, 1975

Dear Mr. Lopez,

This is to confirm our telephone agreement with regard to the appearance of Jean-Marie Straub on Friday, October 24, at Northwestern University in Evanston, Illinois. Enclosed is our check for $300 to cover One half of the payment of $600 to be paid to you at New Yorker Films for Mr. Straub. The remaining money ($300) should be received by you within the next two to three weeks.

I would also like to confirm our agreement to have Straub's Machora Muff for screening prior to Mr. Straub's visit. Your prompt action will be greatly appreciated as this film will provide a good introduction to Straub's work.

Also we would like notification of the availability of a 16mm print of Moses and Aaron as soon as it is ready.

Finally I would like to give you, Mr. Lopez, our sincerest gratitude for the kindness and cooperation you have displayed in all of our conversations. It has truly been a pleasure to have worked with you.

Yours truly,

Bruce

Bruce Jenkins

P.S. Please send a confirmation of this letter in the form of a contract or a receipt. Thank you again.

—Also, does Mr. Straub want a translator to be present? If so, what is the preferred language?

/NU northwestern university norris center/ student activities office

the Straubs   Oct 21 - 75

Not a party, but worth record —
Gregory's friends Jean-Marie &
Danielle Straub have come to
the USA and are staying in this
609 Clbs. Br for a "spotty" visit —
Greg is in Rome — Joan/Mich in Savannah
Vicky Bus in Bloomfield Conn. Mara
& Marie in Bklyn — Pam (& will in Orange
twp NY) Mary A came for a visit
tonight — Plenty of food in the "Frigid
aire"
Just a welcome for!
        Mary A Barone.

Hoping to come alive next week to be
here again! And with so many thanks
already for today *

Each.   Danièle
Woods is much better
than are Hollywood!
* many thanks + amitiés
                Jean-Marie Straub
                21 october 75 *

October 22, 1975

Mr. Daniel Talbot
New Yorker Films
2409 Broadway
New York, New York

Dear Dan:

I was distressed today to learn that there might be a possible misunderstanding about the amount of funding we had available for Jean Marie Straub and Daniele Huillot's visit here. We cannot spend more than $500, including travel, rentals and fee.

When we first discussed it on the telephone, I informed you that $400 was what we could really afford, but agreed to $500 and commented, in fact, that the sum would leave very little of a fee after travel for two persons and rentals.

I'm dropping this note now because Mrs. Marguerite Knowles, my administrative assistant, told me that Mr. Lopez was under the impression that the Center was paying $500 plus travel expenses. Please make sure that he is aware of our agreement.

Best wishes,

Gerald O'Grady
Director

CMS
GO'G:MWK

correct address

Xale

file

~776-831-2304

6/II/76

Dear Dan,

 thank you for <u>Partisan Review</u> and for sending
the script of <u>Hi</u>story Lessons to Paris: my mother got
it!

 Bill DM 2772 for fine grain of <u>Not Reconciled</u>
is to be paid directly to the Bavaria, Munich.
 I think it is very much okay if you charge
Inter Nationes with $ 100 per print "as a service";
problem is only, that I don't hear from them any more -
they have probably seen <u>Introduction to...Schoenberg</u> in
the meantime!?!

 Your document about 35mm release in the States
has interested us very much - I think, it is great from
you to fight on this field, for nobody else will do it:
they are all thinking of profit, in terms of money,
not in terms of profiting to the films and (consequently)
to the filmviewers!!!

 I'm sending your proposal to Straschek: he MMM
should try with the television. His address (just in
case) is still for a while c/o Janet Dawson

 3 Dover Court / 104 Southgate Road
 London N 13JA9 England

 If <u>Les Contrebandières</u>, which was such a good
film, had no success at all, then <u>we</u> have to be ashamed
every time we got some success, don't you think?!

 You are really very nice to exhibit Moses und
<u>Aron</u> in L.A. with a benefit for The Schoenberg Institute!
Let's hope that Schoenberg's boys won't do any harm
again with the dedication! We have now obtain that the
film will be running in some cinemas in the German
Federal Republic <u>with</u> dedication ("Prokino" distribution;
they are new, have only till now <u>Céline et Julie vont en
bateau</u>, which is a very good film, <u>Allonsenfan</u> and
<u>Le milieu du monde</u>, which are not so good...). But don't
tell them! Maybe they won't even see the dedication,
it is very quick - 48 images = 2 seconds!

 We were very happy to hear that Susan is
going on well, and about what Emilie de Brigard told you
on the phone.

 Much love to you, but also to Toby,
and Sandra and Jose....
 Danièle *

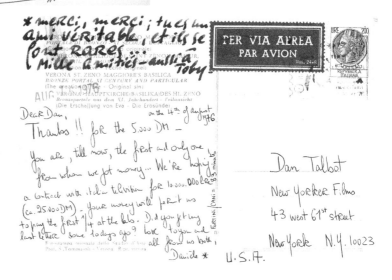

* merci, merci; tu es un
ami véritable, et ils se
font rares ...
mille amitiés - aussi à
Toby

VERONA ST. ZENO MAGGIORE'S BASILICA
BRONZE PORTAL XI CENTURY AND PARTICULAR
(The creation) - Original sin
VERONA - HAUPTKIRCHE-BASILIKA DES HL. ZENO
Bronzeportale aus dem XI. Jahrhundert - Einzelansicht
(Die Erschaffung von Eva - Die Erbsünde)

Dear Dan,
 on the 4th of august
 1976
Thanks !! for the 5.000 DM -

You are, till now, the first and only one
from whom we got money... We're hoping
a contract with italian television for 10.000 DDollars
(ca. 25.000 DM) - your money will for it us
to pay the first 1/4 at the labs. Did you get my
last letter some 10 days ago? love to you and
 all from us both,
 Danièle *

Fotocomposit... mensile dello Studio d'Arte
Prof. S.Tommasoli - Verona - Repr. vietata

PER VIA AEREA
PAR AVION

LIRE 200
REPUBLICA
ITALIANA

Dan Talbot
New Yorker Films
43 West 61st Street
New York N.Y. 10023

U.S.A.

to Dan Talbot
   New Yorker Films   AUG 30 1976
   43rd West 61st street   24th of august !
   New York

   Dearest Dan,
                 yesterday, coming back from two weeks in the country
   (40 miles from Rome, but no phone and no "autos"!) we saw on the street
   Gianni Amico - and heard of yours and Toby's being here...! We missed
   you and we heard that you had to be back on the 26th because of one
   of your daughter; it's a pity, really, and we are very sorry. But
   we want to tell you and Toby, as "compagnons" -even if we are living
   together since 21 years and not 25!!- that we want you both to be
   happy for twice 25 years again together, even if, or because,
   happiness is becoming more and more rare in the world around!

                 We are going to mix FORTINI/CANI tomorrow; if everything
   goes well, we shall be in Paris on monday next, to make the photograph
   sound by Eclair; then back here for the reversal and the prints...
   But till the first english subtitled print be ready, it will last
   a bit (december?)...

                 Please do me the friendship to order at your lab (Capital
   a 16mm color print of MOSES AND AARON (a good one - we shall see the
   print at Cologne in november, that you can tell Mr. Crane, and there
   see, if the good opinion we have about american labs is right or not!
   and have it sent pre-paid ("contre-remboursement", "per Nachnahme")
   to Leo Schönecker
      Filmkundliches Archiv
      D 5ooo Cologne 41
      Berrenrather Str. 423. Please let me know as soon as the print
   has been sent, thanks.

                 Did M&A run in L.A. ??? Or are you afraid to tell us?

                 Again much love to you both,

                                    Danièle *

   don't forget!

   How is Susan ?
   How is Richard ?

                                    nos pensées in jeventez

'SOLA D'ELBA
/eduta aerea
Vue aérienne
Aerial view
Luftansicht
Conc. S.M.A. 364 - Fot. 27661

JAN 7 1977

28 . XII. '76

Happy New year to you and
yoyes !
Don't forget to answer precisely my last letter
(about RiveRosel -CRi- FORTINI(CAN:) in
January '77 !
Hoping to see you again in 77...
Danièle + Jean-Marie
here, cut from the World, without neighbours, phone,
letters — to work —write...

562 — Ediz. Vannucci Ivana - Portoferraio - Tel. 93.131

Riproduzione vietata

AIR MAIL
V.A AEREA

Dan TALBOT
New Yorker Films
43 West 61st Street

NEW YORK
N.Y. 10023

SAR U.S.A.

DA FOTOCOLOR KODAK EKTACHROME

Rome, october 7, 78

Dear Dan,

please take 5 minutes for me, for I have 2 questions:

1st) what happened with TOUTE RéVOLUTION EST UN COUP DE DéS: you
said, you wanted to have, from the copy you get from us
with subtitles, a 16mm negative made, from which you
could make new prints -16-. Did you do it? How did it
work? How is the soundtrack on the 16mm Print??? The photo?

2nd) We have finished editing the last film DALLA NUBE ALLA
RESISTENZA (FROM THE CLOUD TO THE RESISTANCE); 35mm,
color, 104 minutes. I want you to think a little bit
about it already now, even if we are not going to have the
first print before 3 or 4 weeks, because I have to plane
the next things to be done, when and how: do you want to
have in that case too a 16mm negative made from the new
subtitled 35mm print you will get from us (1.450 subtitles
for the whole film)? And, if yes, as the sound is very
important (!) in this new film, is there a possibility of
making a separate optical sound negative to print with it
from your 16mm negative, so that the sound will be much
better?
    Think about it and write the answer to me.
JM. wants to try to go to Cannes with it, even if we hate
Cannes, for it is the only way to break the silence...
We are very, very tired, but somehow proud about this
film.
    Next week we are in Paris, to make the optical
sound (by ECLAIR) and I have to settle my mother's things.
In 2 weeks back here - to fight with the lab for the
first prints...
    Let's hear from you, love to you and
Toby from us both,

Danèle

P. Thanks for the Calculations - lists about our films - I'm sorry,
also sorry, that it is going on so slowly!!

Straub-Huillet   22nd June 1981
via dell'Imbrecciato 257
I-00148 ROMA (Trullo)

                                              Dan Talbot
                                              New Y rker Films

Dearest Dan,

          First of all: did you manage to get a 16mm negative
from the 35mm print of DALLA NUBE ALLA RESISTENZA ? Is it good?
Colour? Sound? Have they not damage the print?

          In case you have now, as we hope, a good 16 negative:
would you be friendly enough to order ne good 16mm print from it,
english subtitled as it is, to have it prepaid by Leo Schönecker
                                              Berrenratherstr. 423
                                              D-5 o Köln 41
                                                     West Germany
- and to let him get the print then through the Goethe-Institute
in New-Y rk, so that he does not have to pay the flight n r the
customs? He will give us 5.000 DM for the right to show the print
in West-Germany; and we are badly in need of money, after the
shooting in Egypt of the second part of TOO EARLY, TOO LATE -
particularly since the italian TV let us fall without giving us
any contract at the last minute!!

          Please let me know, as soon as possible, if this can
be done; thank you.

          And: included a copy of my answer t the School of
Art Institute of Chicago; maybe you can help us there too... Please
excuse us for involving you as much, because we always think of
you as of a friend, you know that. We have 200.000 F debts with
the last film, and we have just paid the last one for DALLA NUBE..
I know that you have little time, so do what you can. Thank you.

How is Toby? Give my love to her, and keep some for you!

                              Danièle *

PS. If this trip is possible, and we go to New York, we will
    need somebody to help us with a car for 2 or 3 days, driving u
    around New York to find a road and a landscape for this next
    film. D you know anybody who has a car and some time and who
    likes what we do, so that he would like to help us?
    What was the name of a young man, admiring very much John F rd
    and liking our work? I think, an irish name? He had a nice
    16mm print of Donavan's Reef, which we saw at his home... Do
    you see whom I mean? Maybe, he will help us - if he has a car,
    or a friend with a car... Thanks, Dan.

Were the films shown at the Public Cinema? When?

January 22; '82

JAN 2 9 1982

Dear Fred,
           you will not believe it, but to-day I received together
the copy of your letter from Decem 18 (the 'original' must havem
arrived in Paris on the same day we left it to Rome - and should be
on its way beetween Paris and Rome with all the other letters since
about two weeks!) and your letter from January 14! As you see, the
misteries of the italian mail are very profound...

           In the meantime, after discussing with Jean-Marie, things
are becoming clearer :

1) - we will fly directly from Rome to Chicago (that is: flight Panam
      from Rome -11.15- to New York / Kennedy -14.30 N.Y.Time-; then from
      New York / La Guardia flight American Airlines 377 -18.00- arriving
      in Chicago at 19.34 american time; if we want to stop in New York
      for example on our way back from Chicago to Rome, we have to pay
      some 20.000 italian lire more than the "excursion" price -more than
      7 days, less than 60- of 1.180.000 lire each)
      for example on April 1st, arriving then in Chicago at 19.34 local
      time. If you want us to arrive already on March 31, tell us...

    - And back flying from Chicago to Rome, but stopping then in New York
      (so that eventual film-showings in New York could be arranged for
      example during the last April week).

2) - We would like then to go by day-train from Chicago to Saint-Louis
      and from Saint-Louis to Kansas City (the important part for us is
      St.Louis-Kansas City by train, if there exist any passenger train!;
      so that, if more practical/in order to get a day-train from St.Louis to
    x Kansas City, we could also first fly from Chicago to St.Louis!
      Eventually spending a night in St.Louis, if necessary to get a day-
      train from St.Louis to Kansas City).

      And then by day-train from Kansas City to Norman/Oklahoma,
      as you proposed. Even if they don't pay much, it's important for us,
      since it is the only possibility to get the old train-track from
      New York to Oklahoma! So you can tell them that we are interested
      in coming to Norman...

    - Then to come back to Chicago possibly the same (day-train) way,
      in order to see it a second time, even the direction which
      interests us is to Oklahoma and not from Oklahoma, but it can be
      useful to see it from the other direction to control what we found.

      If there is absolutely no possibility by train from St.Louis to
      Kansas City(?), then we could also fly directly from Chicago to
      Kansas City and from there take the day-train to Norman/Oklahoma,
      and then back by (day) train from Norman to Kansas City and fly
      from Kansas City to Chicago...

      What we want to film next year is: 3 shots: two young men (Karl and
      Giacomo) sitting in the train, then Karl alone, then the landscape
      from the window of the moving train going to Oklahoma (did you read
      AMERIKA by Franz Kafka? That is it. All the rest -but the first
      shot : the Liberty statue from a ship- will be filmed in Hamburg
      (if the money, 600.000. DM, has been raised until then!) during the
      summer -11 weeks- of '83!

3) - Afterwards, being back in Chicago, we could go (by day train - so
      that we can see the landscape anyway!) to Minneapolis; don't book
      it with Richard Peterson too near the days in Norman, so that we
      have some time -reserve- for our train adventures before (for
      example, during the third april weekM in Minneapolis?).

4)   - And then, as last part of the journey, fly to New York on the way
back, having eventually some showings there (please speak with Dan
Talbot: he is the only one who can lend us the prints - and he
wanted to show eventually a whole retrospective in New York in his
cinema when we are there - so speak with him as soon as possible!
Tell him, that the last April week will be ok. On May we have to
be back in Rome. For lodgings in New York we will porbably have a
possibility by some french friends being there at that time, if
there is no other one; we want to stop in New York on the way back
first for the "Liberty", second for seing again the architecture
there and a lot of small details to refresh our memory... And we
have some people there, among them Dan, whom we would like to see
again!

(handwritten left margin: DAN!)

- We will bring the print of the last film (TOO EARLY, TOO LATE;
will be shown in 2 weeks in 2 cinemas in Paris; can you get the
February Number of the Chiers du Cinéma?) with us, english version
if Dan can fetch us at the Kennedy Airport when we arrive from
Rome on 1st April(?), in case we have any problem with the customs,
it will be very nice; also, we will have some 3 hours free time
beetween Kennedy arrival and La Guardia departure, so that we
could see each other a little!
This print will be then Dan Talbot's "property"; tell him also, we
are ready to take some print of the other films (16mm!) (not too
much, but 1 or 2 are possible!) with us from Chicago to Norman or
Minneapolis or..., if more practical than to send them), as we
did 1975!

(handwritten left margin: DAN! o / PRICE OF THE PRINT - LTC PARI! 6.000 F. If you can pay it to us in April, it will help!!)

- Last two things: 1) we can buy the flight tickets here, and you
will pay them back to us in Chicago; it would
have the vantage that, by that way, we won't
have to change money in the USA: as you
probably know, changing italian lires to get
dollars is murderous!
If it is not possible for administrative
reasons and you have to send us the tickets
(Rome-Chicago-Rome, more than 7 days, less
than 60, stop in New York on the way back),
think how slow the offices are working here...

2) We need a (simple) official letter inviting
us, which we could give to the american consu-
late here in Rome to get the visas; don't
send it too late either...
But go on writing normal letters, not express,
nothing but normal, it is still the best way!

Did you get the still you needed with JM. and me?

I hope that everything is clear now! And I won't write any (long)
letter to you again, take so much of your time in reading them!

We both hope that you and people around you didn't suffer too much
with that awful cold which came over America; here it was nearly
spring, and we had bad conscience of being so warm with so much people
suffering cold in East and North Europe and America!

                Amicalement,

PS. You are right: aside from Minneapolis, Norman and N.Y., no
"tour"; the only other possible would be in St.Louis, if there
is any interest and if it helps for the journey...

Can you find a friend of us now, in Chicago: Bernard Rubenstein; he
was living before in Evanstone (Illinois), School of music, Northern
University, tel.212/864/7515; is probably now in Chicago? Was the
"right arm" of Michael Gielen; conductor on our MOSES AND ARON...

cop

Danièle Huillet-Foussarigues
Jean-Marie Straub
6 rue Cavallotti
F 75018 Paris

18th November 1982

Miss Diane Elliott
AMTRAK
One Penn Plaza
New York City

N.Y.10001

Dear Miss Elliott,

we are going to shoot next summer in
Hamburg (Westgermany) a film after a novel by Franz Kafka
(with the help of the Ministery of Education in Westgermany --
for the anniversary of 100 years after Kafka's Birthday in 1883)
and we want to have 3 shots in the USA for the end of the film,
when the young "hero", Karl Rossmann, goes west to seek his
fortune.

Exactly: we want to film the countryside
(the river and the landscape) along the Missouri through the
(closed!) window of the normal train leaving in the morning
St.Louis to Jefferson City.

We will buy our tickets (2 people for the
camera, 1 soundrecordist, Straub and I, that means 5 people),
sit normally in a 4-seats-corner, and photograph through the
glass window, without lights or lamps, with a hand-camera, as
any tourist or amateur could do. We'll be also very quiet and
disturbing nobody, since we want to register the sound together
with the image. And that should happen at the end of september,
at the latest at the very beginning of october next year (1983).
We know exactly what we want, since we (Straub and I) already
journeyed three times beetween St.Louis and Jefferson City,
in order to know which parts of the countryside were the best
for us. Also: there are few people on this section of the train,
even on saturdays. Only on Sundays it is more crowded, and we
don't intend to shoot on a sunday.

And, even if people from the Amtrak on the
train told us that 'this was a free country and everybody was
allowed to photograph what he wanted to", we are writing to you
to ask for a permit, because we will be coming to the States
just for this shooting and do not want any difficulty or problem
at the last minute!

Hoping in your understanding and help to
"smoothen" our way as much as possible and avoid bureaucratic
complications, and thanking you in advance for doing so,
we remain sincerely,

(Jean-Marie Straub)   (Danièle Huillet)

Dearest Dan,

can you do something for me: find 2 (two) Auto-
numbers (the identification numbers you have to have or
to put on a car) from New York State, but the ones
for the <u>front</u> of a car, not the number for behind,

and send them quickly to me (so that I get them
before the end of this month) well packed, so they
are not destroyed when they arrived, to Hamburg:

Straub,
Zeughaus Strasse 46
D 2000 Hamburg 11
                Westgermany   ????

                I suppose you can guess
                that we need that forthe
                KAFKA-FILM. We begin on
                July 1st.

        Please remember Mrs Barbare Marsmhall XXXX thht we're
        AMTRAK-waiting... Many thanks,

                        much love to you and
                        Toby from your both
                        Straubs,

June 1st, '83 — (40)city code
Telephone #312681 O.K.

                                    D*
                                How are you both?

Dearest Dan, Thanks for your letter to JM. Let's hope, you will succeed   may 1st, 86*
and open CLASS-RELATIONS in theaters... We <u>are</u> patient, but (nearly)
everything seems to go wrong in the world, so wrong, that we will soon have
no desire any more to fight for ... our work!
        Still = please do something very important for me (for my
birthday = today I am 50... as the chief-code in CLASS-RELATIONS!):
manage to find out the address of STEFAN BRECHT, and make sure
he gets my letter and the 2 reviews annexed. Maybe you
could even speak to him about it (Read my letter to him, so you know
                                    what's about!)

if you can avoid the 7 lawyers!
        Excuse me for boring you with that, but you are the only one
I trust for helping me (and it's JM's favourite film, together with
                                        DAHIA NUBE...)
                Much love to you and Toby,
                                            D***
From May 26th to June 26th = STRAUBS, Hotel MIRAMARE, Room 201
                    Lungomare ANDREA DORIA
                    I - 97100 MARINA di RAGUSA (sicily)

Dear Dan,

        send the contract - as you
will,

      but to this address before
the 16th of november:

          Straub c/o Renate Merck

          Glashüttenstrasse 20 A

         D 2000 Hamburg 4

              Westgermany

And let us hope, that the Death of
Empedocles will be a hit, so that
you and we don't have to go to prison
for debts!

      You will get the print
in some days now, it will be sent to
you next week; with the contract tell
us if you got it, so that we don't
have to worry about the print at
least; thanks; love,

               D.

oct.24, '87

Ted Fendt

Dividing Lines
The Distribution and Reception of Jean-Marie Straub and Danièle Huillet's Films in the English-Speaking World

Jean-Marie Straub and Danièle Huillet are not filmmakers who have ever enjoyed wide popularity. Their works have tended to be marginalized to what Straub has sarcastically called the "art cinema ghetto." This is the case just as much in Europe as in the Anglo world. Yet, there was a time when their films, if not widely seen in commercial theaters, did garner a level of support similar to that of other major "art film" makers of their generation. Early on, they gained and benefited from the support of a small, dedicated and diverse group of critics, programmers, and exhibitors. While this has fluctuated and shifted over the years, it has allowed their films to be shown and discussed consistently. The once thriving non-theatrical circuit of university film clubs and small film societies provided venues in which the films could be shown regularly, exposing new, generally younger audiences to their work. The story of the distribution and reception of their films begins in 1965 when their second film, *Not Reconciled*, crossed the Atlantic for the New York and London film festivals.

1 Richard Roud, "Cut rate cinema," *The Guardian* (London), July 22, 1965. It should be noted that, as in Europe, it would take a number of years before critics recognized Huillet's role as equal co-author of the films. Until the mid-1970s, Straub is almost exclusively referred to as the filmmaker.

Not Reconciled caused a scandal at the Berlinale when it was premiered at an unofficial screening during the festival in early 1965. One German critic declared it the "worst film since 1895." Not only German critics attended the screening, however. Richard Roud was also present. An American-born Francophile critic and co-founder of the New York Film Festival as well as a programmer for the London Film Festival, Roud (1929–1989) was an influential voice in English-language film culture. Between the early 1960s and the mid-1980s he was instrumental in bringing much of the era's more daring European cinema to England and the United States. Particularly knowledgeable about French cinema, he would have been aware of the fervent defenses of *Not Reconciled* in the pages of *Cahiers du cinéma* after it came under attack by the German press.

Attempting to convey some of the controversy in the first piece of criticism written in English on the film, Roud[1] proposed aesthetic causes for the outrage: "Some thought [Straub] had no right to tamper with the novel. Others were annoyed because he has directed his non-professional cast to speak in a deliberately unexpressive manner, something between the intoning of a Bresson and the alienation technique of a Brecht. This was resented all the more be-

Ted Fendt

cause, it would seem, no Frenchman has the right to tamper with the German language." These criticisms would continue to be levied at Straub and Huillet with each successive film. But *Not Reconciled*'s affront to mainstream German tastes valorized it for foreign critics who could also appreciate its formal qualities.

In New York, the film received little attention, although a few years later Susan Sontag would tell Jonas Mekas in *The Village Voice* that when she first saw the film, she wanted to "go and kiss the screen."[2] Though Straub and Huillet did not travel to New York for the festival, they did go to London. A brief biographical sketch in *The Guardian* describes Straub as "a thin, anxious-eyed Frenchman," with the "pale, frozen, inward look of a young Samuel Beckett."[3] Critics reviewing the film were split. In his festival preview for *The Observer*, Kenneth Tynan found the film incomprehensible and castigated the filmmakers: "movies like this discredit the cause they profess to serve. They encourage the belief [...] that much of 'art cinema' is a playground where the fantasies of a few neurotics are patiently transferred to celluloid by hundreds of skilled and dedicated technicians."[4] *The Times* was far more positive, emphasizing "performances of a strange hieratic intensity and formality" and especially noting the film's handling of time: "What M. Straub has done is to take the various elements of present and past, fragment them and reassemble them in such a way that they immediately interact and fuse before our eyes."[5] A week later the paper declared the film the "principle discovery" of the festival and a "hopeful sign that

the rigid compartments in which German filmmakers have so long been confined are beginning to break down."[6]

The London Film Festival was an important occasion for the filmmakers personally. One evening, Misha Donat, a young film and television composer, was telling Roud how much he loved the film when Roud pointed the filmmakers out to him, having a drink alone at the bar, and suggested he introduce himself. He did so, contact information was exchanged, and a two years later Huillet got in touch to see if he would help translate the subtitles for their next film, *Chronicle of Anna Magdalena Bach*, beginning a collaboration that has continued to the present.

Although the New York press had given no attention to *Not Reconciled*, the summer 1966 issue of *Film Quarterly* published a long review by Gideon Bachmann. The critic had a unique perspective: he was born in Germany but raised in Eastern Europe, spoke German and saw the film at the first Berlin screening. His review explicates the German cultural situation, clarifying the environment in which the film was made. There is "a great wave of consciousness in German cultural circles about the Nazi past,"

2 Jonas Mekas, "Movie Journal," *The Village Voice*, October 30, 1969, p. 66
3 "London Letter: 'Refugee' film director," *The Guardian*, November, 17, 1965
4 Kenneth Tynan, "Charlton's Chapel," *The Observer*, October 31, 1965
5 "Interesting New Talents in London Film Festival," *The Times* (London), November 18, 1965
6 "The German Cinema," *The Times* (London), November 27, 1965

he writes, but the critical reception suggests "it is most unlikely that a German could have made this film."[7] Like other critics, Bachmann is most struck by the film's complex handling of multiple time periods: "By eliminating time in the traditional sense, Straub has found a first avenue towards realizing the motion picture as the sole art form to work in the fourth dimension: to change, eliminate, recreate, abstract, control – in short, use as a creative element – the factor of time."[8] He describes the filmmakers' methods of adaptation (taking the text unaltered from the source material) and the documentary quality of the cinematography ("Straub *cites* reality") and, of course, does not ignore their politics: "Just as punishment and destruction were handed out by the Nazis without explanation, Straub hands out pangs of consciousness without explanation."[9]

Thanks to Roud's programming and support, Straub and Huillet had entered the radar of American and British film culture. The film was shown again in New York in January 1967 in a Museum of Modern Art series on contemporary cinema, programmed with Peter Kubelka's *Unsere Afrikareise*.

Their next film, *Chronicle of Anna Magdalena Bach*, premiered at a small festival in the Netherlands, the second edition of Hubert Bals' Cinemanifestatie in Utrecht, before gaining wider

recognition internationally when it was selected for the 1968 Berlinale alongside Werner Herzog's *Signs of Life*, Godard's *Weekend*, Welles' *The Immortal Story* and Claude Chabrol's *Les Biches*. Andrew Sarris, reviewing the festival in *The New York Times*, found *Chronicle* to be one of "the more interesting films of the festival [...] though far removed from the country's film industry, which now seems to specialize in dull sex films."[10] Sarris expresses some concern that Straub "seems at times too conscious of his deliberate intellectuality and stylistic austerity," but ultimately praises the film for coming to terms with "Bach's essence as a musical genius," ranking it with Herzog's entry as the best film in the festival. The newly expanded selection committee of the New York Film Festival, which included Sarris and Susan Sontag, invited the film to screen in its 1968 edition.

Another American paying attention to Straub and Huillet's films was Daniel Talbot, the co-owner (with his wife Toby) of the New Yorker Theater at 88th St. and Broadway as well as the distribution company New Yorker Films, which had a growing catalogue of European and American art films. In the summer of 1968, before *Chronicle*'s New York premiere, Talbot contacted the filmmakers at their apartment in Munich to inquire about distributing their first two films, *Machorka-Muff* and *Not Reconciled*. Straub and Huillet were happy to accept. In their response on August 13, 1968 (in Straub's handwriting but with Huillet's English) they go over details of prints and subtitles: "subtitles cannot be printed in Munich, because the German never show a film with titles: all pictures

7 Gideon Bachmann, "Nicht versöhnt," *Film Quarterly*, vol. 19, issue 4, Summer 1966, p. 52

8 Ibid.

9 Ibid., p. 54

10 Andrew Sarris, "Festival Without Fuss," *The New York Times*, July 14, 1968

here are german-synchronized..."[11] Another distributor, Robin von Joachim, had already contacted them about distributing *Chronicle* but as he could not promise a theatrical release, they preferred Talbot distribute that film as well. The subtitled print, paid for by MoMA rather than the German distributor Telepool ("too miserly to pay"), was on its way to the Lincoln Center in New York. The filmmakers asked Talbot to contact Amos Vogel, director of the festival, about seeing the film prior to its public premiere, but suggest he take his time: "I am very patient – and very glad that you like the films."

As the festival got under way in New York, two lasting, general critical approaches to Straub and Huillet's films were quickly established. The mainstream press tended to dismiss them out of hand, while they found support among younger critics writing in film journals or alternative press. Allen Hughes, a dance and music critic for *The New York Times* who had reviewed some recordings by the film's lead actor, Gustav Leonhardt, two years earlier, found the film "cheerless," and although the performances were "mostly very good," he concluded that "some will find it deadly dull."[12] In *The New Yorker*, Penelope Gilliat suggested one could spend the screening thinking about "dinner, and what to do with your life, and how bitterly cold the air-conditioning can be in America."[13]

A young J. Hoberman, writing in what was ostensibly his own college paper, the *Harpur Film Journal*, was paying closer attention to the film when he saw it at the press screening: "Nothing written can really describe its strange and beautiful quality and any plot synopsis will make it seem boring as a bitch. Straub fuses selections from the letters of Bach's second wife (stoical descriptions of domestic tragedies and artistic frustrations), dramatizes a few short anecdotes, but concentrates most of the film on the music. The camera rarely moves but when it does the effect is tremendous. The whole film is suffused in Vermeer-like light & if you let it this film can do fine things for your head."[14] *Chronicle* also received enthusiastic support again from *Film Quarterly*: "Most of the long shots as well as many closer ones are taken at an angle. The angles themselves as well as the restless curve of the Baroque interiors give such a strong impression of movement that I was several times surprised to realize that the camera had not actually moved at all. [...] But of course there *is* movement within the individual shots, though always of a slow and subtle kind. Hands move on harpsichord and organ keys, and one remarkable shot shows feet moving over the organ pedals."[15]

After New York, the film was shown in San Francisco in Leonhardt's presence before the

11 Except where noted, all correspondence between Huillet and Talbot and other correspondence by (and to) Talbot comes from his personal papers. Spelling and grammatical errors in the originals have not been corrected.

12 Allen Hughes, "Bach as Seen in His 2nd Wife's Memories," *The New York Times*, September 20, 1968

13 Penelope Gilliat, "The Current Cinema: A Report on a Party," *The New Yorker*, September 21, 1968, p. 148

14 J. Hoberman, "Report on the New York Film Festival 1968," *Harpur Film Journal*, reprinted online by *Film Comment* [www.filmcomment.com/blog/nyff-j-hoberman-1968-report]

15 Harriet R. Polt, "Anna Magdalena Bach," *Film Quarterly*, vol. 21, no. 2, Winter 1968/1969, p. 55–56

print was shipped across the Atlantic to London. Awarded the festival's top prize, *Chronicle* also received more attention in the British press. John Russell Taylor highlighted the film's minimalism and the qualities it shared with early cinema: "Much of it consists simply (if that is the word) of performances of the music by musicians in costumes of Bach's day and in the original settings, photographed in long takes, either completely fixed or with one simple camera-movement. It sounds as though it could not be 'cinema', but in practice it could not be anything else. Straub himself says that one should observe in his film the hands on the keyboard, the musicians' wigs moving as they play, in the same spirit of wonder with which the first spectators of Lumière's first films saw the leaves moving on the trees."[16]

A British distributor interested in releasing the film planned to dub the narration in English. With the help of Misha Donat, Straub and Huillet found a French actress to record an English narration under their own direction. They also took the opportunity to record the narration in four other languages (French, Dutch, Spanish and Italian). Although the subtitled print ultimately became the preferred version for distribution, this was an opportunity to experiment with the use of foreign accents, a practice they would substantially develop in their subsequent films.

Dan Talbot bought the subtitled version of

the film for distribution in North America and soon wrote to see if he could acquire, sight unseen, a short film for which the couple had won a prize when it premiered in October at the Mannheim Film Festival, *The Bridegroom, the Actress, and the Pimp*. The filmmakers agreed without hesitation: "Enormous Daniel, coming back from Cologne, I find your letter… Okay, my decision is made. […] My God, man, what a price (for a short!) – and what a man, who is planing a war against the whole American system, alone!" Another letter ten days later firmed up plans with Talbot for making and shipping new prints to New York and announced their intention to leave Germany in February to move to Rome where they would make their next film.

In February 1969, *Machorka-Muff, Not Reconciled* and *The Bridegroom, the Actress, and the Pimp* received a week-long run at the New Yorker Theater. *Chronicle of Anna Magdalena Bach* was shown for one week in April. They were part of a four-month series of films New Yorker was distributing, including premiere runs of films by Ousmane Sembène (*Black Girl*), Robert Bresson (*Pickpocket*), Luc Moullet (*The Smugglers*), Agnès Varda (*The Creatures*), Robert Frank (*Me and My Brother*) and Jean Eustache (*Bad Company*). Admission to all screenings was $1. The indifference and bafflement of the mainstream press remained the same as during the festival. A.H. Weiler, reviewing the shorts in *The New York Times*, felt *Machorka-Muff* displayed Straub's "potential as an imaginative filmmaker," but otherwise the films leave "a viewer more often perplexed than convinced."[17] His review in April of

16 John Russell Taylor, "Enter Charm, exit tricks," *The Times*, December 7, 1968
17 A. H. Weiler, "German Newcomer's 3 Films," *The New York Times*, February 24, 1969

Ted Fendt

Chronicle was also negative. These reviews did not bother the filmmakers much, however. German reviews, they told Talbot, "were much more stupid and vulgar (and not funny at all)."

A postcard Straub and Huillet sent in August 1969 announced their arrival in Rome in July. They thank Talbot for helping their new British distributor, Andi Engel, acquire prints of their films for his company PolitKino and mention that, "with God's help," they will begin to shoot their next film on August 27, an adaptation of Pierre Corneille's *Othon*. Writing in *The Guardian* that summer, Richard Roud reported on a few films then in production in Italy, including the new Straub-Huillet project. The film was to be shot in color 16mm with a cast of mainly Italian non-actors and would be their first film in French: "Straub is fascinated by the effect a foreign accent can have in renewing a language, the very strangeness of intonation and pronunciation can give, he feels, a new life to a classic text."[18]

Like the Bach film, *Othon* did not premiere at a major festival. Unlike *Chronicle*, however, it did not subsequently play at a larger festival and therefore received less notice internationally. It was first shown in January 1970 at the Rapallo Film Festival in Italy, a festival focusing primarily on experimental 8mm and 16mm work. A month later, Roud praised the film in *The Guardian*, evoking a Brechtian influence in the way the film continually bounces viewers "back and forth, between movement and repose, between action and reflection, between life and art,"[19] explaining the logic behind using direct sound to capture the performances and the con-

stant whir of Roman traffic in the background. When it was shown in the 1970 New York Film Festival, the film was mainly ignored or dismissed as an "imbecile experiment…and undeniably dull."[20] Surprisingly, praise came from *The New York Times* where a young critic named Roger Greenspun reviewed it. He notes ironically that: "This year, as in the past, the festival paid Straub its greatest tribute (the only valuable, though not infallible, objective test of a film's importance I know of) when at the press screening of 'Othon' half the audience got up and walked out."[21] He praises the performances and cinematography and optimistically suggests that a love for Straub and Huillet's films would come with time.

Despite the lack of critical support, Talbot remained faithful to the filmmakers and acquired *Othon*. Although the film was shot on 16mm, making a 16mm print with subtitles (necessary for non-theatrical distribution) was an issue at the time and Talbot proposed making a 16mm print from the 35mm blow-up that had screened in the festival. When they saw a test reel, Huillet and Straub were greatly disappointed. The "bicolour (red and green)" picture and a soundtrack described by Huillet as "completely… 'kaputt'" would not do and they came close to deciding not to show the film at all in such a state.

18 Richard Roud, "East is West and West is East," *The Guardian*, July 22, 1969
19 Richard Roud, "Verse against Vespas," *The Guardian*, February 11, 1970
20 Harold Clurman, "Film Festival I," *The Nation*, October 5, 1970
21 Roger Greenspun, "Straub's 'Othon' Plumbs Love and Drive for Power," *The New York Times*, September 14, 1970

190

But preferring the film be seen, and knowing it could not be shown without subtitles, they agreed to a compromised print. They insisted, however, that "in seven years, when you have no more THE EYES DO NOT WANT... in your distribution, you destroy or give us back your 16mm negative and every print." *Othon* opened commercially for one week in New York at the St. Mark's Cinema in the East Village on November 18, 1971. *The New York Times* reprinted Greenspun's review without alteration.

A small wave of writing and interviews promoting and defending the filmmakers' work was published around 1970. The first English-language interview, conducted by Andi Engel, was published in a British journal called *Cinemantics* and Engel wrote a chapter on their films for the 1970 book *Second Wave*. These were followed in 1971 by the publication of a book-length study of all the films by Richard Roud titled simply *Straub*.[22]

Engel's essay highlights three decisive aspects of the films, three qualities which make them unique and essential works: "their political impact, their simplicity, and their honesty." He also explains the filmmakers' use of direct sound and the absolute necessity of every element they include in each film: "if you take anything, one minute detail away from any Straub film, you can see how the whole thing crumbles under your fingers."[23]

In *Straub*, Roud develops and expands upon ideas sketched in his reviews, covering each film through *Othon* and providing important biographical information about the filmmakers and a translation of the script for *Not Reconciled*. The image of the filmmakers that emerges is that of creators of austere, minimalist works influenced most heavily by modernist filmmakers like Robert Bresson and Carl Dreyer (although Roud does also note the importance to Straub of the then-obscure Jean Grémillon) who seek to counter the conventions of mainstream cinema. Roud is also keen on comparing their films to music, particularly in their structure. His perspective – complementing the already dominant view of their work as "difficult" and "challenging" – calcified into a foundation for Straub-Huillet criticism over the next decade. One reviewer at the time, Joel Gersman, writing in the student film magazine *The Velvet Light Trap*, criticized the book for not doing enough to familiarize the "uninitiated" with these films, observing that at the time Straub remained "much discussed in elite film circles" without public recognition.[24] Nonetheless, Roud's book did provide a point of entry for those interested in discovering more about Straub and Huillet's work and remained the most comprehensive and available book on them in English for the next two decades.

The walkouts during the press screening for *Othon* were probably nothing compared to the walkouts when *History Lessons* hit the screen at the 1973 New York Film Festival. Roud brought Straub and Huillet's adaptation of an unfinished Brecht novel to the festival along with a short

22 Richard Roud, *Straub*, London: BFI, 1971. Reprinted New York: Viking, 1972
23 Andi Engel, "Jean-Marie Straub," in *Second Wave*, New York: Praeger, 1970, p. 130
24 Joel Gersman, *The Velvet Light Trap*, Summer 1973, p. 54

made in April 1973 for West German television, *Introduction to Arnold Schoenberg's "Accompaniment to a Cinematographic Scene."* In *The New York Times*, Paul Gardiner proposed that it "may well be the festival's most teasingly irritating film. It is impossible to like Straub's austere vision of a Brecht novel about Julius Ceasar [sic] – even for many dedicated Straubists."[25] One Straubist who remained dedicated and, in fact, saw the film twice, was George Robinson, a Columbia University student and critic for the student paper, the *Columbia Daily Spectator*. He had read Roud and Engel and had written an enthusiastic and perceptive review of the short films earlier in the year after a screening at the university. Robinson describes the "orgasmic intensity" of some of the cutting and camera movements and the relevance of the drama to the historic moment: "the impression of behind the scenes wheeling and dealing... Very apt indeed for the year of Watergate."[26]

Audiences had trouble seeing *History Lessons* after the festival, however. Talbot planned to distribute it but not long after, Brecht's German publisher, Suhrkamp Verlag, contacted the filmmakers, threatening legal action if they continued to screen the film. Straub and Huillet had not cleared any rights before shooting, believing they would likely be prevented from using the book if they tried. For the following two years, a long, slow back and forth of letters, phone calls and meetings took place between the lawyers and Talbot in the United States and the filmmakers and the publisher in Europe as they tried to reach an agreement that would allow for future screenings. In a March 1975 letter to

Suhrkamp Verlag, Talbot's frustration is palpable: "I find this whole matter very discouraging at this point less for practical reasons than for moral ones. Two things I know: I am anxious to distribute the film and Jean-Marie Straub is anxious for me to distribute the film, and I am sure that if Bertolt Brecht were alive today he would also want to see this film exhibited." An agreement was eventually reached giving Brecht's son Stefan – apparently only partially informed of the situation – a percentage of royalties from rentals. This lasted through 2002, when Talbot contacted Stefan Brecht and asked him to give up the royalties. Brecht wrote back simply: "You can have it," and the matter was settled.

In the meantime, Straub and Huillet had continued to work. They realized their long-planned project of adapting Arnold Schoenberg's opera *Moses und Aron*. Financing for the film had been difficult to raise. In the early 1970s, Talbot put them in touch with Claude Nedjar, a French producer in Paris, who ended up investing in the project, paying for the sound mix, and much of the remaining budget eventually came from television and radio.

In the winter of 1975 *Moses and Aaron* premiered at the Rotterdam Film Festival (founded by Hubert Bals in 1972 after giving up his Cinemanifestatie events in Utrecht) where Roud wrote very enthusiastically on it. The following summer it was shown, along with *History Lessons* (finally having its UK premiere), at the Ed-

25 Paul Gardiner, "Anticinematic 'History Lessons'," *The New York Times*, October 1, 1973
26 George Robinson, "Straub's Brechtian Lessons," *Columbia Daily Spectator*, October 2, 1973

inburgh International Film Festival, with Straub and Huillet in attendance. *Moses and Aaron* was presented in the main festival and *History Lessons* as part of a sidebar conference organized by the British journal *Screen* on the topic "Brecht and Cinema/Film and Politics." By the mid-1970s, Straub and Huillet's films had become important references for the cultural theory-inflected criticism whose influence had been steadily growing since the 1960s as film studies entered the academic sphere. In the conference, Stephen Heath presented a paper on *History Lessons* and Nagisa Oshima's *Dear Summer Sister*, "From Brecht to Film: Theses, Problems," that was followed by a discussion transcribed in the journal. Heath proposes several definitions of "realism" as defined in Brecht's writings, illustrating them with examples drawn from the two films.[27]

History Lessons proved as challenging for radically-minded critics as it did for the mainstream press. Reflecting a common criticism of Straub and Huillet's work at the time, some at the conference felt the films were not politically en-gaged enough, that they lacked a clear-cut message. Colin MacCabe expressed problems with the filmmakers withholding information that he felt was "necessary for the audience to understand" the film.[28] James Pettifer criticized the driving sequences for having the "aesthetic effect of inducing a semi-hypnosis."[29] In response, Heath and his colleague Martin Walsh[30] argue that the filmmakers are using Brechtian strategies of distanciation meant to provoke critical reflection in viewers. In opposition to commercial cinema, Walsh feels the film makes viewers work; being bored "is simply a cop-out."[31] The driving sequences are an opportunity "to engage with all kinds of issues, the issue of representation [...] the notion of what is history."[32] Walsh and Heath valorize the serious, rigorous aspects of the film, emphasizing formal elements over dramatic content and those qualities that made the film stand out from the mainstream cinema they rejected. A year earlier, Walsh had already pursued these issues in an article published in the American journal *Jump Cut*, discussing the hostility towards Straub and Huillet's films in North America as well as their "reflection on film expression" and "deconstruction" of the language of "illusionist" cinema.[33]

Continuing his commitment to the filmmakers, Roud invited *Moses and Aaron* to the 1975 New York Film Festival. He had first seen the film at a private screening in Paris in December 1974 with Sontag, Jacques Rivette, Michael Gielen (the opera's conductor) and Louis Devos (Aaron) and his family. Upon its premiere in Rotterdam, he devoted a full-page review to it

27 Stephen Heath, "From Brecht to Film: Theses, Problems (on *History Lessons* and *Dear Summer Sister*)," *Screen*, vol. 16, no. 4, Winter 1975/6, p. 34–45
28 "Brecht Event III: Thursday, August 28. Discussion," *Screen*, p. 44
29 Ibid.
30 In several essays written during the 1970s, Walsh theorized a possible Brechtian cinema, drawing heavily on Straub and Huillet's films. These were collected after his untimely death in 1977 in *The Brechtian Aspect of Radical Cinema*, London: BFI, 1981
31 "Brecht Event III," op. cit.
32 Ibid.
33 Martin Walsh, "Political formations in the cinema of Jean-Marie Straub," *Jump Cut*, issue 4, 1974, p. 12

Ted Fendt

in *The Guardian*, providing a detailed description of the complicated process of the sound recording. He hoped Schoenberg's music would make the film more accessible and give the filmmakers a wider audience who would be helped "over the austerely stony ground of Straubian mise-en-scène."[34] In the summer of 1975, *Film Comment* published his review of the Rotterdam Film Festival, in which he further elaborated on his views of the film, declaring it Straub and Huillet's "most accomplished, most achieved work, and possibly their most accessible."[35]

In January 1975, Huillet told Talbot that they had been contacted by the Goethe-Institut in New York about going to the United States to screen their films. She asks that Talbot look into helping arrange travel. Planning for the trip continued throughout the year as they worked out the details for Talbot's acquisition of *Moses and Aaron*. Roud's budget for the festival had been cut so that he could not pay to bring the filmmakers to New York. The West German government would not provide money since they were French nationals. In April, it seemed the trip might not happen. Huillet wrote to Talbot: "But don't worry: we are not longing so much for going to the States, and in some way, if we cannot go because nobody can afford to pay for it, we'll be happy: M&A does not need us, it speaks for itself alone." Eventually, their German producer Klaus Hellwig of Janus Film paid for one plane ticket and Talbot bought the other.

Straub and Huillet felt the trip would be worthwhile only if they could stay for several weeks – "don't kill us, not too much! We don't

want to stay 39 days, not longer than 1 month," Huillet wrote. Talbot decided to organize a traveling retrospective of the films, allowing the filmmakers to see the country and engage with American and Canadian audiences for the first time. The filmmakers requested that of the films shown, each program include *History Lessons* and *Introduction*. Huillet told Talbot as well, regarding places they'd like to visit: "the only thing [Jean-Marie] really wants to see is the Mississippi… Can you arrange it in your program? […] I would like evidently, to see the Grand Canyon, but there is no university there!!!"

Moses and Aaron was shown in New York in the company of Truffaut's *The Story of Adèle H.*, Fassbinder's *Fox and His Friends*, Herzog's *The Enigma of Kaspar Hauser* and Marguerite Duras' *India Song*. The mainstream press reacted as usual. *The New York Times* published a pan, even referring to the film by the wrong title. George Robinson, again in the *Columbia Daily Spectator*, wrote briefly about it: "The film's complexity, I confess, staggers me on a single viewing, but one of the strongest impressions I took away from it is its profoundly mystical strain in the midst of a singularly materialistic mise-en-scène."[36]

The strongest, most articulate writing on the film came from the pen of Manny Farber and Patricia Patterson, reviewing the festival in *Film*

34 Richard Roud, "Golden Bull," *The Guardian*, February 26, 1975
35 Richard Roud, "Rotterdam Journal," *Film Comment*, vol. 11, no. 3, May/June 1975, p. 2
36 George Robinson, "Selections from This Year's New York Film Festival," *The Columbia Daily Spectator*, October 17, 1975

Comment. They evoke Straub and Huillet's "concern for Thingness over illustration," the palpable immediacy of each character, landscape and object in front of their camera in a way no one had yet done. Instead of bafflement, they express the powerful and striking originality of the film: "The delicious and joyful *Moses and Aaron* […] is a very sensual experience, from its voluptuous 360-degree pan around the oval-shaped Roman arena in the Abruzze mountains to the Cézanne-like sculptural insistences which make every crack in the arena's walls seem extraordinary, a physical reality that reverberates in the mind. […] this is one of the few times when weather, sound, and physical setting have been united with such tactile objectivity."[37]

Known for their confrontational Q&As, at Lincoln Center's Alice Tully Hall, the night of October 7, the couple did not disappoint. Straub swaggered back and forth on stage giving a declamatory reading of *The New York Times* review ("a motionless screen in an empty theater with angry, monotone voices on the soundtrack reading out pamphlets in music"), castigating the paper for calling the film "Aaron and Moses." While in New York, the filmmakers met a number of their American admirers for the first time: Talbot, Farber, and Patterson, as well as Tag Gallagher, a young critic who had the filmmakers and Roud over to his apartment where he projected 16mm prints of John Ford's *Pilgrimage* and *Donovan's Reef.* Straub confused Roud when he proclaimed a love for the films of the very out-of-fashion Ford and his desire for his own work to achieve a "combination of John Ford and Kenji Mizoguchi."[38]

Following the festival, the filmmakers set off on a fourteen-city tour across the United States and Canada. They screened their films at museums, universities and cinemas in Berkeley, San Francisco, Santa Barbara, Los Angeles, Fresno, San Diego, St. Louis, Buffalo, Chicago, Toronto, Boston and Lafayette, PA, in addition to screenings in New York at the Goethe-Institut and the release of *Moses and Aaron* at the New Yorker Theater. Many of the small, growing band of fervent Straub-Huillet supporters worked in museums and academia and were instrumental in helping arrange the visits and find stipends. The British filmmakers and theorists Peter Wollen and Laura Mulvey were teaching at Northwestern University in Chicago at the time and hosted the filmmakers at the school. In Chicago, they stayed with Bernard Rubenstein, Michael Gielen's assistant during the recording and shooting of *Moses and Aaron.* Manny Farber evidently went through a great deal of trouble to bring them to UCLA, writing to Talbot: "You have no idea how many asses have to be licked. Only for Straub would I do this again."[39]

37 Manny Farber and Patricia Patterson, "The New York Film Festival Review: Breaking the Rules at the Roulette Table," *Film Comment*, vol. 11, no. 6, November/December 1975, p. 34. Reprinted in *Negative Space.*

38 Tag Gallagher, "Lacrimae Rerum Materialized," in *Die Früchte des Zorns und der Zärtlichkeit. Werkschau Danièle Huillet/Jean-Marie Straub und ausgewählte Filme von John Ford*, ed. Astrid Johanna Ofner, Vienna: Viennale and Austrian Film Museum, 2004. Republished in *Senses of Cinema*, issue 37, October 2005 [sensesofcinema.com/2005/feature-articles/straubs]

39 Letter, Manny Farber to Talbot, 1975, Dan Talbot Papers, Rare Book & Manuscript Library, Columbia University in the City of New York

In Chicago they reiterated their love of John Ford at a screening at Northwestern, remembers Dave Kehr, timidly telling a student – almost as if embarrassed – that their favorite Ford film was *Donovan's Reef*. Bruce Jenkins, a graduate student at the university at the time, recalled a few years later Straub and Huillet's interests as tourists: "they wanted to see the factories; they wanted to see the neighborhoods where the black people live; and they wanted to see the Cézannes at the Art Institute – the Cézannes and only the Cézannes."[40] Years later, Huillet recounted: "the first thing that we did upon arriving in New York was to go to the Museum of Modern Art, to see...Cézanne."[41] Tag Gallagher recalls that while in New York, they hitchhiked to Merion, PA to visit the Barnes Foundation, the location of some Cézanne paintings which were legally bound not to travel.

At the turn of the year, *Jump Cut* published an interview the filmmakers had done in New York as well as a Martin Walsh article on *Moses and Aaron*, and, in London, Andi Engel published the first issue of *Enthusiasm*, which he devoted solely to Straub and Huillet's work, including two interviews and a journal kept during the shooting of *Moses and Aaron* by Gregory Woods, a production assistant and the translator of the subtitles, with lengthy annotations by Huillet. The interviews gave the filmmakers an opportunity to clarify further for English readers their attitudes and ideas about their films. Contradicting some of the notions put forward in *Screen* the previous summer, Straub told *Jump Cut*: "I could say that the deconstruction one

makes in *The Bridegroom, the Actress, and the Pimp* is interesting, but the whole film is the history, the story, of a hatred and that is all. [...] And in *History Lessons* the film does not consist really of those parts of it that would interest someone like Michael Snow for example." Straub denied their films were primarily formal experiments: "...the reflection on the 'language' – I'll use that term although I don't really believe in it – actually, reflection on the instrument and the methods you use in cinema are only interesting because in *History Lessons*, for example, it is the story of a crisis of conscience. [...] The film tells the story of the birth of anger, which explodes at the end."[42]

In his piece on *Moses and Aaron*, Martin Walsh analyses the film's organization of shots and unconventional cutting patterns and what distinguishes them from the "transparent" cutting of Hollywood films, preventing audiences from establishing identification with the characters. Later in 1976, he participated in a conference on film theory at Purdue University where he presented a paper on *Introduction to Arnold Schoenberg's "Accompaniment to a Cinematographic Scene."* Two other participants,

40 Bruce Jenkins, "Adaptation and Ideology: Two Films by Straub and Huillet," unpublished screening introduction, 1981 [Revised and included in *Film at the Public* program, ed. Jonathan Rosenbaum, Buffalo: Media Studies Center, 1982]

41 Danièle Huillet, "Quite A Lot of Pent-Up Anger," in Jean-Marie Straub and Danièle Huillet, *Writings*, edited and with an introduction by Sally Shafto, New York: Sequence Press, 2016

42 Joel Rogers, "*Moses and Aaron* as an object of Marxist reflection," *Jump Cut*, no. 12/13, 1976, p. 61–64

Maureen Turim and Bruce Jenkins, presented papers on Straub and Huillet as well, elaborating the ways in which their films deviated from, questioned and overturned conventions of commercial narrative cinema.

Back in Italy, the filmmakers began pre-production on their next project, a film based on Franco Fortini's 1967 book *The Dogs of Sinai*. Despite a significantly smaller budget than *Moses and Aaron* and working again with the more economical 16mm format, raising money was as difficult as ever. Initially, Italian television would not finance the film, and money was cobbled together from friends: Andi Engel, Stéphane Chalgadjieff and Talbot, who provided (the equivalent of) 5,000 DM. Letters and postcards written throughout the summer of 1976 kept him abreast of the film's progress: "We are editing Fortini/Cani now; shooting was very tiring – much more than M&A – because of Fortini himself and because of all the journeys, and the elections and and and; but I think we got something interesting." Talbot and his wife were in Rome in August to celebrate their 25th wedding anniversary, but the filmmakers were away in the countryside during their trip. "We missed you and we heard that you had to be back on the 26th because of one of your daughter; it's a pity really, and we are very sorry. But we want to tell you and Toby, as 'compagnons' – even if we are living together since 21 years and not 25!! – that we want you both to be happy for twice 25 years

again together, even if, or because, happiness is becoming more and more rare in the world around!"

Over the next months, Huillet sent several detailed letters to Talbot with instructions for making the best subtitled 16mm prints (still a technical challenge). A New Year's postcard sent from Elba ("cut from the world, without neighbours, phone, letters – to work – write...") reminds him to update her on the progress of the lab work.

Fortini/Cani had its world premiere at the Pesaro Film Festival. For the first time since 1965, however, the New York Film Festival did not invite Straub and Huillet to screen their latest film. Richard Roud and Susan Sontag saw the film in Paris in early 1977 and did not care for it. Roud later described it as "their least successful film, largely because the text by Fortini did not provide a sufficiently lyrical springboard to contrast dialectically with the dryness of the *mise en scène*. The original text is already too Straubian."[43] Fortini's addressing of the contentious Arab-Israeli relations could also have posed a problem for the American programmers, in addition to the film being their first in Italian and completely severing them publicly from the German cinema with which they'd long disassociated themselves personally and professionally. Huillet was not surprised. She wrote Talbot: "I had some idea, that it would be like that, but please keep it for you: it seems, that the 'malentendu' between Richard and our films, which begun with NOT RECONCILED and went on till MOSES AND AARON, was finally destroyed by FORTINI/CANI... Richard never had

43 Richard Roud, "Jean-Marie Straub," *Cinema: A Critical Dictionary*, New York: Viking, 1980, p. 970

a 'political' head, and Fortini says some things, which are going to be seen very badly in N.Y. – particularly by some american jews... [...] we should find that right in a certain way, that the festival, after showing [Bernardo Bertolucci's] 1900, should refuse to show FORTINI/CANI."

The film debuted in the English-speaking world in the summer of 1977 at the Edinburgh International Film Festival and received a small US premiere at Jackie Raynal's Bleecker Street Cinema in October as part of a *Cahiers du cinéma* week programmed by Serge Daney, Louis Skorecki and Jonathan Rosenbaum. The film had only a handful of screenings over the following months, including a West Coast premiere in December at the Pacific Film Archive. Andi Engel had founded a new distribution company in the UK, Artificial Eye, and acquired prints of each of the films through *Fortini/Cani* and a short film the couple had completed in the meantime and sent Talbot in December, *Every Revolution is a Throw of the Dice*. Gilbert Adair saw the film, a recitation of Mallarmé's *A Throw of the Dice Will Never Abolish Chance*, in Paris and wrote a column on it for *Sight and Sound* in the spring of 1978: "one of Straub's most striking attempts to remove the kind of patina that encrusts all great art."[44]

Far less was written about *Fortini/Cani* than any previous Straub-Huillet film. The only major reflection to appear following these first screenings was an article by Mark Nash and Steve Neale. Writing about the Edinburgh festival's conference on "History/Production/Memory," they devote several pages to the film, considering it in relation to a number of theoretical issues raised in the conference regarding cinema and history.

The film did receive significant attention the following year when *Artforum* published Gilberto Perez's article "Modern Cinema: The History Lessons of Straub-Huillet." Perez, writing not only on *Fortini/Cani* but on most of the other films as well, offers a perspective very different from the piece by Nash and Neale, whose analysis tends to be more descriptive. Perez develops an interpretation that places Straub and Huillet in a tradition of modern artists from Cézanne to Brecht and Joyce whose concern with form "lay[s] bare the device" without neglecting content. He draws parallels between their work and that of filmmakers like Griffith, Dovzhenko and Jean Renoir, especially for their "refusal to enforce the acceptance of any mode of presentation [...] and their endeavor, instead, to bring their formative activity under our scrutiny, having us entertain the alternative and ponder conflicting ways of regarding things."[45] He argues that the films are self-reflexive but do not avoid drama; form and content are given equal weight.

For Christmas 1977, Straub and Huillet received a book on Cézanne as a gift from New Yorker Films. Huillet and the distributor corresponded regarding details regarding the Mallarmé film as well. She mentions that the last remaining copy of their translation of the subtitles is in the possession of American Mallarmé scholar David Degener in San Francisco (De-

---

44 Gilbert Adair, "Journals: Gilbert Adair from Paris," *Film Comment*, vol. 14, no. 2, March/April 1978, p. 6
45 Gilberto Perez, "Modern Cinema: The History Lessons of Straub-Huillet," *Artforum*, October 1978

gener wrote film criticism in the 1960s and 1970s, co-authoring with Tom Luddy, curator of the Pacific Film Archive, the first New Yorker Films catalogue).

During the summer of 1978, Straub and Huillet shot their second film in Italian, *From the Cloud to the Resistance*. In October, following the editing, Huillet contacted Talbot to ask about the quality of the 16mm prints he had made of *Every Revolution is a Throw of the Dice* and to go over details regarding the new film. She mentions that "even if we hates Cannes," Straub wanted to try to screen the film at the festival in order to "break the silence" they felt had begun to surround their work.

From the Cloud to the Resistance did premiere in Cannes in 1979, out of the main competition in the Director's Fortnight. In spite of the bigger premiere, it was not invited to the New York Film Festival, denying it the attention crucial to a foreign film's theatrical success. Nevertheless, Talbot acquired it, perhaps with the understanding that the film would do business on the non-theatrical circuit where the other films continued to be booked regularly (it did receive a belated, weekend run in Chicago in 1981). Huillet recognized the challenges of distributing their films in a letter to Talbot: "Our main problem is, more and more, to get people to see the films we're making – and this battle becomes always harder and more hopeless. That is what is destroying us!"

The 35mm print of *From the Cloud to the Resistance* arrived in the US in July 1979. Talbot immediately made a 16mm print for non-theatrical screenings. However, aside from a screening

at NYU for a class taught by Jonathan Rosenbaum, the film remained unseen publicly for nearly two years. The first public screening was in April 1981 at SUNY Buffalo, together with *Every Revolution is a Throw of the Dice*, as part of a series focusing on adaptations programmed by Bruce Jenkins.

In June 1981, returning from Egypt where they were filming the second part of *Too Early, Too Late*, Straub and Huillet received a letter from Fred Camper, a professor at the School of the Art Institute of Chicago, asking if they would attend a retrospective the following April. Huillet told Camper they would be glad to come – though only after a retrospective so that his students could ask them "concrete questions."

The trip was also an opportunity to scout locations for their next film, *Class Relations*, for which they planned to film several shots in America. They asked Camper to help plan for them to travel by train from Chicago to St. Louis as well as to New York. In April 1982, they arrived in Chicago, a print of the English-language version of *Too Early, Too Late* in their luggage (the film had premiered at the Kino Arsenal in Berlin in November 1981 and was also shown at the 1982 Berlinale Forum). From Chicago, they scouted locations along the Missouri River aboard an Amtrak train, and traveled to Kansas City, Norman, Oklahoma, and Columbus, Ohio for university screenings and to Madison, WI for a conference on German film. During their time in St. Louis, Straub and Huillet met Barton Byg, a PhD candidate at Washington University, and in Ohio the American filmmaker Thom Andersen. They would go on to cast both Byg and Andersen in *Class Relations* and Byg helped to translate the subtitles for the film into English. The filmmakers then traveled to New York where they screened *Too Early, Too Late* at the Collective for Living Cinema on April 30, leaving the print with New Yorker Films before returning to Europe.

Straub and Huillet were in New York again the following November for a complete retrospective at the Public Theater organized by Jonathan Rosenbaum. It included the North American premiere of a new short film shot over the summer, *En rachâchant*, and a selection of films by filmmakers whom Straub and Huillet admired. Through SUNY Buffalo's Media Study Center, Rosenbaum and Bruce Jenkins published a 20-page dossier on the filmmakers, including Perez's *Artforum* piece, articles by Rosenbaum, Jenkins, Tony Rayns and Luc Moullet as well as an interview with the filmmakers discussing the films they had programmed to complement their own (the selection included Glauber Rocha's *Antonio das Mortes*, Dreyer's *Day of Wrath*, Chaplin's *A King in New York*, Stroheim's *Blind Husbands* and Renoir's *This Land is Mine*, among others).

The retrospective led to a positive write-up of the new features in *The Village Voice*. J. Hoberman characterized *Fortini/Cani*, *From the Cloud to the Resistance* and *Too Early, Too Late* as "political pastorals" and compared their juxtaposition of a text with a landscape to the work of a young American filmmaker, James Benning. He found *From the Cloud* to be the "most mysterious and beautiful of the new features."[46] An interview with the filmmakers by Phil

Mariani, which also included a transcript of parts of a Q&A at the Public Theater, was soon published in the first issue of *Wedge*, a short-lived New York art and critical theory magazine.

From September 21–25, 1983, the filmmakers made their fourth and final trip to the United States, joined by a small crew and actors to film shots for *Class Relations*, including two on the Amtrak train they had ridden the year before and a shot of the Statue of Liberty in New York. The scene in the film featuring the Americans, Barton Byg and Thom Andersen, was shot in Hamburg. Andersen, who does not speak German, learned his lines phonetically (like another member of the cast, Laura Betti), following closely the pauses and stresses marked by Huillet and Straub in the script. He recalls Huillet directing him to try not to act until "the text is in your blood."

Class Relations premiered at the 1984 Berlinale where it received the most positive reviews of any of their films in years. Writing in *The Guardian*, Richard Roud criticized the title, wondering if it indicated a "masochistic desire to keep people away from the box-office, or a patronizing nudge to the audience," but praised the film's cinematography, proclaiming: "each shot is a marvel of austere pictorial splendor."[47] For the first time in nine years, a Straub-Huillet film screened at the New York Film Festival where it received surprisingly positive reviews

46 J. Hoberman, *The Village Voice*, November 16, 1982
47 Richard Roud, "Berlin bows to backstage drama," *The Guardian*, February 24, 1984

from the local press. Although he expresses a fair degree of caution and does not feel Straub and Huillet's style is suitable to the material, Vincent Canby praised the acting in *The New York Times* and Ed Sikov, writing in the *New York Native*, found it to be a visual "knockout" and quite humorous.[48] J. Hoberman wrote a long essay on the film for *Artforum*, "Once Upon a Time in Amerika," and Gilbert Adair praised it in *Sight and Sound*.

The film opened in London in 1985, distributed by Artificial Eye and shown at Andi Engel's Camden Theater (Engel had a role in the film too) where it ran for a week. With no US release planned, however, Straub's patience with New Yorker Films began to run thin. In March 1986, he wrote to Talbot, in French: "I gave you the present (among others) of two wonderful films: *From the Cloud to the Resistance*, which is the best Italian film since *Paisan*; *Class Relations*, which is the only German film since *The Thousand Eyes of Doctor Mabuse*. And I see that you don't have the courage to offer them the smallest commercial release in New York. Yet you impose on the inhabitants of the city in your own theaters, the artificial and, in any case, non-existent and – even commercially – stale products of Fassbinder and the Tavianis." Despite a few belated, short runs in a few art houses without any promotion, the brief attention Straub and Huillet had again received in the early 1980s had quickly dissipated.

Public screenings of their films became more rare as the decade advanced, and academic interest followed suit. Although Maureen Turim published two pieces on their work in 1984 and 1986, the decline of much of the theoretical debates of the mid-1970s that had kept discussion of their work active (if inaccessible to a wider public) was reflected in a general decrease in scholarly writing on Straub and Huillet.

In 1987, Talbot acquired their next film *The Death of Empedocles*. It had premiered at the Berlinale but divided critics sharply. Many who had seen *Class Relations* as some kind of move towards a more commercial style, found *Empedocles* to be a step in the opposite direction. Reporting from Berlin for the *Chicago Tribune*, Dave Kehr called it a "disappointment,"[49] though in a second dispatch ten days later he described it as an effort to reach a "filmmaking degree zero," capturing "some of the startling beauty of the first, primitive film experiments of the 1890s."[50] Not selected for the New York Film Festival, the film received its North American premiere in September 1987 at the Festival des films du monde in Montreal. In the US, it premiered in November 1988 at the Pacific Film Archive and was given a week long run in Chicago at the Facets Media Center, on the condition that Jonathan Rosenbaum would devote his *Chicago Reader* column to the film that week.

Rosenbaum's review notes the difficulty that *Empedocles* had crossing the Atlantic and the lack of interest from his colleagues who had generally "dismissed it as Straub-Huillet's least

48 Ed Sikov, "Class Relations," *New York Native*, October 22, 1984
49 Dave Kehr, "'Platoon' Invades Europe Festival," *Chicago Tribune*, March 5, 1987
50 Dave Kehr, "Berlin Barometer," *Chicago Tribune*, March 15, 1987

rewarding and/or most 'punishing' feature." He commends the performances and recitation of the text as well as the intense presence of the actors and locations. "Part of Straub-Huillet's achievement is to dramatize this text well beyond any possible silent reading of it by giving it a maximal physicality in sound, emotion, and gesture. And because so much of the text is concerned with the physicality of nature (as well as the four elements), the static camera setups function musically in a way that is analogous to pedal points; like sustained or suspended chords, they allow the melodies of the verse and the countermelodies of the surrounding natural sounds to take root."[51] Despite Rosenbaum's efforts, however, attendance at Facets was low.

The film premiered in London in 1990 at the Goethe-Institut during a Straub-Huillet retrospective. In his review of the screening for *Sight and Sound*, Julien Petley notes that the film was not going to receive a release at Andi Engel's theater. But the screening at the Goethe-Institut, he writes, was attended by a large, enthusiastic crowd, most of whom stayed for a "well-informed debate with the filmmakers."[52] They spoke about editing the film, particularly working with long takes (Huillet: "don't believe it is easier to edit when you have long-held shots: you have to be even more precise than in the short ones."[53]) and the distribution of their work (Straub: "We are not naive, we know that in the present state of distribution and exhibition such films as ours will have only a very small audience in the 'communal' cinemas. But when *Moses and Aaron* was shown on television, even

at 11 at night, it got almost two million viewers. *Empedocles* was shown at 11:30 and that got 800,000."[54])

The landscape of film distribution and exhibition had radically shifted by the late 1980s. A review by Rosenbaum or a piece in a film magazine could not counter the indifference to Straub and Huillet's work or foreign films in general. Non-theatrical bookings were decreasing and continued to decrease in the 1990s as the distribution of films on video – New Yorker still only had film prints – increased exponentially. After *The Death of Empedocles*, New Yorker Films never acquired another Straub-Huillet film.

Talbot proposed the filmmakers make an English-language version of *Cézanne* in 1989, but they declined, feeling it would not be the same film. It was shown in London without subtitles in March 1991 at the National Film Theater, receiving a brief, but very positive, mention in *The Guardian* after the screening. The following two films (*Antigone*, *Lothringen!*) were neither distributed nor shown in the English-speaking world.

The first major study of Straub and Huillet's films in English since the 1982 Rosenbaum catalogue appeared in the midst of this indifference: *Landscapes of Resistance*, Barton Byg's study of about their German language work.

51 Jonathan Rosenbaum, "The Sound of German," *Chicago Reader*, December 2, 1988 [Reprinted in *Essential Cinema: On the Necessity of Film Canons*, Baltimore: Johns Hopkins University, 2004]
52 Julien Petley, "Etna & Ecology," *Sight and Sound*, Summer 1990, p. 150
53 Ibid.
54 Ibid.

An attempt to shed light on the films and re-introduce the filmmakers to Anglo audiences, Byg provides important background information on Straub-Huillet and their working methods. He describes the critical reception of their films and challenges many of the earlier interpretations. Drawing on the aesthetic theories of Adorno, Benjamin, and Brecht, among others, he situates the films in a German cultural and literary context, draws parallels with the work of other modernist artists and develops the evaluations of Farber and Patterson, Perez, and Rosenbaum by stressing Straub and Huillet's "strategy of rediscovering the fundamental visual pleasure of cinema."[55] Byg draws on his first-hand experience in order to discuss their relationship to translation, comparing their methods of adapting texts to Benjamin's translation theories in his chapters on *Empedocles, Black Sin,* and *Antigone.*

Perhaps in connection with the book or the presence of Jonathan Rosenbaum on the selection committee, in 1997, the New York Film Festival screened *From Today Until Tomorrow,* their adaptation of the Schoenberg opera. Reviews in the mainstream press differed little from those of the earlier films. Writing for *Variety,* Godfrey Cheshire was relieved the film lacked the "political overtones"[56] of *Moses and Aaron* and commended the music and performances. He advised viewers interested in truly adventurous cinema to look elsewhere, however. The film did not have other festival screenings but the Harvard Film Archive and the Pacific Film Archive, thanks to the efforts of their curators John Gianvito and Edith Kramer, acquired subtitled prints. Another major contribution to Straub-Huillet studies came the following year with the publication of Gilberto Perez's book *The Material Ghost: Films and their Medium* which included a greatly expanded and updated version of his *Artforum* essay, discussing *Not Reconciled, History Lessons,* and *Fortini/Cani* in greater detail.

The couple's following film, *Sicilia!,* premiered in the Director's Fortnight at Cannes in 1999 and came to the New York Film Festival as well. The film's one and only screening was packed, according to Phillip Lopate, reporting in *Film Comment.* The English-language press generally ignored the film, however. Academics like Perez who were continuing to write on the films tended to focus on the earlier ones which remained in distribution through New Yorker Films, not writing on anything following *The Death of Empedocles.* Although it was not distributed theatrically, the Harvard and Pacific film archives again acquired prints of *Sicilia!* for their collections. The film received a Canadian premiere in 2000 in a Best of the Decade series programmed by James Quandt.

Straub and Huillet did not attend these US screenings in the 1990s, having not returned to the US since 1983. This was in part due to their disgust with US foreign policy, as Huillet told John Gianvito: "following the NATO bombings in Kosovo in 1999, they declared they would

55 Barton Byg, *Landscapes of Resistance: The German Films of Danièle Huillet and Jean-Marie Straub,* Berkeley: University of California, 1995, p. 2
56 Godfrey Cheshire, "From Today Until Tomorrow," *Variety,* September 29, 1997

never again come to the United States."[57] But it was also due to the feeling that they had too much work related to their own projects. In a letter from 2004, Huillet declined an invitation from Ahn C. Park, a programmer in South Korea, to attend screenings of their films in Seoul: "…we're working, and we need our strength and concentration. Going to the end of the world for three days like jet-setters – we've never done this and we won't start at our age… Moreover, we ourselves are not important, what we have to say is in the films."[58]

After *Sicilia!*, five years and two films passed before a new film of theirs was shown in the English-speaking world. In the meantime, a partial retrospective – everything in the New Yorker Films catalogue – took place in October 2004 at Anthology Film Archives in New York, and a year prior, in January 2003, the Talbots and Straub and Huillet met in Paris for the first time since the 1980s, discussing a possible DVD release of *Chronicle of Anna Magdalena Bach* and, eventually, *Moses and Aaron*. A Japanese company had already released those films and some others on VHS and Laserdisc in the 1990s and Huillet hoped they could use the same video masters. *Chronicle* was released on DVD three years later, in 2006.

2004 also saw the publication of two major studies of their work: Ursula Böser's book *The Art of Seeing, the Art of Listening* and Tag Gallagher's essay "Lacrimae Rerum Materialized." Commissioned by the Viennale and the Austrian Film Museum for the catalogue of the 2004 Straub-Huillet retrospective in Vienna (complemented by the filmmakers' selection of

27 films by John Ford) and re-published online the following year on the Australian film website *Senses of Cinema*, Gallagher's essay marks a radical departure from much of what had been written on the filmmakers since the 1970s. Foregoing theory, Gallagher's piece is an auteurist study disputing many of the prevailing notions in Straub-Huillet criticism, defiantly not taking it as a given that their films are difficult or challenging. Rather than introducing modernist art theory, he compares them to Ford and Kenji Mizoguchi, seeking to draw attention on the traditional roots of their oeuvre, not their modernism. He argues that "what is wonderful is the sensuality and passion"[59] expressed visually and through the rich performances.

In contrast, Ursula Böser's work – to date the last book-length study of Straub and Huillet's films in English (published by a German press) – takes a neo-formalist approach to several of the filmmakers' German-language films. Informed by the theories and writings of Viktor Shklovsky, David Bordwell, Kristin Thompson, and Noël Burch, Böser considers the ways in which Straub and Huillet create formal patterns in the editing and performances (her account of speech patterns in *Class Relations* and attention to the filmmakers' intervention in Kafka's text are particularly noteworthy for English-lan-

---

57 John Gianvito, "From Yesterday Until Today," *Undercurrent*, issue 3, November 2011 [old.fipresci.org/undercurrent/issue_0306/huillet_gianvito.htm]
58 Letter, 2004, Dan Talbot Papers, Rare Book & Manuscript Library, Columbia University in the City of New York
59 Tag Gallagher, op. cit.

guage speakers) and jolt viewers into seeing anew through their repetition and disruption.

After six years of disinterest, the 2005 London and New York film festivals again programmed a new Straub-Huillet film. *A Visit to the Louvre* (2004) was shown without subtitles as they did not have time to prepare a translation with Misha Donat. In New York, reflecting the changing status of Straub and Huillet's work, the film was shown in the festival's experimental sidebar, Views from the Avant-Garde. At its single screening, at 11 a.m., a printed translation of the film's narration was handed out to the audience. Jared Rapfogel, reviewing Views for *Senses of Cinema*, deemed the film's inclusion alone to make that year's program "essential" and noted the near impossibility of seeing Straub and Huillet's films. The only English-language review of the film at the time, Rapfogel's text highlights the film's formal rigor; "but [it is] not without a certain flexibility; while more often than not the paintings are shown in their entirety, sometimes their physical frames are included within the cinematic frame, sometimes cropped out, and in a handful of instances Straub/Huillet break their self-imposed rule against re-composing the artwork to focus on a certain part of the canvas."[60]

60 Jared Rapfogel, "Stop Motion: Transformation and Stasis at the NYFF's Views from the Avant-Garde," *Senses of Cinema*, issue 39, May 2006 [sensesofcinema.com/2006/festival-reports/views_avant_garde2005]
61 Mary Rinebold, "Orchard Underground," *Artnet* [www.artnet.com/magazineus/features/rinebold/rinebold9-6-06.asp]

A resurgence of Straub and Huillet criticism occurred between 2005 and 2007, bolstered by the DVD release of *Chronicle*. Translations of articles by Jacques Aumont and Dominique Païni appeared in print and online, and the blog of critic Andy Rector, *Kino Slang*, began to make available older, unavailable essays on the filmmakers in addition to original criticism.

After the release of the Bach DVD, Huillet wrote Talbot to let him know she was working on a new video master of *Moses and Aaron* for a Japanese release with *Introduction to Arnold Schoenberg's "Accompaniment to a Cinematographic Scene."* She hoped New Yorker Films would want to release that film on DVD as well. The company announced its upcoming release in 2008 but it was delayed until 2011 after they briefly went out of business in 2009.

New York cinephiles had another opportunity to see a previously unseen Straub-Huillet film in 2006. Miguel Abreu was first exposed to Straub and Huillet's work while attending the California Institute of the Arts in the 1980s, where Thom Andersen taught and screened their films. He opened his Lower East Side gallery in March 2006 with 35mm screenings of *The Death of Empedocles* and *Cézanne* (the North American premiere). The screenings in the small gallery were free and crowded. Paintings by contemporary artist Blake Rayne were hung on the walls and Abreu handed out copies of the Dominique Païni essay, "Straub, Hölderlin, Cézanne": "a distant confrontation of the masters," in Abreu's words.[61]

In her final letter to Talbot, in August 2006, Huillet, sick with cancer, informed him they would not be attending the Venice Film Festival for the premiere of their latest film *These Encounters of Theirs*, shot over the summer: "too many police." In October, Huillet passed away. Obituaries published in *The New York Times* and *The Guardian* characterized her as the "softer, more conciliatory personality" to Straub's "bad cop" at screenings.[62] Miguel Abreu Gallery hosted a memorial screening at the end of the month with *Too Early, Too Late* and *Fortini/Cani* and a number of tributes appeared online and in print, notably a dossier in *Undercurrent* and a review of *These Encounters of Theirs* and a dialogue between Portuguese filmmaker Pedro Costa and Thom Andersen published in the Canadian magazine *Cinema Scope*.

In March 2007, *These Encounters of Theirs* received its North American premiere at New York's Lincoln Center in the series Film Comment Selects. Aside from some strong recommendations from critics online, there was little mention of it in the press. In September, Wavelengths, the experimental section of the Toronto International Film Festival, screened *Europa 2005, 27 October*, a short film shot on mini-DV (their first) in collaboration with Jean-Claude Rousseau and Christophe Clavert, the last film the couple completed together. The following year, Straub completed two short films planned with Huillet just prior to her death – *Itinerary of Jean Bricard* and *Artemide's Knee*. Both works were shown in the Directors Fortnight at the 2008 Cannes Film Festival and reviewed very positively by a handful of English-language critics, including Daniel Kasmen, writing in Mubi Notebook, and Andréa Picard,

who reviewed *Artemide's Knee* for *Cinema Scope* and showed it in her Wavelengths program at the Toronto Film Festival in September, pairing it with a silent 16mm film by American experimental filmmaker Nathanial Dorsky. Both *Itinerary* and *Artemide's Knee* were also shown at the London Film Festival the following month. Perhaps due to the lack of prints with English subtitles (therefore requiring digitally projected, manually-operated soft-titles at each screening), the films were not widely seen despite the small but positive reception in the international press.

A year later came *The Witches, women among themselves*, another adaptation of one of the Pavese dialogues and Straub's last film in 35mm. The film was seen in fewer festivals than the previous two and consequently received less press coverage. After a screening in Wavelengths in September, it was shown in Los Angeles at AFI Fest, selected by Pedro Costa to screen with his feature *Ne change rien*. It was not until May 2010 that *The Witches* and the previous two films came to New York, where they were presented to a packed house at Anthology Film Archives during Migrating Forms, a festival of experimental film and video work programmed by Nellie Killian and Kevin McGarry. In *The New Yorker* the following week, Richard Brody reviewed the films, lamenting their delayed arrival to the United States but concluding it was better late than never.

As Straub moved to digital filmmaking, his production pace picked up and from 2009 on-

62 Dave Kehr, "Danièle Huillet, 70, Creator of Challenging Films, Dies," *The New York Times*, October 12, 2006

wards he began making around two short films a year. Barbara Wurm, reviewing the 2009 Viennale for *Senses of Cinema* described one of the first digital shorts, *Corneille-Brecht*, a recitation and reading of excerpts from two Corneille plays and Brecht's *The Trial of Lucullus*, as a "radically sublime lesson in remobilising the 'demos'."[63] That film – in three different versions – and one of Straub's two previous digital films, *Oh Supreme Light*, was shown in Views from the Avant-Garde in 2010. Richard Brody publicized the noon screening on his blog for *The New Yorker*, writing primarily on *Oh Supreme Light*, which he found to be a "short film of extraordinary provenance and import."[64] Critic Michael Sicinski wrote at length on *Oh Supreme Light* on his website, *The Academic Hack*, in early 2011. Sicinski attends closely to the film's aesthetic elements, and Straub's use of Edgar Varèse music at the beginning: "This could be said to rhyme, in a broad sense, with Straub's cinematic use of space and landscape. There is a radical particularity in the land formations Straub commits to film or video; in using the camera to register a place's sonic existence, or its reflected light, Straub is also giving us a concrete segment of its accumulated physical history, practically a core sample. So in that regard, [Varèse's] *Déserts* is music that hints at pure sound, the sound between sounds, and the molecular level of deep listening."[65]

Views from the Avant-Garde continued to be the main venue in the Anglo world for Straub's new work in 2011, premiering three digital shorts (*An Heir, The Inconsolable One* and *Jackals and Arabs*), as well as the 1994 film *Lothringen!*. Robert Koehler, reviewing the program, which had also screened at the Locarno Film Festival, notes the prescience of screening the newer *An Heir* with the older *Lothringen!*, both shot in the Lorraine region of France (where Straub is from) and based on books by Maurice Barrès. In a curious echo of reviews of *Not Reconciled* from over forty years before, Koehler writes that Straub "doesn't much like Germans, and it seems that with *Un héritier*, he returns to *Lothringen!* and its ringing call against German psychic and cultural occupation."[66] These programs – again held early in the morning – were decently attended despite receiving almost no coverage in the New York press, not surprisingly given the general lack of coverage of avant-garde cinema.

After a Canadian premiere of *A Tale by Michel de Montaigne* in 2012 in Wavelengths, no more new Straub films would be programmed in North America for three years. *Mubi Notebook*, in a piece on each film in the Wavelengths program, continued its support of Straub's latest work with reviews by both Michael Sicinski and

63 Barbara Wurm, "Leftist Glamour? or, Home Runs and Explorations: The 47th Viennale: Vienna International Film Festival," *Senses of Cinema*, issue 54, April 2010 [sensesofcinema.com/2010/festival-reports/vienna-international-film-festival]

64 Richard Brody, "Light Viewing," *The New Yorker*, October 1, 2010 [www.newyorker.com/culture/richard-brody/light-viewing]

65 Michael Sicinski, "Reviews of New Releases Seen, January 2011," *The Academic Hack* [academichack.net/reviewsJanuary2011.htm]

66 Robert Koehler, "Locarno 2011. Old and New Straub," *Mubi Notebook* [https://mubi.com/notebook/posts/locarno-2011-old-and-new-straub]

Daniel Kasman. Perhaps because it was shown in the festival without English subtitles, Sicinski focused again on the film's formal elements – "much of the meaning of this lovely film resides in the strict separation of elements, those parts of conventional cinema that are usually combined without a second thought" – although he moves beyond the level of description and suggests an interpretation of the various ways Straub uses on- and off-screen sound: "So why does Straub place his insisted-upon use of sound in a context where it is one choice among several? Perhaps because being modern means recognizing the vulnerability Montaigne describes, the fact that your project is perennially under assault from other competing visions."

Although the next two films Straub made – *Dialogue of Shadows* and *Concerning Venice* – did not make it to North America and were only belatedly shown in the UK, they did receive some coverage in English-language film journals. Daniel Fairfax, in his report on the 2013 Viennale for *Senses of Cinema*, found *Dialogue of Shadows* to be "the richest, most beautiful viewing experience" he had at the festival. Of the actors, he writes: "The physicality of their on-screen presence and the musicality of their recitations are performative high-points of Straub/Huillet's work."[67]

A program of the digital shorts at the Goethe-Institut brought all of them to London in 2014, and in 2015, Straub's feature-length film *Communists* and its accompanying short *The Algerian War!* came to Montreal for the Festival du nouveau cinéma. The film also traveled to the Melbourne International Film Festival, making it the first new Straub film to screen in Australia in many years.

The fact that only a handful of critics have given these recent films any attention in English, says more about the state of their exhibition than it does about the films themselves – few screenings and often in marginalized avant-garde programs whose visibility in the press is already close to non-existent. Relatively strong attendance at the scarce screenings of the new work in London, New York and Toronto, especially from a younger, more adventurous cinephilic audience, suggests there is more interest in Straub's work than the limited exhibition would indicate.

In 1976, Straub told *Jump Cut*: "You have to have methods of dividing. Dividing not only the public, but also the ways that you choose, the instruments that you choose. But if it's only to divide cinema, to divide itself, that is not very interesting. That's like the serpent biting its tail."[68] Since *Not Reconciled*, Straub and Huillet have made films that divide through their formal and dramatic risks, through their political and ethical beliefs. Films that fearlessly divide audiences, programmers, critics and, finally, cinema. This may have led to the loss of certain supporters who were instrumental in assuring that their films were seen, although the loss of

67 Daniel Fairfax, "October Love Song: The 51st Viennale," *Senses of Cinema*, issue 69, November 2013 [sensesofcinema.com/2013/festival-reports/october-love-song-the-51st-viennale]
68 Joel Rogers, "*Moses and Aaron* as an object of Marxist reflection," *Jump Cut*, no. 12/13, 1976

D. H. & J.-M. S. on the road

the non-theatrical distribution chain played a significant role as well. Nevertheless, when supporters were lost, new, interested viewers turned up. Straub and Huillet's work has attracted a diverse array of critical approaches and caused many to walk out. Recent screenings suggest, however, that despite a lack of decent prints and only rare occasions to see the films, new or old, interest could be greater than ever.

69 Danièle Huillet, "Quite A Lot of Pent-Up Anger," in *Writings*, op. cit.

One has always had to go to their films – to book the prints or seek out the ever rarer screenings. Yet, this is what Huillet said pleased her most about the Barnes Foundation, the art museum in Merion, PA to which they had hitchhiked in 1975 to see some Cézannes: "we were happy to have finally found a museum where it was considered normal for people to come to the paintings – which can always be achieved if you really want even with hardly any money (we're the proof!) – and not the paintings to the people."[69]

Barbara Ulrich

Straubian Reproductions

Organizing and preparing the North American Tour

I am very grateful for the opportunity to re-count the circumstances and choices that have led to the 2016/2017 traveling North American retrospective. The first presentation of the complete works of Jean-Marie Straub and Danièle Huillet – films from 1962–2015, 53 years of work and 46 titles – is a fantastic, unprecedented event that would never have been possible without the help of many friends and unknown "Straubians" who would prefer to remain anonymous.

As unprecedented as it is in its current form, the retrospective nevertheless fits within the very old association that links the Straubs to the United States, notably through their friendship with Dan Talbot who, by buying and distributing every film with English subtitles, from *Machorka-Muff* (1962) to *Der Tod des Empedokles* (*The Death of Empedocles*, 1986), brought attention to the first part of this singular body of work.

Just as there was a pause in Hölderlin's life between the first and third versions of his *Empedocles*, there is an American pause after the first of two corresponding Hölderlin films by the Straubs: from *Schwarze Sünde* (*Black Sin*, 1988) onward, there was no more distribution. While the sixteen films from the first period continued and continue to circulate, the films after 1987 have only been shown sporadically in the United States.

In 2013, in a discussion with Sally Shafto about a translation for the DVD box set of the Bach film, we said that it would be great to organize a major retrospective to fill the gap. She soon sent out an e-mail that quickly received enthusiastic and positive responses from many American institutions. The project was entirely possible.

But could it be done?

The first inventory seemed reassuring. Sixteen films at New Yorker Films and a dozen films shot on video/HD, already subtitled, with problems only for the middle section: around fifteen 35mm films for which prints had to be found or newly struck and subtitled.

We began by inspecting the New Yorker prints at MoMA, thanks to Josh Siegel. It was very moving to discover the historic prints that bore the traces of decades of screenings as well as the care and respect of generations of projectionists.

We watched them in chronological order, beginning with the German films. Then came *Othon* (1969), Danièle's favorite film: Rome, the south after the north, an explosion of color after black and white. Here is the explosion of 1969 in 2014:

Scratches are part of the life of a print. The alteration of the color, however, seemed to us to prohibit their use, all the more so since *Othon* was not an isolated case. Almost all the color prints from this period, notably the five in 16mm, were equally red or worse. The reassuring inventory now appeared in a different light. We decided to scan and digitize the 16mm films and three of the 35mm films.

~

The digital transfer of a movie shot on film is inevitably a new movie. The scan does reproduce the information in the film stock, but it forms and transforms it according to its own nature. Take the example of a 2K scan of a 16mm negative. The surface of a frame is 10.26 mm × 7.49 mm. The scanner reads each frame in >3 million pixels, 2048 pixels on the horizontal axis and 1556 pixels on the vertical axis. The pixels question the original material.

Our tiny film frame is thus being questioned around three million times. The scanner records the responses from the negative as a positive image composed of approximately three million pieces of data.

This is fundamentally different than direct digital capture, like with our smartphones, and it is fundamentally different from a positive film print struck from a negative. In the first case, the subject, a blooming flower, for example, is "perceived" directly in 2 (or 4, or 8!) million questions and rendered, hence the sometimes brutal sharpness of the result.

In the case of a positive print from a film negative, we remain in the same universe (photochemical) and everything goes smoothly. In the enormous enlargement of a 16mm print when it is projected on a big screen, we're used to accepting the lack of definition – because there isn't so much detailed information on the small film – and the often surprising amounts of grain, depending on the sensitivity of the film stock and the developing solution.

But what about our digital scan of the film negative, a hybrid somewhere in the middle? Between the limitations and the possibilities, what is it really?

We worked from the original negatives and 2K scans of the 16mm and 4K scans of the 35mm films, as well as the magnetic soundtracks. The restoration work was done in 2K.

A word about the "levels" of the restoration. Some of the negatives were in a rather good state, while others were in incomprehensibly poor condition. On one negative, there was a hole in the emulsion in the lower part of the image, on every frame of every reel for the entire film. Another negative had scratches towards the end of a reel that became deeper and deeper until the reel ended brutally with black film leader spliced in where the soundtrack continued. What had happened? Buried lab secrets, nasty surprises.

The "restoration" that was needed was tedious, sometimes nearly impossible. It was similar to the work of a cabinet-maker who is restoring an old piece of furniture. The main question that one asks is: do we want an entirely new, clean film or do we accept the persistence of a few scratches and specks of dirt that bear witness to the film's earlier life? These are artisanal choices and the results, once a decision is made, depend on the knowledge, experience, ingenuity and sensitivity of the person doing the work.

But there is a second, much more complex level, not technical, far from it, but "moral," "political." With my digitized negative, which is already a positive, I can essentially do whatever I want. The computer offers tools that do not exist with film. "To photoshop" is a verb that has come into use and we all know what it means. Why am I talking about this? Because there is obviously the temptation to "improve" our new film. Improve? In what sense? The scan (let's stick with the 2K example of 16mm film) contains and shows more than a print made from the same negative. The clouds in the sky in *Othon* appeared with details that had never been seen on the film prints. Of course, we weren't going to artificially overexpose them under the pretext of wanting a result as close as possible to the original prints. The grain in the long traveling shots in *Geschichtsunterricht* (*History Lessons*, 1972), with the extreme oscillations of light between the burning sun and the quieter shadows, will perhaps dance and burn even more than on a film print. Patches of color appear that are in the layers of the negative's emulsion but were not visible on the prints. Should we intervene? It is very easy to put a mask over the image and "correct" what might look strange! Everyone will have his or her own opinion in this regard. We decided to forego this "restoration" solution – a step that is possible and so often used – because it seemed simply not "Straubian" to us.

~

For the Straubs, aesthetics, politics and morality are one and the same. "Beauty" is the work with the frame, the abundance that appears in an image and is the fruit of the preparatory work. It is the surprise of changes in the light, a lizard running by, the movement of the wigs, an unexpected smile like the young man's in *History Lessons* when a leaf falls on his hand and he lifts it off before beginning his lines. The Straubs kept these unforeseen moments in the editing: being open to and welcoming the unexpected is a crucial moment of the Straubian aesthetic-political credo. The famous absence of lighting continuity between shots is one example: if a shot is done outside in the evening and the following shot, which comes immediately after in the text, is done the next morning, the light will obviously not be the same. But that is the reality of the moment of shooting. It is always about the greater presence of the reality of the world in which the reality of the film is not only inscribed but to which it is subordinate. This is why during the color timing the lighting is never matched between shots. The reality of the shoot is there and must remain visible.

We worked with all of this in mind, trying to carry it into the digital world. "We," meaning Renato Berta and Robert Alazraki, who guided the color grading with Pierre Sudre. Jean-Pierre Laforce mixed the sound. Jean-Marie Straub was present, participated in the first color grading sessions, and saw the group – a mix of very old accomplices and specialists in these new worlds – fall into place. At the center was Olivier Boischot, who, since the beginning of the adventure, assured us of his commitment until the end and did not waver even when the work to be done proved incomparably vaster than planned. It is not nothing to locate by hand a hole in the emulsion on 138,000 frames and it is nearly impossible to replace missing frames from the original negative with frames from an inter-negative without the change in texture being noticeable. But he did it. For this retrospective he has provided not only his great experience and his network of acquaintances, but also, it must be said, all of his time for an entire year and all of his sensitivity and patience.

We have therefore tried to make "new" films that remain faithful to Straubian choices.

A word on the subtitling. We found and used the original translations and have only corrected obvious mistakes. It goes without saying that we also respected the initial choices of omissions, meaning that long parts of the spoken text are sometimes left without subtitles in order to allow the eyes to concentrate on the image.

Since it has not been possible to find the old typefaces, we chose the very neutral Helvetica

Neue for all of the digital versions. We used the layout of the original prints everywhere that we were able to find them, meaning the spacing of the lines even where breaks in the lines do not correspond to pauses in the breathing, but only to the technical necessities of subtitling, especially for the 16mm films. Thank you to Christophe Clavert and all those, known and unknown, who transcribed and re-read the many documents, not only in English but in German, French, and Italian as well.

So these are the 8 DCPs – in addition to *Chronicle*, made previously in an entirely different context. The latter received support from the French Film Archive and the Swiss Cinémathèque and *Fortini/Cani* and *Too Early, Too Late* from the CNC. Along with the six prints from New Yorker, they form the first part of the body of work.

Then there are the fourteen 35mm films from *Black Sin* to *Le Streghe, Femmes entre elles* (*The Witches, women among themselves*, 2009) – five release prints, four new prints from the private Straub-Huillet collection and, thanks to the Cinemateca Portuguesa, four newly struck prints. For the print of *Operai, contadini* (*Workers, Peasants*, 2001), we thank the Cineteca di Bologna. Thank you as well to the Viennale and Stadtkino Wien. All of these prints have subtitles and will remain in distribution in the United States after the tour. It is in honor of all those who can still project film and do it well.

Additionally, there is a new, identical collage/edit with higher quality materials of *Proposta in quattro parti* (*Proposal in Four Parts*) – many thanks to the Museum of Modern Art Department of Film for the Griffith! – and a DCP that regroups the two shorts *L'arrotino* (*The Knife Sharpener*, 2001) and *Il viandante* (*The Wayfarer,* 2001), the more or less unseen *Dolando* (2002) and *Incantati* (2002), a last minute discovery!

Now visible in its entirety for the first time, the Straubian corpus is ready for the big tour!

The tour has been organized by Thomas Beard. The films will be accompanied by *Writings*, texts by Danièle Huillet and Jean-Marie Straub, published by Sequence Press, edited and with an introduction by Sally Shafto, and this book, which owes its existence to Ted Fendt who tackled the project head on, with love and perseverance. Thank you as well to Alexander Horwath for having welcomed it into the collection of the Austrian Film Museum and to the Goethe-Institut for supporting its publication. Thank you, finally, to the Contemporary Art Fund of the city of Geneva and Miguel Abreu and Katherine Pickard whose support, not only with logistics, has been decisive.

Filmography (1962–2015)

This filmography was originally published in French and assembled by Benoît Turquety for his book *Jean-Marie Straub et Danièle Huillet: « objectivistes » en cinéma* (2009). It was approved by Danièle Huillet and incorporates information used in a 1977 filmography she edited. It has been updated, revised, expanded, and translated by Ted Fendt. The format follows the credits that appear in each film. Information in brackets has been added for clarity.

All films edited by Straub-Huillet and all films mixed in mono except where noted.

Following Danièle Huillet and Jean-Marie Straub's own practice, the films have been dated according to their years of production, not their first public screening.

1962
Machorka-Muff
WEST GERMANY, 35MM, 1.37:1, B&W, 18'

[Opening credits in German, white text on black]
- "Ein bildhaft abstrakter Traum, keine
  Geschichte. Jean-Marie Straub."
  ["A metaphorically abstract dream, not a story."
  – Handwritten]
[Black text on white]
- Atlas Filmverleih GmbH. presents
- A film by Danièle Huillet and Jean-Marie Straub
- In the Cineropa-Film, Walter Krüttner
  Production
- Based on the story by Heinrich Böll "Haupt-
  städtisches Journal" [1957], published by
  Kiepenheuer & Witsch in the collection
  Dr. Murkes gesammeltes Schweigen with the
  author's permission
- Machorka-Muff
- With: Renate Langsdorff [Inn], Dr. Johannes
  Eckardt [Priest], Dr. Rolf Thiede [Murcks-
  Maloch], Günther Strupp [Heffling],
  Heiner Braun [Minister], Gino Cardella [Waiter],
  Julius Wikidal [Mason]
- Direction: Jean-Marie Straub,
  Assistance: Danièle Huillet
- Camera: Wendelin Sachtler,
  Assitance: Hans Christof Brüning
- Lighting: Franz Schinabeck,
  Sound: Janos Rozmer, Window Dressing:
  E. A. Luttringhaus
- Production Manager: Hans von der Heydt,
  Location Manager: Hansdieter Seel
- Editing: C.P. Lemmer
- Organ: François Louis, from his piece
  Permutations, 1957

Lead actor Erich Kuby (as Erich von Machorka-
Muff) is uncredited. **ADDITIONAL MUSIC:** J. S. Bach,
The Musical Offering, BWV 1079, "Ricercar a 6."
PRODUCTION DATES AND LOCATIONS: 10 days,
September 1962, Bonn and Munich. **BUDGET:**
31,000 DM. **EQUIPMENT:** 1 Arri Blimp 120 camera,
1 Nagra. **FILM STOCK:** Kodak Double-X (6,000 m.)
FINAL LENGTH: 480 m. **ENGLISH SUBTITLES** by
Herman G. Weinberg, **FRENCH SUBTITLES** by
Danièle Huillet. **FIRST SCREENING:** 1963 Inter-
national Short Film Festival Oberhausen
(February; out of competition); New Yorker
Theater (February 23, 1969); 1969 London Film
Festival (November 18). **TV PREMIERE:** August 25,
1969 (ARD, West Germany).

———

1964/65
Nicht versöhnt oder
Es hilft nur Gewalt, wo Gewalt herrscht
*(Not Reconciled, or Only Violence Helps
Where Violence Rules)*
WEST GERMANY, 35MM, 1.37:1, B&W, 52'

[Opening credits, white text over a shot of
Klingelpütz Prison and the monument to victims
of the Gestapo, Cologne]
- Nicht versöhnt oder Es hilft nur Gewalt,
  wo Gewalt herrscht
- By Danièle Huillet and Jean-Marie Straub,
  based on the novel *Billard um halbzehn* [1959]
  by Heinrich Böll
[White scrolling text over shot of Gerhard Marcks'
statue *The Mourning Woman* in Cologne]
- Cast: Henning Harmssen [Robert Fähmel,
  40 years old], Georg Zander [Hugo, hotel boy
  and Ferdinand "Ferdi" Progulske], Ulrich
  Hopmann [Robert Fähmel, 18 years old],
  Ernst Kutzinski [Schrella, 15 years old], Jochen
  Grüner, Günter Göbel, Peter Berger, Klaus
  Weyer, Eberhard Ellrich, Norbert Pritz, Bernd
  Wagner, Michael Krüger, Joseph Vollmert,
  Dieter Hornberg, Egbert Meiers, Ralf Kurth,
  Jürgen Beier, Michael Holy, Engelbert Greis,
  Wolfgang Kück, Herbert Gammersbach,

Rolf Buhl, Peter Kneip, Gerd Lenze, Erdmann Dortschy, Piero Poli, Margrit Borstel [blond who knits], Diana Schlesinger, Karin Kraus, Claudia Wurm, Frouwke van Herwynen, Ise Maassen, Dagmar von Netzer, Hartmut Kirchner, Jürgen Kraeft, Achim Wurm, Max Dietrich Willutzki, Hannelore Langhoff, Johanna Odry, Günther Becker, Willy Bruno Wange, Stefan Odry, Anita Bell [old woman playing cards], Erika Brühl [Edith, Schrella's sister], Werner Brühl [Trischler], Helga Brühl [Mrs. Trischler], Paul Esser, Hans Zander, Karl Bodenschatz [porter], Heiner Braun [Nettlinger], Heinrich Hargesheimer [Heinrich Fähmel, Robert's father, 80 years old], Huguette Sellen [Robert Fähmel's secretary], Ulrich von Thüna [Schrella, 35 years old], Walter Brenner, Chargesheimer [= Carl-Heinz Hargesheimer, as Heinrich Fähmel, 35 years old], Rudolf Thome, Claudio Domberger, Lutz Grübnau [first abbot], Hans Schönberger, Karsten Peters, Kai A. Niemeyer, Danièle Straub [young Johanna], Franz Menzel, Martin Trieb [second abbot], Kim Sachtler, Walter Talmon-Gros, Joe Hembus, Max Zihlmann, Maurie Fischbein, Martha Ständner [Johanna Fähmel, Robert's mother, 70 years old], Christel Meuser, Wendelin Sachtler [Mull], Eva Maria Bold [Ruth Fähmel, Robert's daughter], Joachim Weiler [Joseph Fähmel, Robert's son], Hiltraud Wegener [Marianne, Joseph's fiancée], Kathrin Bold [Ferdinand's sister], Annie Lautner, Johannes Buzalski, Eduard von Wickenburg [M.], Gottfried Bold [M.'s colleague], Victor von Halem [M.'s other colleague], Beate Speith
- "Anstatt den Eindruck hervorrufen zu wollen, er improvisiere, soll der Schauspieler lieber zeigen, was die Wahrheit ist: er zitiert. Bertolt Brecht." ["Instead of wanting to create the impression that he is improvising, the actor should instead show what is the truth: he is quoting. Bertold Brecht."]

- Camera: Wendelin Sachtler, Gerhard Ries, Christian Schwarzwald, Jean-Marie Straub, Negative: Kodak XX [5222] Rochester USA, Rear Projection: Bavaria, Trick-Atelier, Print timers: R. Iblherr, D. Kain
- Sound: Lutz Grübnau and Willi Hanspach, Neumann Miniature Condenser KM 56, Sound Mix: Paul Schöler, Aventin, Munich
- Technician: Herbert Martin, Assistance: Charlie Putzgruber, Hartmut Koldewey, Wilhelm Eschweiler
- Editing: Danièle Huillet and Jean-Marie Straub, Music conducted by François Louis, Geneva
- Production Manager: Danièle Huillet. Assistance: Max Dietrich Willutzki, Uschi Fritsche
- Direction: Jean-Marie Straub

MUSIC: Béla Bartók, *Sonata for Two Pianos and Percussion* (first movement, measures 1–10); J. S. Bach, *Orchestral Suite No. 2 in B Minor*, BWV 1067 (opening). **PRODUCTION DATES AND LOCATIONS:** August–September 1964 and April 1965 (6 + 2 weeks), at 45 different locations, in and around Cologne, Eifel, and Munich. **EQUIPMENT:** 1 Arri Blimp 120 camera, 1 Nagra. 19,000 m. of negative exposed. **FINAL LENGTH:** 1500 m. Budget: 117,000 DM. **ENGLISH SUBTITLES** by Huillet and Misha Donat, **FRENCH SUBTITLES** by Huillet, **ITALIAN SUBTITLES** by Huillet and Adriano Aprà. **FIRST SCREENING:** 1965 Berlin Film Festival (July 4), unofficial; 1965 Bergamo Film Festival (Grand Prize); 1965 New York Film Festival (September 18); 1965 London Film Festival (November 15); released in Munich, Theatiner-Filmkunst, February 11, 1966; 1966 *Cahiers du cinéma* Week, Paris; 1966 Pesaro Film Festival (Young Critics Prize and New Film Prize – jury: Gianni Amico, Marco Bellocchio, Bernardo Bertolucci, Jean-Luc Godard, Joris Ivens, Jaromil Jires and Pier Paolo Pasolini). **TV PREMIERE:** August 25, 1969 (ARD, West Germany). Originally shown in the New York and London film festivals as *Unreconciled*.

1967
Chronik der Anna Magdalena Bach
(Chronicle of Anna Magdalena Bach)
WEST GERMANY/ITALY, 35MM, 1.37:1, B&W, 93'

[Opening credits, white text on a black]
- Chronik der Anna Magdalena Bach
- By Danièle Huillet and Jean-Marie Straub
- With Gustav Leonhardt [Johann Sebastian Bach], Christiane Lang-Drewanz [Anna Magdalena Bach]
- Paolo Carlini [Dr. Hölzel, advisor], Ernst Castelli [Steger, court advisor], Hans-Peter Boye [Born, advisor to the religious chapter], Joachim Wolf [rector], Rainer Kirchner [superintendent], Eckart Brüntjen [Kittler, choir prefect], Walter Peters [Krause, choir prefect], Kathrien Leonhardt [Catharina Dorothea Bach], Anja Fährmann [Regina Susanna Bach], Katja Drewanz [Christiana Sophia Henrietta Bach]
- Bob van Asperen [Johann Elias Bach], Andreas Pangritz [Wilhelm Friedemann Bach], Bernd Weikl [singer, BWV 205], Wolfgang Schöne [singer, BWV 82], Karl-Heinz Lampe [singer, BWV 42], Christa Degler [voice of Anna Magdalena Bach for BWV 244a], Karlheinz Klein [bass of the duet BWV 140]
- Orchestras: Concentus Musicus, Ensemble für Alte Musik, Vienna; conducted by Nikolaus Harnoncourt [orchestra at the court of Cöthen, with Nikolaus Harnoncourt in the role of Prince Leopold of Anhalt-Cöthen]. Konzertgruppe der Schola Cantorum Basiliensis [Basel]; conducted by August Wenzinger [church orchestra in Leipzig]
- Choirs: Knabenchor, Hannover, conducted by Heinz Hennig [chorus of the Saint-Thomas school]. Sopranos: Bernhard Wehle of the Regensburger Domspatzen [for BWV 140]
- Costumes: "Casa d'arte Firenze," Vera Poggioni, Renata Morroni, Wigs: "Parrucche Rocchetti," Todero Guerrino, Harpsichords, spinet and clavichord from Martin Skowroneck, Bremen, and Carl August Gräbner, Dresden
- Image: Ugo Piccone, Saverio Diamanti, Giovanni Canfarelli, Hans Kracht (Defa), Uwe Radon (Defa), Rear projection: Thomas Hartwig
- Sound: Louis Hochet, Lucien Moreau, Sound Mix: Paul Schöler
- Main locations: Eutin (castle [Prince of Anhalt-Cöthen's castle]); Preetz (monastery church [organ loft no. 3, Cöthen Cathedral]; Stade ([churches] St. Wilhaldi and St. Cosmae [organ loft no. 1, St. Thomas Church in Leipzig; organ loft no. 2, at the university]); Leipzig (facade of the city hall [Leipzig marketplace]); Lüneburg (Lüne Abbey [St. Thomas School: refectory, Cantor's lodgings]); Haseldorf (castle [Cantor's lodgings: composition room; superintendent's lodgings]); Lübeck (Füchting court [municipal counsel's room, Leipzig Town Hall]); Nuremberg (National Germanic Museum [Cantor's lodgings: music room]); Freiberg in Saxony (cathedral [organ loft no. 5, Notre-Dame of Dresden church]); Grosshartmannsdorf (church [organ loft no. 4, St. Sophie of Dresden church]); [East] Berlin (Opera House ["Apollo" room]). Bach's manuscripts and original prints have been kindly placed at our disposal by the Tübingen University Library, the West German Library of Marburg, the State Library of the Stiftung Preussischer Kulturbesitz in Berlin-Dahlem, the Berlin State Library unter den Linden and by the Bach-Archiv Leipzig. We also thank professors Christhard Mahrenholz, Georg von Dadelson, Alfred Dürr, Friedrich Smend and Werner Neumann
- Technicians: Hans Eberle, Max Jörg, Walter Eder, Max Strobl, Heinz Krähnke (Defa), Peter Algert (Defa), Jürgen Zanner (Defa), Jürgen Schlobach (Defa)
- German-Italian Co-production, Franz Seitz Filmproduktion [Munich], Gianvittorio Baldi IDI Cinematografica [Rome], Straub-Huillet,

Kuratorium Junger Deutscher Film [Munich], Hessischer Rundfunk [Frankfurt], Filmfonds e.V. [Rome]; Telepool [Munich]
- Production Manager: Danièle Huillet, Assistance: Georg Föcking, Aldo Passalacqua, Joachim Wolf, Horst Winter (Defa), Günter Maag (Defa)
- Editing: Danièle Huillet, For: Jacques Rivette, Jean-Luc Godard, Michel Delahaye, Peter Nestler, and many others. Jean Marie-Straub

MUSIC BY J. S. BACH: *Brandenburg Concerto No. 5*, BWV 1050, first movement (allegro 1), measures 147–227, harpsichord and orchestra (1720–1721) • *Little Clavier Book for Wilhelm Friedemann Bach*, BWV 128, Prelude no. 6, clavichord, 1720 • *Little Clavier Book for Anna Magdalena Bach ANNO 1722*, BWV 812, French Suite No. 1 in D minor, Minuet II, spinet • *Sonata No. 2 in D major for Viola da Gamba and Harpsichord*, BWV 1028, adagio, ca. 1720 • *Organ Sonata No. 2 in C minor*, BWV 526, largo, organ, 1727 • *Magnificat in D major*, BWV 243, no. 11 and no. 12 through measure 19 ("Sicut locutus est" and Gloria), 1728–1731 • *Little Clavier Book for A.M.B.*, BWV 830, Tempo di gavotta of the Partita No. 6 in E minor, spinet, 1725 • *Cantata* BWV 205, "Der zufriedengestellte Aeolus," recitative for bass ("Ja! ja! Die Stunden sind nunmehro nah") and aria ("Wie will ich lustig lachen"), 1725 • *Cantata* BWV 198 (Funeral Ode), final chorus, 1727 • *Cantata* BWV 244a (Funeral music for Prince Leopold), aria "Mit Freuden sei die Welt verlassen," measure 25 until the end, 1729 • *St. Matthew's Passion*, BWV 244, opening chorus, 1727 • *Cantata* BWV 42, "Am Abend aber desselbigen Sabbats," Sinfonia (da capo, measures 1 to 53) and Tenor Recitative, 1725 • *Prelude and Fugue in B minor*, BWV 544, 1727–1731 • *Mass in B minor*, BWV 232, first Kyrie eleison, measures 1–30, 1733 • *Cantata* BWV 215, first chorus, measures 1–181, 1734 • *Ascension*

Oratorio, BWV 11, second part of final chorus, 1735 • *Clavier-Übung III*, "Kyrie, Gott heiliger Geist," BWV 671, 1739 • *Clavier-Übung II, Italian Concerto*, BWV 971, andante, 1735 • *Cantata* BWV 140, first duo, measures 1–36, 1731 • *Goldberg Variations*, BWV 988, 25th variation, 1741–1742 • *Cantata* BWV 82, "Ich habe genug," final recitative and final aria, 1727 • *The Musical Offering*, BWV 1079, Ricercar a 6, measures 1–39, harpsichord, 1747 • *Art of the Fugue*, BWV 1080, Contrapunctus XIX, measures 193–239, clavichord, 1750 • *Choral Preludes*, "Vor deinen Thron tret' ich," BWV 668, first part, measures 1–11, 1750. **MUSIC BY LEO LEONIUS:** *Conventional Sunday motet (11th after Trinity)* from the "Florilegium Portense" by Erhard Bodenschatz. **TEXT:** Carl Philipp Emanuel Bach and J. F. Agricola, *Necrology* (1754), letters and memoirs by Johann Sebastian Bach and other period documents. **PRODUCTION DATES:** August 20 to October 14, 1967. **EQUIPMENT:** 1 Mitchell BNC 300, 1 Nagra III, Neumann microphones, Kodak 4-X (5224) film stock, Rochester, USA. 28,500 m. of negative exposed. **FINAL LENGTH:** 2,558 m. **BUDGET:** 470,000 DM. In addition to subtitled versions, there exist 4 versions with the voice-over commentary read in different languages. **FRENCH VERSION:** dialogue subtitled by Danièle Huillet, commentary read in French with a strong German accent by Christiane Lang; **DUTCH VERSION:** dialogue subtitled with Henk de By, commentary read in Dutch by Margret Schumacher; **ITALIAN VERSION:** dialogue subtitled with Adriano Aprà, commentary read in Italian with a slight German accent by Rita Ehrhardt; **ENGLISH VERSION:** dialogue subtitled with Misha Donat, commentary read in English with a slight German accent by Gisela Hume. **FIRST SCREENING:** 1968 Cinemanifestatie Utrecht (February 3); 1968 Cannes Film Festival, Critic's Week (May); 1968 Berlin Film Festival (June 30); 1968 New York Film Festival (September 19); 1968 London Film

Festival (Grand Prize); 1968 Prades Film Festival (Special Prize). German Critics' "Bambi" Prize: Best German Film of 1968. **TV PREMIERE:** September 29, 1969 (HR III, West Germany).

———

1968

Der Bräutigam, die Komödiantin und der Zuhälter
(The Bridegroom, the Actress, and the Pimp)
WEST GERMANY, 35MM, 1.37:1, B&W, 23'

[Opening credits – white text over a shot of graffiti: "stupid old Germany I hate it over here I hope I can go soon Patricia 1.3.68"]
- [With] Irm Hermann [Désirée], Kristin Peterson [Irene], Hanna Schygulla [Lucy], Peer Raben [Alt/Willy], Rudolf Waldemar Brem [Petrell]
- James Powell [James]
- Lilith Ungerer [Marie/Lilith], Rainer W. Fassbinder [Freder/the Pimp]
- Der Bräutigam, die Komödiantin und der Zuhälter
- By Jean-Marie Straub
- [Image] Klaus Schilling, Hubs Hagen, [sound] Peter Lutz, Klaus Eckelt [theater sequence], Herbert Linder
- [Technicians] Herbert Meier, Heina Pust, Dietmar Müller, Bernward Wember, Jan Bodenham
- [Texts] Juan de la Cruz, Ferdinand Bruckner, Helmut Färber
- [Production] Danièle Huillet and Klaus Hellwig, Janus Film und Fersehen [Frankfurt]

TEXT: Ferdinand Bruckner, *Krankheit der Jugend* (*Pains of Youth,* 1926), condensed by Jean-Marie Straub; Juan de la Cruz (1542–1591), "Romance on the Gospel," "Spiritual Canticle," stanza 22 (first version) or stanza 29 (second version), translated into German by Straub, Huillet and Helmut

Färber. **MUSIC:** J. S. Bach, *Cantata* BWV 11, "Du Tag, wenn wirst du sein… Komm, stelle dich doch ein." **PRODUCTION DATES AND LOCATIONS:** half-day in the Action Theater (Munich), April 1, 1968, four days in Munich, May 1968. **EQUIPMENT:** 1 Arriflex 300, 1 Nagra, Kodak 4-X (5224) and Double-X (5222) film stock (7,000 m.). **FINAL LENGTH:** 630 m. **BUDGET:** 17,500 DM. **ENGLISH SUBTITLES** by Danièle Huillet and Bernard Eisenschitz, **FRENCH SUBTITLES** by Huillet. **FIRST SCREENING:** 1968 Mannheim Film Festival (October 10); New Yorker Theater (February 23, 1969); 1969 London Film Festival (November 28).

———

1969

Les yeux ne veulent pas en tout temps se fermer ou Peut-être qu'un jour Rome se permettra de choisir à son tour
(Eyes do not want to close at all times or Perhaps one day Rome will permit herself to choose in her turn)
WEST GERMANY/ITALY, 16MM, 1.33:1, COLOR, 88'

[Opening credits, white text on black]
- Les yeux ne veulent pas en tout temps se fermer
- ou Peut-être qu'un jour Rome se permettra de choisir à son tour
- Based on *Othon* [1664] by Pierre Corneille
- Film by Jean-Marie Straub and Danièle Huillet
- Assisted by Leo Mingrone, Anna Raboni, Sebastian Schadhauser, Italo Pastorino, Elias Chaluja
- Hairdresser: Todero Guerrino
- Photography: Ugo Piccone, Renato Berta
- Sound: Louis Hochet, Lucien Moreau
- Production: Janus-Film, Klaus Hellwig
[End credits, scrolling, white text on black]
- Othon: Adriano Aprà, Plautine: Anne

Brumagne, Galba: Ennio Lauricella, Camille:
Olimpia Carlisi, Vinius: Anthony Pensabene,
Lacus: Jubarite Semaran [Jean-Marie Straub],
Martian: Jean-Claude Biette, Albin: Leo
Mingrone, Albiane: Gianna Mingrone, Flavie:
Marilù Parolini, Atticus: Edoardo de Gregorio,
Rutile: Sergio Rossi [1st soldier: Sebastian
Schadhauser, 2nd soldier: Jacques Fillion]
- Processing and prints: LV di Luciano Vittori
- This film is dedicated to the very great number
of those born into the French language who
have never had the privilege to get to know
the work of Corneille; and to Alberto Moravia
and Laura Betti who obtained permission for
me to shoot on Palatine Hill and in the gardens
of the villa Doria-Pamphilj in Rome. J.-M. S.

PRODUCTION DATES AND LOCATION: four weeks
in Rome, August–September 1969. **EQUIPMENT:**
1 Éclair-Coutant, 4 lenses, 1 Nagra. **FILM STOCK:**
Eastman 7254 (13,920 m.), blown up to 35mm.
FINAL LENGTH: 2,400 m. **BUDGET:** 170,000 DM.
SUBTITLED IN ENGLISH by Huillet and Misha
Donat, **IN ITALIAN** by Huillet and Adriano Aprà,
IN GERMAN by Huillet and Herbert Linder. **FIRST
SCREENING:** 1970 Rapallo Film Festival (January 4);
1970 Mannheim Film Festival (October 8); 1970
New York Film Festival. Released for one week in
New York at St. Mark's Cinema and Film Forum,
November 1971. **TV PREMIERE:** January 26, 1971
(ZDF, West Germany), followed by a discussion
with Jean-Marie Straub, Ulrich Gregor,
Ivan Nagel, Karsten Peters, and Rudolph Ganz.

1972

Geschichtsunterricht *(History Lessons)*
ITALY/WEST GERMANY, 16 MM, 1.33:1, COLOR, 85'

[Opening credits, black text on white, in German]
- Adapted from the novel fragment
Die Geschäfte des Herrn Julius Caesar
[1937–39] by Bertolt Brecht
- Geschichtsunterricht
- Film by Jean-Marie Straub and Danièle Huillet
- Renato Berta, Emilio Bestetti, Image
- Jeti Grigioni, Sound
- Leo Mingrone, Sebastian Schadhauser,
Benedikt Zulauf, Assistance
[End credits, scrolling, black text on white]
- Gottfried Bold, the Banker; Johann Unter-
pertinger, the Peasant; Henri Ludwig, the
Lawyer; Carl Vaillant, the Writer; Benedikt
Zulauf, the Young Man; Color: LV di
Luciano Vittori

PRODUCTION: Straub-Huillet, Rome; Janus Film
und Fernseh-Produktion, Frankfurt. **MUSIC:**
J. S. Bach, *Saint Matthew's Passion*, BWV 244.
PRODUCTION DATES AND LOCATIONS: three
weeks in Rome, Frascati, Trentino-Alto Adige
and on Elba, June–July 1972. **EQUIPMENT:**
1 Éclair-Coutant, 4 prime lenses, 1 zoom lens and
1 Nagra. **FILM STOCK:** Eastman 7254 (7,560 m.).
FINAL LENGTH: 961 m. **COST:** 65,000 DM.
SUBTITLED IN ENGLISH by Huillet and Misha
Donat, **IN FRENCH** by Huillet, **IN ITALIAN** by
Huillet and Adriano Aprà, Leo and Gianna
Mingrone, **IN DUTCH** by Huillet and Frans van de
Staak. **FIRST SCREENING:** private, 1972 Mannheim
Film Festival (October 10); 1973 New York Film
Festival. **TV PREMIERE:** May 20, 1974 (ARD,
West Germany).

Filmography

1972
Einleitung zu Arnold Schoenbergs Begleitmusik zu einer Lichtspielscene
(Introduction to Arnold Schoenberg's "Accompaniment to a Cinematographic Scene")
WEST GERMANY, 16MM, 1.33:1, COLOR/B&W, 15'

[No opening credits;
end credits, white text on red]
- Einleitung zu Arnold Schoenbergs Begleitmusik zu einer Lichtspielscene
- By Jean-Marie Straub with Günter Peter Straschek, Danièle Huillet and Peter Nestler
- Photography: Renato Berta, Horst Bever; Lighting: Karl-Heinz Granek
- Sound: Jeti Grigioni, Harald Lill; Sound Mixing: Adriano Taloni
- Production: Straub-Huillet; commissioned by Südwestfunk [third TV station in Baden-Baden]
- Color: LV di Luciano Vittori

TEXTS: Arnold Schoenberg, letters to Wassily Kandinsky, April 20 and May 4, 1923; Bertolt Brecht, extract from a speech to the International Congress in Defense of Culture, 1935. **MUSIC:** Arnold Schoenberg, *Begleitmusik zu einer Licht-spielscene*, opus 34, 1930. **PRODUCTION DATES AND LOCATIONS:** one day in Rome and one in Baden-Baden (TV studios), June and October 1972. **EQUIPMENT:** 1 Éclair ACL, 1 Nagra. **FILM STOCK:** Eastman 7254 (Rome), Agfa-Gevaert color and black and white reversal (Baden-Baden). **BUDGET:** 7,500 DM. **SUBTITLED IN ENGLISH** by Huillet and Misha Donat, **IN FRENCH** by Huillet, **IN ITALIAN** by Huillet and Gianna and Leo Mingrone, **IN GERMAN** by Huillet and Sebastian Schadhauser. **FIRST SCREENING:** 1973 International Short Film Festival Oberhausen (April 9); 1973 New York Film Festival. **TV PREMIERE:** March 29, 1975 (HR III/WDR III/NDR III, West Germany).

1974
Moses und Aron
(Moses and Aaron)
AUSTRIA/WEST GERMANY/FRANCE/ITALY
35MM (TWO SHOTS ORIGINALLY IN 16MM)
1.37:1, COLOR, 105'

[Opening credits, black text on white, in German]
- A co-production of Austrian Radio and Tele-vision and the ARD (including West Berlin)
- Under the direction of Hessen Radio
- Produced by Janus-Film & Fernsehen with financing from Straub-Huillet, RAI, ORTF and Taurus-Film
- A German-French co-production of Janus Film & Fernsehen with NEF Diffusion
- Production Management, Direction, Editing: Danièle Huillet, Jean-Marie Straub
- Musical Direction: Michael Gielen; Assistance: Bernard Rubenstein
[Red handwriting on white, 48 frames]
- For Holger Meins, J.-M. S., D. H.
[white text on black]
- Moses und Aron. Opera in three acts by Arnold Schoenberg. Publisher B. Schott's Söhne
[End credits, white text on black]
- Moses: Günter Reich, Aron: Louis Devos
- Young girl: Eva Csapó, Young Man: Roger Lucas, Other Man: Richard Salter
- Priest: Werner Mann, Ephraimite: Ladislav Illavsky, Sick Woman: Friedl Obrowsky
- Austrian Radio Choir, Preparation: Gottfried Preinfalk
- Austrian Radio Symphony Orchestra
- Sound: Louis Hochet, Ernst Neuspiel, Georges Vaglio, Jeti Grigioni
- Image: Ugo Piccone, Saverio Diamanti, Gianni Canfarelli, Renato Berta
- Technicians: Francesco Ragusa, Alvaro Nannicini, Gianfranco Baldacci
- Assistants: Paolo Benvenuti, Hans-Peter

Böffgen, Leo Mingrone, Basti [Sebastian]
Schadhauser, Gabriele Soncini, Harald Vogel,
Gregory Woods
- "Cantini" Costumes: Renata Morroni,
Augusta Morelli, Mariateresa Stefanelli,
Hair: Guerrino Todero, Shoes: Ernesto Pompei
- Choreography: Jochen Ulrich, Dancers:
Helmut Baumann, Jürg Burth, Nick Farrant,
Wolfgang Kegler, Michael Molnar
- Processing and Prints: LV di Luciano Vittori

Arnold Schoenberg's opera *Moses und Aron* was
written primarily between May 1930 (Berlin) and
March 1932 (Barcelona). The third act remained
unfinished. **SCRIPT DATED:** Berlin, late 1959–
Rome, early 1970. **PRE-CREDITS:** fragment of page
of Luther's translation of the Bible (1523): Exodus,
32, 25–28. **PRODUCTION DATES AND LOCATIONS:**
2 shots in Louxor (Egypt) in May 1973 (shots
42 and 43; pans over the Nile Valley), in 16mm;
recording of the orchestra in Vienna, 6 weeks;
in the amphitheater in Alba Fucense (Abruzzo,
Italy) and Lake Matese (last shot, Act III) in
August–September 1974, 5 weeks. **EQUIPMENT:**
Beaulieu 16mm camera (Louxor shots), Mitchell
BNC 300 Blimp camera, 2 Nagra IV and 1 Nagra
III. **FILM STOCK:** Kodak 16mm color reversal
(Louxor) and Eastmancolor 5254 (35mm, color).
BUDGET: 720,000 DM and the support (orchestra
and choir in Vienna) of Austrian Radio and Tele-
vision (ORF): about 600,000 DM. **SUBTITLED IN
ENGLISH** by Huillet, Gregory Woods, and Misha
Donat, **IN FRENCH** by Huillet, **IN DUTCH** by
Huillet and Frans van de Staak. **FIRST SCREENING:**
1975 Rotterdam Film Festival (February); 1975
Edinburgh Film Festival; 1975 New York Film
Festival. **TV PREMIERE:** March 29, 1975 (HR III/
WDR III/NDR III, West Germany)

1976
Fortini/Cani
ITALY, 16MM, 1.33:1, COLOR, 83'

[Pre-credits, shot of the book cover]
- *Dissensi 5, Franco Fortini, I cani del Sinai,
De Donato Editore* [1967]
[Opening credits, white text on black]
- Film by Jean-Marie Straub and Danièle Huillet
- Franco Lattes [= Franco Fortini],
Luciana Nissim, Adriano Aprà
[End credits, white text on black]
- Éclair-Coutant: Renato Berta, Emilio Bestetti
- Nagra: Jeti Grigioni
- Assistants: Leo Mingrone, Gabriele Soncini,
Gregory Woods, Bernard Mangiante
- Processing/Prints: LV Luciano Vittori
- Production: Straub-Huillet
- Financing: André Engel, Artificial Eye,
Daniel Talbot, New Yorker Films, Stéphane
Tchalgadjieff, Sunchild, Polytel International,
Radiotelevisione Italiana, seconda rete

The film is known as *Fortini/Cani*, but the title
does not appear in the film. **PRODUCTION DATES
AND LOCATIONS:** 3 weeks (June 1976) in Coton-
cello (Elba), Marzabotto, Sant'Anna di Stazzema,
San Terenzo, Vinca, San Leonardo/Frigido,
Bergiola (Apuan Alps), Florence, Milan, Rome.
FILM STOCK: Eastman 7247. **BUDGET:** 22,000,000
lira. **SUBTITLED IN ENGLISH** by Huillet and Misha
Donat, **IN FRENCH** by Huillet, **IN GERMAN** by
Huillet, Manfred Blank, and Andrea Spingler.
FIRST SCREENING: 1976 Pesaro Film Festival
(September 19); Second Salon du Cinéma,
Paris (November 1976); Bleeker Street Cinema,
New York (October 1977).

1977
Toute révolution est un coup de dés
(Every Revolution is a Throw of the Dice)
FRANCE, 35MM, 1.37:1, COLOR, 10'

[Opening credits, white text on black, in French]
- Toute révolution est un coup de dés.
  (Jules Michelet)
[Multicolored handwriting on white]
- For Frans van de Staak, Jean Narboni,
  Jacques Rivette and some others.
  J.-M. S. May 77
[End credits, white text on black]
- Photography: Willy Lubtchansky,
  Dominique Chapuis
- Sound: Louis Hochet, Alain Donavy
[Reproduction of the title page,
black text on white]
- Poème *Un coup de dés jamais n'abolira le hasard*
  par Stéphane Mallarmé [1897]
[Photograph of the poet posing at his table,
then white text on black]
- (Re)citers: Helmut Färber, Michel Delahaye,
  Georges Goldfayn, Danièle Huillet
- Manfred Blank, Marilù Parolini, Aksar Khaled,
  Andrea Spingler, Dominique Villain

PRODUCTION DATES AND LOCATIONS: May 9–10,
1977 in Père-Lachaise cemetery, Paris. **EQUIP-
MENT:** Arriflex 120, 1 Nagra. **BUDGET:** 55,000 F.
SUBTITLED IN ENGLISH by Huillet, Misha Donat,
and Gregory Woods, **IN GERMAN** by Huillet,
Manfred Blank, Andrea Spingler, and Helmut
Färber, **IN ITALIAN** by Huillet. **FIRST SCREENING:**
Released in Paris, December 7, 1977 (with Jean-
Claude Biette's *Le Théâtre des matières*); Albright-
Know Art Gallery, Buffalo, NY (April 1981).

1978
Dalla nube alla resistenza
(From the Cloud to the Resistance)
ITALY/WEST GERMANY, 35MM, 1.37:1, COLOR, 105'

[Opening credits, black text on white]
- L'Institut National de l'Audiovisuel presents
  [in French; the rest of the credits are in Italian]
- A production by Danièle Huillet and
  Jean-Marie Straub
- With RAI-TV, Rete 2, Janus Film & Fernsehen
  and Artificial Eye
[White text on black]
- Dalla nube alla resistenza
- Texts by Cesare Pavese: *Dialoghi con Leucò*
  [*Dialogues with Leucò*], Einaudi 1947;
  La luna e il falò [*The Moon and the Bonfires*],
  Einaudi 1950
[Black text on white]
- First Part
[Titles preceding each dialogue]
- 1 The Cloud: Olimpia Carlisi,
  Ixion: Guido Lombardi
- 2 Hippolochus: Gino Felici,
  Sarpedon: Lori Pelosini
- 3 Oedipus: Walter Pardini,
  Tiresias: Ennio Lauricella
- 4 First Hunter: Andrea Bacci,
  Second Hunter: Lori Cavallini
- 5 Lityerses: Francesco Ragusa,
  Hercules: Fiorangelo Pucci
- 6 Father: Dolando Bernardini,
  Son: Andrea Filippi
[Title announcing the second part (shot 91),
then an introductory shot, shot 93 is scrolling
text]
- The Bastard: Mauro Monni, Nuto: Carmelo
  Lacorte, Cinto: Mario di Mattia, Valino:
  Luigi Giordanello, The Cavalier: Paolo Cinanni,
  People at the Bar: Maria Eugenia T., Alberto
  Signetto, Paolo Pederzolli, Ugo Bertone,
  Gianni Canfarelli, Domenico Carosso,

Sandro Signetto, Antonio Mingrone,
The Priest: Gianni Toti
[End credits, black text on white]
- Music conducted by Gustav Leonhardt
- Sound: Louis Hochet, Georges Vaglio,
  Transcription: Fono Rete
- Photography: Saverio Diamanti,
  Gianni Canfarelli, Processing and prints:
  LV Luciano Vittori
- Gaffer: Francesco Ragusa,
  Grip: Gianfranco Baldacci
- Assistants: Leo Mingrone, Isaline Panchaud,
  Manfred Blank, Rotraud Kühn;
- Vincent Nordon, Stéphanie de Mareuil,
  Paolo Pederzolli
- Hairdresser: Silvana Todero, Costumes: Cantini,
  Shoes: Pompei
[Blue handwriting on white]
- In memory of Yvonne without whom there
  would be no Straub-Films. J.-M. S.

MUSIC: J. S. Bach, *The Musical Offering*, BWV
1079, trio sonata "Sonata sopr'il soggetto reale."
PRODUCTION DATES AND LOCATIONS: June–
July 1978, 5 weeks in Maremme, Mount Pisano,
Tripalle near Pisa, in the Langhe (Piedmont).
BUDGET: 200,000 DM. **SUBTITLED IN ENGLISH**
by Huillet, Misha Donat, and Gregory Woods,
IN FRENCH by Huillet, **IN GERMAN** by Huillet and
Andrea Spingler, **IN DUTCH** by Huillet and Frans
van de Staak. **FIRST SCREENING:** 1979 Cannes Film
Festival, Un Certain Regard (May); Pacific Film
Archive, Berkeley (February 5, 1980).

1980/81
Too Early, Too Late
*Zu früh, zu spät – Trop tôt, trop tard –
Troppo presto, troppo tardi*
FRANCE/EGYPT, 16MM, 1.33:1, COLOR, 100'

[Opening credits, white text on black,
location sound of bells and chirping]
- Zu früh, zu spät, Trop tôt, trop tard,
  Too Early, Too Late, Troppo presto, troppo tardi
- A: Friedrich Engels
- [Script, direction, editing, production]
  Danièle Huillet, Jean-Marie Straub
- [Photography] Willy Lubtchansky,
  Caroline Champetier
- [Sound] Louis Hochet, Manfred Blank
- [Assistants] Radovan Tadic, Vincent Nordon,
  Leo Mingrone, Isaline Panchaud
[Credits before second part]
- B: Mahmud Hussein
[Script, direction, editing, production:
Danièle Huillet, Jean-Marie Straub]
- [Narration] Bahgat el Nadi, Gérard Samaan
- [Sound] Louis Hochet, Manfred Blank
- [Photography] Robert Alazraki,
  Marguerite Perlado
- [Assistants] Mustafa Darwish, Magda Wassef,
  Gaber Abdel-Ghani, Bahgat Mostafa
[No end credits]

TEXTS: letter from Friedrich Engels to Karl Kautsky
(February 20, 1889); excerpt from *Die Bauernfrage
in Frankreich und Deutschland* by F. Engels
("The Peasant Question in France and Germany,"
Die Neue Zeit, 1894–95); statistics in first part
excerpted from the *Cahiers de doléance*;
M. Hussein, postface to *La Lutte de classes en
Égypte de 1945 à 1968* (*Class Struggle in Egypt
from 1945 to 1968*, Paris, F. Maspéro, 1969).
PRODUCTION DATES AND LOCATIONS: first part –
2 weeks in France, June 1980, second part –
3 weeks in Egypt, May 1981. Budget: 400,000 F.

225

FOUR SOUNDTRACKS EXIST: in German, French, English and Italian. Huillet reads the commentary of the first part in all versions; Bhagat el Nadi reads the commentary for the second part in French and English, Gérard Samaan in German and Italian. **FIRST SCREENING:** Kino Arsenal, Berlin (November 8, 1981); 1982 Berlin Film Festival, Internationales Forum des jungen Films (February); released in Paris, Forum des Halles and Action République, February 17, 1982; Collective for Living Cinema, New York (April 30, 1982).

———

1982
En rachâchant
FRANCE, 35MM, 1.37:1, B&W, 7'

[Opening credits, black text on white, in French]
- L'Institut National de l'Audiovisuel presents
- En rachâchant
- Text by Marguerite Duras
- Film by Danièle Huillet and Jean-Marie Straub
- [Image] Henri Alekan, Louis Cochet
- [Assistants] Dominique Gentil, Ariane Damain
- [Sound] Louis Hochet, Manfred Blank
[End credits]
- Ernesto: Olivier Straub, The Mom: Nadette Thinus, The Dad: Bernard Thinus, The Schoolmaster: Raymond Gérard
- Laboratory: LTC Saint-Cloud, Production: Straub-Huillet, Diagonale, INA

TEXT: Marguerite Duras, "Ah! Ernesto!" (Boissy-Saint-Léger: Harlin Quist, 1971). **PRODUCTION DATES AND LOCATIONS:** August 1982, Straub-Huillet's apartment in Paris and Saint-Ouen (school). **SUBTITLED IN ENGLISH** by Huillet and Misha Donat, **IN GERMAN** by Huillet and Andrea Spingler. **FIRST SCREENING:** Released in France, March 23, 1983 with Éric Rohmer's *Pauline on the Beach;* Public Theater, New York (November 1983).

1983
Klassenverhältnisse *(Class Relations)*
WEST GERMANY/FRANCE, 35MM, 1.37:1, B&W, 130'

[Opening credits, white text on black, in German]
- Klassenverhältnisse
- Film by Danièle Huillet and Jean-Marie Straub
- Based on the novel by Franz Kafka, *Der Verschollene (Amerika)* (S. Fischer Verlag) [1911–14]
- Camera: Willy Lubtchansky, Caroline Champetier, Christophe Pollock
- Sound: Louis Hochet, Georges Vaglio, Manfred Blank
- Lighting and Grips: Jim Howe, David Scott, Georg Brommer
- Assistants: Klaus Feddermann, Ralf Olbrisch, Berthold Schweiz, Manfred Sommer
[End credits]
- [Cast] Karl Rossmann: Christian Heinisch, Giacomo: Nazzareno Bianconi
- Uncle: Mario Adorf
- Brunelda: Laura Betti
- Delamarche: Harun Farocki, Robinson: Manfred Blank
- Chauffeur: Reinald Schnell, Line: Anna Schnell
- Captain: Klaus Trabe, the Head Treasurer: Hermann Hartmann
- Schubal: Gérard Semaan, Steward: Jean-François Quinque
- Pollunder: Willi Vöbel, Green: Tilmann Heinisch
- Klara: Anne Bold, Mack: Burckhardt Stoelck
- Servant: Aloys Pompetzki, Pollunder's Driver: Willi Dewelk
- Theresa: Libgart Schwarz, Head Cook: Kathrin Bold
- Manager: Alfred Edel, Head Porter: Andi Engel
- Waiter: Alf Bold, Other elevator boy: Salvatore Sammartino
- Police: Klaus Feddermann, Henning Rademacher, Taxi Driver: Franz Hillers
- Inn Keeper: Lydia Bozyk, Student: Georg Brintrup

- Americans: Thom Andersen and Barton Byg
- French-German co-production of Janus-Film [Frankfurt] with Hessischer Rundfunk and NEF Diffusion, co-financed by the BMI, FFA and the Hamburger Filmförderung

PRODUCTION DATES AND LOCATIONS: July 2 to September 20, 1983 (Hamburg and Bremen), September 21–25, 1983 (New York and St. Louis). **EQUIPMENT:** 1 Moviecam 35mm camera, 1 Nagra. **BUDGET:** 600,000 DM. **SUBTITLED IN ENGLISH** by Huillet and Barton Byg, **IN FRENCH** by Huillet, **IN ITALIAN** by Huillet and Domenico Carosso, **IN DUTCH** by Huillet and Frans van de Staak. **FIRST SCREENING:** 1984 Berlin Film Festival, Competition (February, Special Jury Prize); 1984 New York Film Festival (October).

———

1985

Proposta in quattro parti
(Proposition in Four Parts)
ITALY, VIDEO, 4:3, COLOR/B&W, 41'

[Opening credits, red handwriting on white, in Italian]
- A proposition in four parts by Danièle Huillet and Jean-Marie Straub
[Titles preceding each section, in Italian]
- 1. *A Corner in Wheat*, D. W. Griffith, 1909 [14', in its entirety, silent]
- 2. from *Moses und Aron*, Arnold Schoenberg, 1932, Straub-Huillet, 1974
- 3. from *Fortini/Cani*, Franco Fortini, 1967, Straub-Huillet, 1976
- 4. from *Dalla nube alla resistenza*, Cesare Pavese, 1948–50, Straub-Huillet, 1978
[End credits]
- Danièle Huillet, Jean-Marie Straub, End 1985

Video montage, conceived and edited by Jean-Marie Straub for Enrico Ghezzi's TV program *La Magnifca ossessione*, broadcast on RAI 3 over forty hours from December 25 to 26, 1985. It is also titled *Montaggio in quattro movimenti per "La Magnifica ossessione"* (in the program for the retrospective at the 2001 Turin Film Festival).

———

1986

Der Tod des Empedokles; oder: wenn dann der Erde Grün von neuem euch erglänzt
(The Death of Empedocles or When the Green of the Earth Will Glisten for You Anew)
WEST GERMANY/FRANCE
35MM, 1.37:1, COLOR, 132'

[Opening credits, black text on white, in German]
- A French-German co-production of Janus-Film with Les Films du Losange
- Co-financed by Hessischer Rundfunk, the Hamburger Filmförderung, the FFA and the CNC
[White text on black]
- Der Tod des Empedokles
[Black text on white]
- Tragedy in two acts by Friedrich Hölderlin 1798
[White text on black]
- oder: wenn dann der Erde Grün von neuem euch erglänzt
- Film by Danièle Huillet and Jean-Marie Straub 1986
- Text in collaboration with D. E. Sattler (Roter Stern Publishing)
- Sound: Louis Hochet, Georges Vaglio, Alessandro Zanon
- Camera: Renato Berta, Jean-Paul Toraille, Giovanni Canfarelli
- Assistants: Michael Esser, Hans Hurch, Leo Mingrone, Roberto Palí, Cesare Candelotti

- Costumes: Giovanna del Chiappa,
  Costumi d'arte, Hair: Guerrino Todero
[End credits, black text on white]
- Empedocles: Andreas von Rauch,
  Pausanias: Vladimir Baratta
- Panthea: Martina Baratta, Delia: Ute Cremer
- Hermocrates: Howard Vernon,
  Critias: William Berger
- Three Citizens: Federico Hecker, Peter Boom,
  Giorgio Baratta
- Three Slaves: Georg Bintrup, Achille Brunini,
  Manfred Esser
- Peasant: Peter Kammerer
- Processing and Prints: Luciano Vittori
- Color Timing: Sergio Lustri

This is based on the *first version* of the film. Four different versions exist – four edits (by Huillet and Straub) and sound mixes from different takes of the same shots in the same order. The negative (35mm Kodak color) was developed at Luciano Vittori (Rome), the sound mixes were done with Louis Hochet at Éclair, Épinay-sur-Seine (Paris).
FIRST VERSION: edited in Rome, late Summer 1986; timed, printed and stored at Vittori. Length: 3,629 m. Print screened at the Berlin Film Festival. Opening title text aligned to the right. The "Lizard Version."
SECOND VERSION: edited in Rome, Autumn 1986; timed, printed and stored at LTC, Saint-Cloud, France. Length: 3,618 m. Opening credits in French. Prints subtitled in English by Huillet and Barton Byg, in French by Huillet, in Italian by Huillet, Domenico Carosso, and Vladimir Baratta. The "Paris Version."
THIRD VERSION: edited at the Filmhaus of the Friedensallee in Hamburg during a seminar with students, March 1987; timed, printed and stored at Geyer-Werke laboratory in Hamburg. Length: 3,601 m. Opening credits aligned to the left. The "Rooster Version."
FOURTH VERSION: edited in 1987.

The film is based on the first version (1798) of Hölderlin's unfinished *Der Tod des Empedokles*. The text was established by Huillet and Straub in collaboration with D.E. Sattler, the editor of Hölderlin's complete works published by Roter Stern in Frankfurt (1975), the *Frankfurter Hölderlin-Ausgabe*.
MUSIC: J.S. Bach, *Sonata No. 1 in G Minor*, BWV 1001, performed by Andreas von Rauch. **PRODUCTION DATES AND LOCATIONS:** Late May to late July 1986, 8 weeks in a park in Dona Fugata (Ragusa, southern Sicily) and on Mount Etna, near Linguaglossa. **BUDGET:** 800,000 DM. **FIRST SCREENING:** 1987 Berlin Film Festival, Competition (February); 1987 Festival des films du monde, Montreal (August–September); Pacific Film Archive, Berkeley (October 11, 1988); Facets Media Center, Chicago (one-week release, December 1988).

1988
Schwarze Sünde *(Black Sin)*
WEST GERMANY, 35MM, 1.37:1, COLOR, 42'

[Pre-credits: two sculptures by Ernst Barlach: *Mutter Erde (Mother Earth)* and *Der Rächer (The Avenger);* opening credits, black text on white, in German]
- Schwarze Sünde
- Film by Danièle Huillet and Jean-Marie Straub
- Assistants: Francesco Ragusa, Michael Esser, Hans Hurch
- Leo Mingrone, Arnold Schmidt, Roberto Palì
- Camera: William Lubtchansky
- Christophe Pollock, Gianni Canfarelli
- Sound: Louis Hochet
- Alessandro Zanon, Pierre Donnadieu
- Text by Friedrich Hölderlin (Verlag Roter Stern)
[End credits, black text on white]
- Empedocles: Andreas von Rauch

- Pausanias: Vladimir Theye [= Vladimir Baratta]
- Manes: Howard Vernon
- Production: Straub-Huillet with Dominique Païni
- Processed and Printed: Luciano Vittori, Color Timing: Sergio Lustri
- *Mother Earth* and *The Avenger* were filmed in the Ernst Barlach House by Helmut Herbst
- "Der schwer gefaßte Entschluß" was recorded in London in 1935 with Adolf Busch, Gösta Andreasson, Karl Doktor, Hermann Busch

Danièle Huillet's role at the end of the film is uncredited. **TEXT:** from the third version (1799) of *Der Tod des Empedokles*, established with D. E. Sattler. **MUSIC:** Ludwig van Beethoven, *String Quartet No. 16 in F major,* opus 135, "Der schwer gefaßte Entschluß". **PRODUCTION DATES AND LOCATIONS:** late July and August, 1988, three weeks on Mt. Etna (altitude: 1900 m.). **BUDGET:** 300,000 DM. There are also 4 versions of this film. The second was **SUBTITLED IN FRENCH** by Huillet and **IN ITALIAN** by Huillet and Domenico Carosso. **FIRST SCREENING:** 1989 Cannes Film Festival, Un Certain Regard (May).

———

1989

Cézanne. Dialogue avec Joachim Gasquet
(Cézanne. Conversation with Joachim Gasquet)
FRANCE/WEST GERMANY
35MM, 1.37:1, COLOR/B&W, 51'

[Opening credits, black text on white]
- Cézanne
- Dialogue avec Joachim Gasquet
  (Les éditions Bernheim-Jeune)
[White text on black]
- Film by Danièle Huillet and Jean-Marie Straub
- Photography: Henri Alekan
- Lighting: Louis Cochet, Assistant: Hopi Lebel
- Camera: Stefan Zimmer, Michael Esser,

Moviecam by Cinécam, Argenteuil
- Sound: Louis Hochet, Georges Vaglio
[End credits, white text on black]
- We thank Éditions Gallimard for the excerpt from the film *Madame Bovary* by Jean Renoir
- Monsieur Antoine Salomon for the photographs of Paul Cézanne
- and Virginie Herbin for having provoked this film
- The works by Cézanne that we filmed are found in the following museums: National Gallery, London; Musée d'Orsay, Paris; National Gallery of Scotland, Edinburgh
- Kunstmuseum, Basel; Petit Palais, Paris; Courtauld Institute Galleries, Tate Gallery, London; Cabinet des Dessins of the Musée du Louvre
- Production/Copyright 1989, Musée d'Orsay, SEPT, Diagonale, Straub-Huillet
- Visa d'exploitation n° 71526

The film also exists in a German version, co-produced by Hessischer Rundfunk: *Paul Cézanne im Gespräch mit Joachim Gasquet*. The two versions are different (two negative edits), and the German version is 12 minutes longer. **TEXT:** Joachim Gasquet, from "Ce qu'il m'a dit..." in *Cézanne* (Paris: Éditions Bernheim-Jeune, 1921). The film includes a reel of *Madame Bovary* (Jean Renoir, 1934, based on the novel by Gustav Flaubert) centered around the "comices agricoles" as well as two excerpts from *The Death of Empedocles* and various documents (photos of Cézanne by Maurice Denis, paintings by Cézanne). The words attributed to Cézanne are spoken by Danièle Huillet, those of Gasquet by Jean-Marie Straub in both the French and German versions. The French version is subtitled in English. **PRODUCTION DATES AND LOCATIONS:** September–October 1989, three weeks in Paris, London, Edinburgh, Basel, Ascona and Mount St.-Victoire. **BUDGET:** 900,000 F. The film was rejected by the Musée d'Orsay which had commissioned it. **FIRST SCREENING:** Club Publicis, Paris (April 3, 1990, a few days after a

229

TV broadcast on La Sept); National Film Theater, London (February 27, 1991); Miguel Abreu Gallery, New York (March 17, 2006).

————

1991

Die Antigone des Sophokles nach der Hölderlinschen Übertragung für die Bühne bearbeitet von Brecht 1948

(The Antigone of Sophocles after Hölderlin's Translation Adapted for the Stage by Brecht 1948)
GERMANY/FRANCE, 35MM, 1.37:1, COLOR, 100'

[Opening credits]
- Il Teatro di Segesta
[Black text on white, in German]
- Die Antigone des Sophokles nach der Hölderlinschen Übertragung für die Bühne bearbeitet von Brecht 1948 (Suhrkamp Verlag)
- Film by Danièle Huillet and Jean-Marie Straub 1991
- Assistants: Michael Esser, Hans Hurch, Francesco Ragusa, Daniele Rossi, Yu-Jung Nam
- Olivier Moeckli, Stephan Settele, Stefan Ofner, Marco Zappone, Ernaldo Data
- Co-production Regina Ziegler (Filmproduktion, Berlin), Martine Marignac (Pierre Grise Productions, Paris), Hessischer Rundfunk, Straub-Huillet
- Production Manager: Danièle Huillet with Hartmut Köhler, Rosalie Lecan
- Antigone: Astrid Ofner, Ismene: Ursula Ofner
- Elders: Hans Diehl, Kurt Radeke, Michael Maassen, Rainer Philippi
- Creon: Werner Rehm
- Guard: Lars Studer, Haemon: Stephan Wolf-Schönburg, Tiresias: Albert Hetterle, Child: Mario di Mattia
- Messenger: Michael König, Servant-Messenger: Libgart Schwarz
- Costumi d'Arte Ruggero Peruzzi, Hair: Guerrino Todero, Shoes: Pompei

- Sound: Louis Hochet, Georges Vaglio, Sandro Zanon
- Camera: Nicolas Eprendre, Irina and William Lubtchansky
- Negative: Kodak 5245, [Laboratory] Geyer-Werke Berlin, [Camera] Movie-Cam by Cine-Light
- Music by Bernd Alois Zimmermann conducted by Michael Gielen
[End credits]
- The memory of humanity for sufferings borne is astonishingly short. Its gift of imagination for coming sufferings is almost even less. It is this callousness that we must combat. For humanity is threatened by wars compared to which those past are like poor attempts and they will come, without any doubt, if the hands of those who prepare them in all openness are not broken. Bertolt Brecht 1952
[Handwritten]
- Thank you, thank you Marco Müller and Jean-Luc Godard
[White text on black]
- Also made with the support of the Berliner Filmförderung, the Filmförderungsanstalt and the CNC

TEXT: Brecht's 1948 reworking for the stage of Hölderlin's German translation (1800–1803) of Sophocle's tragedy *Antigone* (441 BC) – without Brecht's prologue. The play was performed at the Schaubühne in Berlin (premiere on May 3, 1991), then for a single performance on August 14 at the Teatro di Segesta. **MUSIC:** an extract from *Die Soldaten* (1958–65) by Bernd Alois Zimmermann. **PRODUCTION DATES AND LOCATION:** Summer 1991, 5 weeks at the ancient Teatro di Segesta (Sicily). **BUDGET:** 3,000,000 F. There are two versions of the film. First version subtitled in English, second in French (by Danièle Huillet). **FIRST SCREENING:** 1992 Berlin Film Festival, Panorama (February).

1994
Lothringen!
GERMANY/FRANCE, 35MM, 1.37:1, COLOR, 21'

[Opening credits, black text on white]
- Lothringen!

[White text on black]
- Film by Danièle Huillet and Jean-Marie Straub
- Adapted from the novel *Colette Baudoche* by Maurice Barrès
- Music by Franz Joseph Haydn [performed by the] Amadeus Quartet

[End credits, white text on black]
- Emmanuelle Straub [Colette]
- Narration spoken in French by André Warynski and Dominique Dosdat, in German by J.-M. S.
- Sound: Louis Hochet, Georges Vaglio, Mix: Euro Studios
- Image: Christophe Pollock, Emmanuelle Collinot
- Camera: Golden Panaflex G II, Lenses: Primo, Negative: Eastman 5248, Laboratory: LTC
- Production: Saarländischer Rundfunk (Peter Brugger), Straub-Huillet, Pierre Grise (Martine Marignac)

TEXT: Maurice Barrès, *Colette Baudoche. Histoires d'une jeune fille de Metz* (*Colette Baudoche: Story of a Young Girl from Metz*, Paris: F. Juven, 1909). In the German version, Straub speaks the parts of the narration recited in French by A. Warynski; Emmanuelle Straub's lines and the grandmother's story spoken by D. Dosdat are subtitled. The French Version is subtitled in English. **PRODUCTION DATES AND LOCATIONS:** June 1994, Metz and surrounding areas, Koblenz. **FIRST SCREENING:** 1994 Locarno Film Festival (August); Cinémathèque française, December 1994; 2011 New York Film Festival, Views from the Avant-Garde (October 8, French version). **TV PREMIERE:** Arte, January 12, 1995.

1996
Von heute auf morgen
(From Today Until Tomorrow)
GERMANY/FRANCE, 35MM, 1.37:1, B&W, 62'

[Pre-credit shot: pan over the orchestra and set]
[Opening credits, white text on black, in German]
- Von heute auf morgen
- Opera in One Act by Arnold Schönberg
- Conducted by Michael Gielen
- Libretto Max Blonda 1929

[Shot of a wall with graffiti: "Wo liegt euer Lächeln begraben?!" ("Where does your hidden smile lie?!")]
- Film by Danièle Huillet and Jean-Marie Straub, 1996
- Set Design: Max Schoendorff, J.-M. S./D. H.
- Camera: William Lubtchansky
- Irina Lubtchansky, Marion Befve
- Lighting: Jim Howe, Barry Davis, Andreas Niels Michel
- Sound: Louis Hochet
- Georges Vaglio, Sandro Zamon, Klaus Barm
- Charly Morell, Hans-Bernhard Bätzing, Björn Rosenberg

[End credits, white text on black]
- Frankfurt Radio Symphony Orchestra
- Husband: Richard Salter, Wife: Christine Whittlesey
- Child: Annabelle Hahn
- Friend: Claudia Barainsky, Singer: Ryszard Karczykowski
- Hair Dresser: Jutta Braun
- Music assistants: Till Drömann, David Coleman
- Film assistants: Rosalie Lecan, Jean-Charles Fitoussi, Arnaud Maillet
- Production: Straub-Huillet
- Pierre Grise, Martine Marignac
- In co-production with Hessischer Rundfunk
- Dietmar Schings, Leo Karl Gerhartz, Hans-Peter Baden
- Dedicated to Helga Gielen, Dieter Reifarth, André and Dominique Warynski

PRODUCTION LOCATION: Hessischer Rundfunk Studio, Frankfurt. **SUBTITLED IN ENGLISH** by Huillet and Barton Byg, **IN FRENCH** by Huillet, **IN ITALIAN** by Huillet and Domenico Carosso. Released in France with *Lothringen!*, February 12, 1997; 1997 New York Film Festival (October). **TV PREMIERE:** January 7, 1998 (HR III, Germany). English subtitled prints in the collections of the Pacific and Harvard Film Archives.

————

1998
Sicilia!
ITALY/FRANCE, 35MM, 1.37:1, B&W, 66'

[Opening credits, black text on white, in French]
- For the marmoset and in memory of Barnabé the cat. J.-M.S.

[White text on black]
- Sicilia!
- Film by Danièle Huillet and Jean-Marie Straub 1998
- Assistants: Arnaud Maillet, Jean-Charles Fitoussi, Romano Guelfi, Andreas Teuchert
- Photography: William Lubtchansky
- Irina Lubtchansky, Marion Befve, LTC, Saint-Cloud
- Lighting: Jim Howe, Olivier Cazzitti
- Sound: Jean-Pierre Duret, Jacques Balley
- Mix: Louis Hochet, Sonodi, Épinay-sur-Seine

[End credits, white text on black]
- Gianni Buscarino [Silvestro], Vittorio Vigneri [Knife Sharpener]
- Angela Nugara [Mother]
- Carmelo Maddio [Man], Angela Durantini [his Wife]
- Simone Nucatola, Ignazio Trombello
- Giovanni Interlandi [The Great Lombardo], Giuseppe Bontà [Man from Catania], Mario Baschieri [Little Old Man]
- Production: Straub-Huillet

- French-Italian co-production Pierre Grise Productions, Martine Marignac; Centre National de la Cinématographie
- Alia Film, Enzo Porcelli; Instituto Luce
- Pre-sales ARD Degeto; Hessischer Rundfunk, Dietmar Schings; Saarländischer Rundfunk; Westdeutscher Rundfunk
- Thank you, thank you Salvatore Scollo, Barbara Ulrich, Dominique and André
- Gabriella Taddeo, Anna Barzacchini, Paolo Bernardini, Dario Marconcini, Marcello Landi and his wife
- Piero Spilá, Francesco Grillini, and the rail workers of Messina and Syracuse
- Constellations, dialogues from the novel *Conversazione in Sicilia* by Elio Vittorini 1937–38

[Photograph of Elio Vittorini]

MUSIC: Ludwig van Beethoven, *String Quartet in A Minor,* opus 132. The text was performed at the Teatro Francesco di Bartolo, Buti, Italy, April 1998. **PRODUCTION LOCATIONS:** Buti, Messina, Syracuse, Grammichele. **SUBTITLED IN ENGLISH** by Huillet and Barton Byg, **IN FRENCH** by Huillet. **FIRST SCREENING:** Cannes Film Festival, Un Certain Regard, May 20, 1999; released in France, September 15, 1999; 1999 New York Film Festival (October). There are three versions of the film.

————

2000
Operai, contadini *(Workers, Peasants)*
ITALY/FRANCE, 35MM, 1.37:1, COLOR DTS (RECORDED IN MONO), 123'

[Opening credits, black text on white, in French]
- Operai, contadini | Ouvriers, paysans | Arbeiter, Bauern
- Characters, constellations and text by Elio Vittorini

[White text on black]
- Film by Danièle Huillet and Jean-Marie Straub
- [Image] Renato Berta,
  Jean-Paul Toraille [Marion Befve]
- [Sound] Jean-Pierre Duret, Dimitri Haulet
- [Assistants] Romano Guelfi,
  Jean-Charles Fitoussi, Arnaud Maillet

[End credits, white text on black]
- [Actors] Angela Nugara [Widow Biliotti],
  Giacinto Di Pascoli [Cattarin],
  Giampaolo Cassarino [Pompeo Manera]
- Enrico Achilli [Cataldo Chiesa],
  Angela Durantini [Elvira La Farina],
  Martina Gionfriddo [Carmela Graziadei]
- Andrea Balducci [Fischio], Gabriella Taddei
  [Giralda Adorno], Vittorio Vigneri [Spine]
- Aldo Fruttuosi [Ventura, "Faccia Cattiva"],
  Rosalba Curatola [Siracusa],
  Enrico Pelosini [Toma]
- "Il Seracino" (Marcello Landi)
- Production: Straub-Huillet
- Martine Marignac, Pierre Grise Productions;
  Charlotte Vincent, Capricci Films
- Teatro Comunale Francesco di Bartolo (Buti),
  Studio National des Arts Contemporains
  (Le Fresnoy)
- Saarländischer Rundfunk, Südwestrundfunk,
  Westdeutscher Rundfunk, Werner Dütsch

[Black text on white]
- Mix: Jean-Pierre Laforce, Jackson, DTS Stereo
  [sound recorded in mono]
- Color Timing: Marcel Mazoyer, LTC Saint Cloud

There are three versions of this film, first version subtitled in English. **TEXT:** Elio Vittorini, *Le donne di Messina*, 1st edition published in 1949, 2nd edition, partially re-written, in 1964. The film uses almost the entirety of chapters XLIV to XLVII from the novel. Performed at the Teatro Francesco di Bartolo, Buti, Italy in June 2000. **MUSIC:** Johann Sebastian Bach, *Cantata* BWV 125, Aria (Duetto). **PRODUCTION DATE AND LOCATION:**

Summer 2000, Buti. **FIRST SCREENING:** 2001 Cannes Film Festival, Director's Fortnight (May); released in France, September 2001.

———

2001
Il viandante *(The Wayfarer)*
ITALY/FRANCE, 35 MM, 1.37:1, B&W, 5'

[Opening credits, black handwriting on white]
- Jean-Marie Straub, Danièle Huillet
  Il viandante (Le Chemineau)
  Angela Nugara, Gianni Buscarino
  For Danièle!

———

2001
L'arrotino *(The Knife Sharpener)*
ITALY/FRANCE, 35MM, 1.37:1, B&W, 7'

[Opening credits, black handwriting on white]
- Jean-Marie Straub, Danièle Huillet
  Le Rémouleur
  Gianni Buscarino, Vittorio Vigneri

Both of these films are re-edited sequences from *Sicilia!* **FIRST SCREENING:** 2001 Torino Film Festival (November 21).

———

2002
Il ritorno del figlio prodigo
(The Return of the Prodigal Son)
ITALY/FRANCE/GERMANY
35MM, 1.37:1, COLOR, DOLBY, 29'

New version of shots 40 to 46 and 63 to 66 of *Workers, Peasants*, focusing on the character Spine.

2002

Umiliati: che niente di fatto o toccata da loro, di uscito dale mani loro, risultasse essente dal diritto di qualcho estranea (Operai, contadini – seguito e fine)
(Humiliated: …that nothing produced or touched by them, coming from their hands, proves free from the claim of some stranger [Workers, Peasants – continuation and end])
ITALY/FRANCE/GERMANY
35MM, 1.37:1, COLOR, DOLBY, 35'

For theatrical distribution, the film was released together with the previous one
(see the entry on *Le Retour du fils prodigue – Humiliés*, 2001–2003).

———

2002

Incantati
ITALY/FRANCE/GERMANY
35MM, 1.37:1, DOLBY, COLOR, 6'

New edit of the end of *Umiliati*

———

2002

Dolando
ITALY/FRANCE/GERMANY
35MM, 1.37:1, COLOR, DOLBY, 7'

[Opening credits]
- Danièle Huillet, Jean-Marie Straub
- [Image] Renato Berta, Jean-Paul Toraille, Marion Befve
- [Sound] Jean-Pierre Duret, Dimitri Haulet, Jean-Pierre Laforce

Film made during the production of *Umiliati*. Three shots showing Dolando Bernardini, an actor in the film, singing *a capella* a few verses of *La Gerusalemme liberata* by Torquato Tasso (Canto 19, strophes 11–12, 25–16 and Canto 20, strophe 73), which he knew by heart. Followed by a new take of the last shot of *Workers, Peasants*.

———

2001–2003

Le Retour du fils prodigue – Humiliés
(The Return of the Prodigal Son – The Humiliated)
ITALY/FRANCE/GERMANY
35MM, 1.37:1, COLOR, DOLBY, 64'

[Opening credits, for both films]
- Grand palm… [handwritten]
- [Text] Elio Vittorini
- Danièle Huillet, Jean-Marie Straub
- [Image] Renato Berta, Jean-Paul Toraille, Marion Befve
- [Sound] Jean-Pierre Duret, Dimitri Haulet, Jean-Pierre Laforce
- [Assisants] Giulio Bursi, Maurizio Buquicchio, Arnaud Maillet, Jean-Charles Fitoussi
- Production: Straub-Huillet
- Associazione Teatro Buti, Fondazione Pontedera Teatro, Regione Toscana, Provincia di Pisa, Comune di Buti
- Martine Marignac, Pierre Grise Productions, Centre National de la Cinématographie
- Werner Dütsch, Westdeutscher Rundfunk
- Studio National des Arts Contemporains, Le Fresnoy
- Camera: Panavision, Negative: Kodak 5279, Lab: LTC
- Music: Edgar Varèse
- Il ritorno del figlio prodigo
- Martina Gionfriddo, Andrea Balducci, Gabriella Taddei
- Vittorio Vigneri, Aldo Fruttuosi
- Umiliati

- Rosalba Curatola, Aldo Fruttuosi
- Romano Guelfi
- Paolo Spaziani, Federico Ciaramella, Daniel Vannucci
- Enrico Achilli, Martina Gionfriddo, Enrico Pelosini
- Angela Durantini, Andrea Balducci, Dolando Bernardini
- Giampaolo Cassarino, Giacinto Di Pascoli
- Gabriella Taddei
- Vittorio Vigneri
- "Il Seracino"

TEXT: Elio Vittorini, *Le donne di Messina,* excerpts (see note for *Operai, contadini*). **MUSIC:** Edgar Varèse, *Arcana* (1925–27). Performed at the Teatro Francesco di Bartolo, Buti, May 31, June 1 and 2, 2002. **FIRST SCREENING:** Cinémathèque française (Palais de Chaillot, March 24, 2003); released in Paris, April 23, 2003; second version screened at the Cinémathèque française, March 9, 2004.

2004
Une visite au Louvre
(A Visit to the Louvre)
FRANCE/GERMANY, 35MM, 1.37:1, COLOR
DOLBY SR, 48' (1ST VERSION), 47' (2ND VERSION)

[Opening credits, black text on white, in French]
- Joachim Gasquet
- Une visite au Louvre
- [Narration] Julie Koltaï
- Danièle Huillet, Jean-Marie Straub
- [Image] William Lubtchansky, Irina Lubtchansky, Jean-Paul Toraille
- [Lighting] André Atellian, Jim Howe, Marc Romani
- [Image] Renato Berta, Marion Befve
- [Sound] Jean-Pierre Duret, Dimitri Haulet, Gérard Delagarde, Jean-Pierre Laforce

[End credits, black text on white]
- Production: Straub-Huillet, Atopic: Christophe Gougeon
- Centre National de la Cinématographie: thank you Frédéric Mitterand and Hugues Quattrone
- Le Fresnoy, Studio National des Arts Contemporains: thank you Alain Fleischer, Frédéric Papon, Christian Châtel
- Fondation de France, Initiatives d'artistes: thank you François Albéra, François Hers, Catia Riccaboni
- Ministere de la Culture, Delegation aux Arts Plastiques: thank you Bernard Blistène, Chantal Soyer, Pascale Cassagneau, Jean-Claude Conesa
- Strandfilm: Dieter Reifarth, Zweites Deutsches Fernsehen: Inge Classen
- RAI Tre, Enrico Ghezzi
- thank you, thank you André Goeminne and Anne Pontégnie
- Bertrand Brouder, Cornelia Geiser
- Régis Michel, Catherine Bélanger, Patricia Oranin-Godin, Claire Herlic, Jeanne Latrobe
- Cinecam, Kodak 5247: thank you Nathalie Cikalovski, LTC: Fabrice Dequeant
- Studio: Daniel Dehayes, Jackson: Dolby SR mono
- Fondspa, Luxembourg: Guy Daleidan, thank you Marie-Claude Beaud
- Fonds Images de France, du Ministère des Affaires étrangères

TEXT: Joachim Gasquet, from "Ce qu'il m'a dit ..." in *Cézanne* (Paris: Éditions Bernheim-Jeune, 1921). Includes an unused take of the first shot of *Workers, Peasants.* **SUBTITLED IN ENGLISH** by Misha Donat and Straub, **IN GERMAN** by Huillet, Peter Kammerer, and Antonia Weiße, **IN ITALIAN** by Huillet and Romano Guelfi. Both versions of the film are shown one after the other. The first version begins with a title card: "Dominique Païni provoked this film in 1990," in Jean-Marie Straub's handwriting and ends with: "Thank you François Albéra, François Hers, Catia Riccaboni." **FIRST SCREENING:** Released in Paris, March 17, 2004; 2005 New York Film Festival, Views from the Avant-Garde (October); 2005 London Film Festival (October; both screenings without subtitles).

————

2005

Quei loro incontri
(These Encounters of Theirs)
ITALY/FRANCE
35MM, 1.37:1, COLOR, DOLBY SRD, 68'

[Opening credits, white text on black, in French, preceded by a projection framing card]
- Regione Toscana, Provincia di Pisa, Teatro comunale du Buti
- "Il Seracino" Marcello Landi
- Martine Marignac, Pierre Grise Productions
- Centre National de la Cinématographie
- Le Fresnoy Studio National des Arts Contemporains, Frédéric Papon, Christian Châtel, Jean-René Lorand, Blandine Tourneux
- Production: Straub-Huillet
- [Image] Renato Berta, Jean-Paul Toraille, Marion Befve
- [Sound] Jean-Pierre Duret, Dimitri Haulet, Jean-Pierre Laforce
- [Assistants] Kamel Belaïd, Arnaud Maillet, Giulio Bursi, Maurizio Buquicchio
- Quei loro incontri, Ces rencontres avec eux
- The last five *Dialogues with Leucò* by Cesare Pavese
- Film by Danièle Huillet and Jean-Marie Straub
[Title cards preceding each dialogue]
- [Cast] 1. Angela Nugara – Vittorio Vigneri
- 2. Grazia Orsi – Romano Guelfi

- 3. Angela Durantini – Enrico Achilli
- 4. Giovanna Daddi – Dario Marconcini
- 5. Andrea Bacci – Andrea Balducci
[End credits]
- 1947–2005
- Archipel, LTC Saint Cloud
- fin

MUSIC: Ludwig van Beethoven, *Quartet no. 11,* opus 59. Performed at the Teatro Francesco di Bartolo, Buti, May 20–23, 2005. First version **SUBTITLED IN ENGLISH** by Misha Donat and Straub. **FIRST SCREENING:** 2006 Venice Film Festival (September); released in France, October 18, 2006; 2007 Film Comment Selects, New York (February). Marguerite Duras Prize, 2007.

————

2006

Europa 2005, 27 Octobre
(Europa 2005, 27 October)
FRANCE, MINIDV, 4:3, COLOR, 10'30''

Shot near the Clichy-sous-Bois power transformer where Zyed Benna and Bouna Traoré died from electrocution on October 27, 2005, while running from the police. Shot and edited by Jean-Claude Rousseau. **ASSISTANT:** Christophe Clavert. **FIRST SCREENING:** Musée contemporain du Val-de-Marne (September 21, 2006), shown before a pre-release screening of *Quei loro incontri*; 2007 Toronto Film Festival, Wavelengths (September); Anthology Film Archives, New York (June 29, 2012); Goethe-Institut, London (March 10, 2015).

2007

Le Genou d'Artémide *(Artemide's Knee)*
ITALY/FRANCE, 35MM, 1.37:1, COLOR, DOLBY SRD
26' (1ST VERSION), 27' (2ND VERSION)

[Red handwriting on white in first version,
blue in second version]
- For Barbara

[Opening credits, white text on black, in French]
- Le Genou d'Artémide
- Film by Jean-Marie Straub
- [Text] Cesare Pavese
- [Cast] Andrea Bacci, Dario Marconcini,
  Teatro Comunale di Buti
- [Producer] Martine Marignac,
  Pierre Grise Productions
- [Image] Renato Berta, Jean-Paul Toraille,
  Marion Befve
- [Sound] Jean-Pierre Duret, Dimitri Haulet,
  Jean-Pierre Laforce
- [Assistants] Arnaud Dommerc,
  Jean-Charles Fitoussi, Romano Guelfi,
  Giulio Bursi, Maurizio Buquicchio
- [Editor] Nicole Lubtchansky
- Blandine Tourneux, Frédéric Papon,
  Le Fresnoy
- [Music] Gustav Mahler

[End credits: white text on black]
- [Music] Heinrich Schütz
- Cine-Stereo/LTC Saint-Cloud

TEXT: Cesare Pavese, "La Belva" ("The Beast") in
Dialoghi con Leucò (*Dialogues with Leucò*). Per-
formed as *Il Ginocchio di Artemide* at the Teatro
Francesco di Bartolo, Buti, May 24–25, 2007.
MUSIC: Gustav Mahler, "Der Abschied," from
Das Lied von der Erde, conducted by Bruno
Walter, soprano: Kathleen Ferrier. First version
SUBTITLED IN ENGLISH by Misha Donat and
Straub, **IN FRENCH** by Jacques Bontemps, Bernard
Eisenschitz, and Straub, **IN GERMAN** by Antonia
Weiße, Barbara Ulrich, Peter Kammerer, and

Straub. **FIRST SCREENING:** March 15, 2008, Ciné-
mathèque française; 2008 Cannes Film Festival,
Director's Fortnight (May 19); 2008 London Film
Festival (October); 2010 Migrating Forms, New
York (May 15).

––––––

2007

Itinéraire de Jean Bricard
(Itinerary of Jean Bricard)
FRANCE, 35MM, 1.37:1, B&W, DOLBY SRD, 40'
(2 VERSIONS)

[Opening credits, handwritten,
black text on white]
- For Peter Nestler

[Black text on white]
- Itinéraire de Jean Bricard by Jean-Yves Petiteau
- Film by Danièle Huillet and Jean-Marie Straub

[End credits, black text on white]
- [Image] Irina Lubtchansky, William and Nicole,
  Jean-Paul Toraille
- [Sound] Dimitri Haulet, Jean-Pierre Laforce,
  Jean-Pierre Duret, Zaki Allal
- [Assistants] André Atellian, Arnaud Dommerc,
  Jean Vivier, Jean-Charles Fitoussi
- Le Fresnoy, Frédéric Papon, Blandine Tourneux,
  Cyril Lauwerier, Christian Châtel,
  Jean-René Lorand
- Martine Marignac, Pierre Grise Productions,
  Centre National de la Cinématographie

TEXT: Jean-Yves Petiteau, "Itinéraire de Jean
Bricard" in *Interlope la curieuse* (Nantes), no. 9/10,
June 1994. **PRODUCTION DATES AND LOCATION:**
December 2007, on and around Coton Island, on
the Loire. **SUBTITLED IN ENGLISH** by Misha Donat
and Straub (first version), **IN GERMAN** by Barbara
Ulrich and Straub, **IN ITALIAN** by Giorgio
Passerone and Straub. **FIRST SCREENING:** 2008
Cannes Film Festival, Director's Fortnight

(May 19, with *Artemide's Knee*, Jean-Marie Straub considering the two films inseparable); 2008 London Film Festival; 2010 Migrating Forms, New York (May 15).

2008
Le Streghe, Femmes entre elles
(The Witches, women among themselves)
FRANCE/ITALY
35MM, 1.37:1, COLOR, DOLBY SRD, 21'

[Opening credits, black text on white, in French]
- Le Streghe, Femmes entre elles
- The first of the *Dialogues With Leucò* written by Cesare Pavese
- Film by Jean-Marie Straub
- [Image] Renato Berta, Jean-Paul Toraille, Irina Lubtchansky
- [Sound] Jean-Pierre Duret, Jean-Pierre Laforce, Julien Sicart, Zaki Allal
- [Assistants] Arnaud Dommerc, Mehdi Benallal, Romano Guelfi, Giulio Bursi, Maurizio Buquicchio
- [Editor] Catherine Quesemand
- [Cast] Giovanna Daddi, Giovanna Giuliani
[End credits, black text on white]
- Production: Straub-Huillet
- Teatro Comunale di Buti, Martine Marignac, Pierre Grise Productions
- Le Fresnoy, Frédéric Papon, Blandine Tourneux, Jean-René Lorand
- LTC Saint-Cloud, Archipel, Dolby SRD

First performed at the Teatro Francesco di Bartolo, Buti, June 5, 2008. **PRODUCTION DATES AND LOCATION:** June 16–20, 2008, Buti. **SUBTITLED IN ENGLISH** by Misha Donat and Straub (first version), **IN FRENCH** by Jacques Bontemps, Bernard Eisenschitz, Barbara Ulrich, and Straub, **IN GERMAN** by Antonia Weiße, Barbara Ulrich,

and Straub. **FIRST SCREENING:** Cinémathèque française, March 9, 2009, with the second version of *Itinéraire de Jean Bricard*; 2009 Toronto Film Festival, Wavelengths (September); 2010 Migrating Forms, New York (May 15).

2009
Corneille–Brecht
FRANCE, MINIDV, 4:3, COLOR
26'43'' (VERSION A, SUBTITLED IN GERMAN)
26'27'' (VERSION B, SUBTITLED IN FRENCH)
26'55'' (VERSION C, SUBTITLED IN ENGLISH)

[Opening credits, black text on white]
- Cornelia Geiser, Jean-Marie Straub, Corneille–Brecht, Christophe Clavert, Jean-Claude Rousseau, Barbara Ulrich

TEXT: Pierre Corneille, *Horace* (1640) and *Othon* (1664); Bertolt Brecht, *Das Verhör des Lukullus* (*The Trial of Lucullus*, 1940). **PRODUCTION DATES AND LOCATION:** July 2009, Jean-Marie Straub's apartment, Paris. **CAMERA:** Panasonic AG DVX-100. **SUBTITLED IN ENGLISH** by Misha Donat and Straub, **IN FRENCH** by Bertrand Brouder, Barbara Ulrich and Straub, **IN ITALIAN** by Giorgio Passerone and Straub. **FIRST SCREENING:** 2009 Viennale (October 31); 2010 New York Film Festival, Views from the Avant-Garde (October 1).

2009
Joachim Gatti
FRANCE, HD, 16:9, COLOR, 1'30''

No credits. **IMAGE:** Renato Berta. Text by Jean-Jacques Rousseau, from the preface to the *Discours sur l'origine et les fondements de l'inégalité parmi les hommes* (*Discourse on the*

Origin and Foundations of Inequality Among Men, 1755). **CAMERA:** Red One. Produced for *Outrage et Rebellion*, a collective film conceived by Nicole Brenez and Nathalie Hubert in response to the blinding of the French filmmaker Joachim Gatti during a peaceful protest in Montreuil in July 2009 when a police officer fired a flash-ball gun into the crowd. Published on the website mediapart.fr on December 10, 2009. **FIRST SCREENING:** 2009 Viennale (October 31)

TEXT: Dante Alighieri, "Canto XXXIII" of *Paradiso, Divina Commedia*. **CAMERA:** Red One. **PRODUCTION DATES AND LOCATION:** Buti, September 7–10, 2009. First version **SUBTITLED IN ENGLISH** by Misha Donat and Straub, based on Henry Wadsworth Longfellow's translation of 1867, **IN GERMAN** by Peter Kammerer and Straub, **IN FRENCH BY** Giorgio Passerone and Straub. **FIRST SCREENING:** 2010 Locarno Film Festival (August); 2010 New York Film Festival, Views from the Avant-Garde (October 1).

2009

O somma luce *(Oh Supreme Light)*
ITALY/FRANCE, HD, 16:9, COLOR, 18'
(2 VERSIONS)

[Opening credits, white text on black]
- First version, Dante, O somma luce, with Giorgio Passerone
- Film by Jean-Marie Straub
- [Image] Renato Berta, Jean-Paul Toraille, Arnaud Dommerc, Franck Ciochetti
- [Sound] Jean-Pierre Duret, [Editing] Catherine Quesemand, [Sound Mix] Jean-Pierre Laforce
- [Le Fresnoy] Florent Le Duc, Baptiste Evrand, Blandine Tourneux, Cyrille Lauwerier
- [Producer] Barbara Ulrich
- [Assistants] Romano Guelfi, Maurizio Buquicchio, Giulio Bursi
- Music: Edgar Varèse, *Déserts*, Théâtre des Champs-Élysées, December 2, 1954
[End credits, white text on black]
- Production: Straub-Huillet, Martine Marignac, Pierre Grise Productions, Cyrille Bordonzotti
- Andrea Bacci, Teatro Communale di Buti
- Frédéric Papon, Le Fresnoy, Studio National des Arts Contemporains

2010

L'Inconsolable *(The Inconsolable One)*
ITALY, MINIDV, 4:3, COLOR
15' (1ST VERSION)
15'17'' (2ND VERSION)

[Opening credits, white text on black]
- L'Inconsolable, first version
- Film by Jean-Marie Straub
- [Dialogue] Cesare Pavese
- [Cast] Giovanna Daddi, Andrea Bacci
- [Camera] Renato Berta, Christophe Clavert
- [Sound] Dimitri Haulet, Julien Gonzalez
- [Assistants] Barbara Ulrich, Arnaud Dommerc
- [Assistants] Giulio Bursi, Maurizio Buquicchio, Romano Guelfi
[End credits, white text on black]
- Music: Robert Schumann
- Editing: Catherine Quesemand
- Sound mix: Jean-Pierre Laforce
- [Production] Les Fées Productions, Sandrine Pillon, Lucie Portehaut, Florence Hugues
- Teatro Comunale di Buti
- La Fémis, Marc Nicolas, Frédéric Papon, Delphine Dumon, Gaël Blondet
- Straub-Huillet, Belva GmbH
- © Les Fées Productions 2011, visa n. 126 666

TEXT: Cesare Pavese, "L'inconsolabile" in *Dialoghi con Leucò*. Performed at the Teatro Comunale di Buti on September 3, 2010. **PRODUCTION DATES AND LOCATION:** September 6–9, 2010, Buti. **CAMERA:** Panasonic AG-DVX 100. **SUBTITLED IN ENGLISH** by Misha Donat and Straub, **IN GERMAN** by Barbara Ulrich, Peter Kammerer, and Straub, **IN FRENCH** by Barbara Ulrich and Straub. **FIRST SCREENING:** 2011 Locarno Film Festival (August); 2011 New York Film Festival, Views from the Avant-Garde (October 8).

———

2010

Un héritier *(An Heir)*
FRANCE, MINIDV, 4:3, COLOR
20'23'' (1ˢᵀ VERSION)
21'5'' (2ᴺᴰ VERSION)

[Opening credits, white text on black]
- Un héritier, first version
- Film by Jean-Marie Straub
- [Dialogue] Maurice Barrès
- [Cast] Barbara Ulrich
- Joseph Rottner, Jubarite Semaran
- [Camera] Renato Berta, Christophe Clavert
- [Sound] Dimitri Haulet, Julien Gonzalez
- [Assistants] Arnaud Dommerc
- Maurizio Buquicchio, Grégoire Letouvet
[End credits, white text on black]
- Editing: Catherine Quesemand
- Sound mix: Jean-Pierre Laforce
- Les Fées Productions, Sandrine Pillon, Lucie Portehaut, Florence Hugues
- With the participation of the Centre National de la Cinématographie and the Region Alsace
- Jeonju Digital Project 2011
- La Fémis, Marc Nicolas, Frédéric Papon, Delphine Dumont, Gaël Blondet
- Thank you, thank you Sylvie and Hubert Bangraz, Maison Forestiere de Rathsamhausen

- the Schreiber family, and the employees of the Domaine du Moulin d'Ottrott
- Straub-Huillet, Belva GmbH
- © Les Fées Productions 2011, visa no. 127 278

TEXT: Maurice Barrès, *Au service de l'Allemagne* (*In the Service of Germany*, 1905), chapter 8. Commissioned by the Jeonju Digital Project. **PRODUCTION DATES AND LOCATIONS:** September 14–22, 2010, Ottrott, France. **CAMERA:** Panasonic AG-DVX 100. Both versions **SUBTITLED IN ENGLISH** by Misha Donat and Straub, first version **IN GERMAN** by Barbara Ulrich, Antonia Weiße, and Straub, **IN ITALIAN** by Peter Kammerer, Marco Ferri, Giorgio Passerone, and Straub. **FIRST SCREENING:** 2011 Jeonju Film Festival (April 28–May 6); 2011 New York Film Festival, Views from the Avant-Garde (October 8).

———

2011

Schakale und Araber *(Jackals and Arabs)*
FRANCE, MINIDV, 4:3, COLOR
10'43'' (1ˢᵀ VERSION)
10'35'' (2ᴺᴰ VERSION)

[Opening credits, black text on white]
- First version, Straub Huillet Films, Belva GmbH
- Present
- Schakale und Araber by Franz Kafka
- [Music] György Kurtag
[End credits, black text on white]
- [Cast] Barbara Ulrich, Giorgio Passerone, Jubarite Semaran
- [Camera] Christophe Clavert, Jean-Marc Degardin, Arnaud Dommerc
- [Sound] Jérome Ayasse, [sound mix] Jean-Pierre Laforce, Gaël Blondet
- Jean-Marie Straub

TEXT: Franz Kafka, *Schakale und Araber (Jackals and Arabs*, 1917). **MUSIC:** György Kurtag, *Kafka-Fragmente* (1987), opus 24, Part IV, No. 7: "Wiederum, wiederum." **PRODUCTION DATES AND LOCATION:** April 22–29 and May 1, 2011, Straub's apartment, Paris. **CAMERA:** Panasonic AG-DVX 100. First version **SUBTITLED IN FRENCH** by Danièle Huillet, originally published in *Cahiers du cinéma*, issue 400, October 1987; second version **IN ENGLISH** by Misha Donat and Straub. **FIRST SCREENING:** 2011 Locarno Film Festival (August 10); 2011 New York Film Festival, Views from the Avant-Garde (October 8); Goethe-Institut, London (March 10, 2015).

———

2011

La madre *(The Mother)*
ITALY, HD, 4:3, COLOR
20'9'' (1ST VERSION, SUBTITLED IN GERMAN)
20'9'' (2ND VERSION, SUBTITLED IN FRENCH)
19'38'' (3RD VERSION, SUBTITLED IN ENGLISH)

[Opening credits, black text on white]
- Third version, Straub Huillet Films, Belva GmbH
- Present
- La madre
- Dialogue by Cesare Pavese
- Film by Jean-Marie Straub
- Cast: Giovanna Daddi, Dario Marconcini, Teatro Comunale di Buti
- Image and editing: Christophe Clavert, color timing: Jean-Marc Degardin
- Assistants: Arnaud Dommerc, Barbara Ulrich
- Sound: Jérôme Ayasse, sound mix: Jean-Pierre Laforce, Gaël Blondet
- Music: Gustav Mahler
[No end credits]

TEXT: Cesare Pavese, "La madre" in *Dialoghi con Leucò*. **MUSIC:** Gustav Mahler, "Ich bin der Welt abhanden gekommen," Daniel Barenboim (piano), Dietrich Fischer-Dieskau (voice). Performed at the Teatro Communale di Buti on September 13, 2011. **PRODUCTION DATES AND LOCATION:** September 4–8, 2011, Acciaiolo, Italy. **CAMERA:** Panasonic AG DVX-100. **SUBTITLED IN ENGLISH** by Misha Donat and Straub, **IN GERMAN** by Barbara Ulrich and Straub, **IN FRENCH** by Aristide Bianchi, Barbara Ulrich, and Straub. **FIRST SCREENING:** all versions, February 28, 2012, La Fémis, Paris; 2012 Viennale (November 4).

———

2013

Un conte de Michel de Montaigne
(A Tale by Michel de Montaigne)
FRANCE, HD, 4:3, COLOR, 34'

[Opening credits, black text on white]
- Un conte de Michel de Montaigne
- Film by Jean-Marie Straub
- With Barbara Ulrich
- Camera, editing: Christophe Clavert, color timing: Jean-Marc Degardin
- Sound: Jérôme Ayasse, sound mix: Jean-Pierre Laforce, Gaël Blondet
- Production: Arnaud Dommerc, Andolfi, Straub-Huillet, Belva
[End credits, white text on black]
- With the help of the CNC and the participation of La Fémis

TEXT: Michel de Montaigne, "De l'exercitation" (book II, chapter 6) in *Essais*. **MUSIC:** Ludwig van Beethoven, *String Quartet No. 15 in A Minor*, opus 132. **CAMERA:** Canon 5D. **SUBTITLED IN ENGLISH** by Misha Donat and Straub, **IN GERMAN** by Peter Kammerer and Straub, **IN ITALIAN** by Giorgio Passerone and Straub. **FIRST SCREENING:** 2013 Locarno Film Festival (August); 2013 Toronto Film Festival, Wavelengths (September; shown without subtitles).

2013
La Mort de Venise *(The Death of Venice)*
FRANCE, HD, 4:3, COLOR, 2'

Commissioned by the Venice Film Festival for the omnibus film *Future Reloaded*. **IMAGE:** Christophe Clavert. **CAMERA:** Canon 5D. **FIRST SCREENING:** 2013 Venice Film Festival (September).

———

2013
Dialogue d'ombres
(Dialogue of Shadows)
FRANCE, HD, 4:3, COLOR/B&W, 28'

[Opening credits, white text on black]
- Dialogue d'ombres,
  by Georges Bernanos, 1928
- Film by Danièle Huillet and Jean-Marie Straub,
  1954–2013
- With Barbara Ulrich, Belva Film
- Françoise: Cornelia Geiser,
  Jacques: Bertrand Brouder
- Image/editing: Renato Berta, Christophe Clavert
- Sound: Dimitri Haulet
- Andolfi production, Arnaud Dommerc
- Assistant: Emilie Richard

[End credits, white text on black]
- Color timing: Jean-Marc Degardin,
  Studio Orlando: Olivier Boischot
- Sound mix: Jean-Pierre Laforce, Gaël Blondet
- Thank you, thank you as well to Marie
  Guyonnet and Daniel Martin for welcoming us
  at La Boderie, Athis-de-l'Orne
- Thank you as well to Marc Nicolas and
  Frédéric Papon for their welcome at La Fémis
- This film has been supported by the participa-
  tion of CNAP – Centre National des Arts
  Plastiques (Image/Mouvement), Ministère de
  la Culture et de la Communication
- La Ruche Studio, Paris

The film opens with an excerpt of *Chronicle of Anna Magdalena Bach* (version with French narration), shots 81–83, including the off-screen performance of BWV 140. **TEXT:** Georges Bernanos, *Dialogue d'ombres* (1928). **PRODUCTION DATES AND LOCATION:** June 15–20, 2013, Sainte-Honorine-la-Chardonne, France. **SUBTITLED IN ENGLISH** by Ted Fendt, Misha Donat, and Straub, **IN GERMAN** by Peter Kammerer and Straub, **IN ITALIAN** by Giorgio Passerone and Straub. **FIRST SCREENING:** 2014 Locarno Film Festival (August); Goethe-Institut, London (March 10, 2015).

———

2013
À propos de Venise (Geschichtsunterricht)
(Concerning Venice [History Lessons])
SWITZERLAND, HD, 4:3, COLOR/B&W, 22'39''

[Opening credits, white text on black]
- À propos de Venise (Geschichtsunterricht)
- Film by Jean-Marie Straub
- With Barbara Ulrich
- Text by Maurice Barrès
- Image and editing: Christophe Clavert
- Sound: Dimitri Haulet
- Sound mix: Jean-Pierre Laforce, Gaël Blondet,
  La Fémis
- Assistants: Arnaud Dommerc, Gilles Pandel

[End credits, white text on black]
- Music by J.-S. Bach, conducted by
  Gustav Leonhardt
- Laboratories: Studio Orlando, Olivier Boischot,
  La Ruche Studio
- Coproduction: Andolfi, Belva Film

The film closes with an excerpt of *Chronicle of Anna Magdalena Bach*, shot 37, performance of BWV 205. **TEXT:** Maurice Barrès, *Amori et Dolori sacrum – La mort de Venise* (1903), extract from

chapter 3. **PRODUCTION DATES AND LOCATION:**
October 12–14, 2013, Rolle, Switzerland. **CAMERA:**
Canon 5D. **SUBTITLED IN ENGLISH** by Ted Fendt,
Misha Donat and Straub, **IN GERMAN** by
Johannes Beringer and Straub, **IN ITALIAN** by
Giorgio Passerone and Straub. **FIRST SCREENING:**
2014 Locarno Film Festival (August); Goethe-
Institut, London (March 10, 2015).

———

2014
Kommunisten *(Communists)*
SWITZERLAND/FRANCE, HD, 4:3, COLOR, 70'

[Opening credits, white text on black]
- Kommunisten
- Film by Jean-Marie Straub
- For Jacques-Henri Michot and
  Giorgio Passerone
- Based on the novel *Le Temps du mépris*
  by André Malraux, music: Hanns Eisler
- Cast: Arnaud Dommerc, Jubarite Semaran,
  Gilles Pandel, Barbara Ulrich
- Image and editing: Christophe Clavert,
  sound: Dimitri Haulet
- Sound mix: Jean-Pierre Laforce,
  color timing: Richard Deusy
[End credits, white text on black]
- 1. Operai, contadini (2001)
  Image: Renato Berta, sound: Jean-Pierre Duret,
  cast: Aldo Fruttuosi, Rosalba Curatola,
  Enrico Pelosini
- 2. Trop tôt, trop Ttard (1981)
  Image: Robert Alazraki, sound: Louis Hochet,
  commentary: Bahgat el Nadi
- 3. Fortini/Cani (1976)
  Image: Renato Berta, sound: Jeti Grigioni,
  commentary: Franco Fortini
- 4. Der Tod des Empedokles (1986)
  Image: Renato Berta, sound: Louis Hochet,
  cast: Andreas von Rauch, Vladimir Baratta

- 5. Schwarze Sünde (1988)
  Image: William Lubtchansky,
  sound: Louis Hochet, cast: Danièle Huillet
- Post-production: Olivier Boischot
- Labs: Omnimago: Olaf Legenbauer,
  Studio Orlando, La Ruche Studio
- Production: Andolfi: Arnaud Dommerc, Jean-
  Baptiste Legard, Belva Film: Barbara Ulrich
- With the participation of the Centre National
  de la Cinématographie
- Extracts from the work *Le Temps du mépris*
  by André Malraux, © Editions Gallimard
- Thank you, thank you Florence Malraux

MUSIC: Hanns Eisler, "Auferstanden aus Ruinen"
(German Democratic Republic national anthem),
lyrics by Johannes R. Becher. **PRODUCTION DATES
AND LOCATION:** Summer/Fall 2014, Rolle, Switzer-
land. **CAMERA:** Canon 5D. **SUBTITLED IN ENGLISH**
by Barton Byg, Misha Donat, Ted Fendt, Huillet,
Straub, Gregory Woods, **IN GERMAN** by Johannes
Beringer, Manfred Blank, Huillet, Peter Kammerer,
Andrea Spingler, and Straub, **IN FRENCH** by
Huillet, **IN ITALIAN** by Vladimir Baratta, Domenico
Carosso, Huillet, Giorgio Passerone, and Straub.
FIRST SCREENING: 2014 Viennale (October 31);
Goethe-Institut, London (March 12, 2015);
2015 Festival du nouveau cinéma, Montreal
(October 11).

———

2014
La Guerre d'Algérie! *(The Algerian War!)*
FRANCE, HD, 4:3, COLOR, 2'

[Opening credits, white text on black]
- La Guerre d'Algérie!
- Film by Jean-Marie Straub
- Based on a story by Jean Sandretto
  (inexploré no. 23)
- Cast: Christophe Clavert, Dimitri Haulet

- Sound: Dimitri Haulet, image and editing: Christophe Clavert
- Sound mix: Jean-Pierre Laforce
- Assistants: Arnaud Dommerc, Barbara Ulrich, Giorgio Passerone
- Production: Andolfi, Belva Film
- Thank you Paul Denizot

Shown preceding *Kommunisten*. **MUSIC:** Franz Schubert, "Der Erlkönig" (1815). **PRODUCTION DATES AND LOCATION:** October 3–4, 2014, Jean-Marie Straub's apartment, Paris. **SUBTITLED IN ENGLISH** by Ted Fendt and Straub. **FIRST SCREENING:** 2014 Viennale (October 31); Goethe-Institut, London (March 12, 2015); 2015 Festival du nouveau cinéma, Montreal (October 11).

2015
L'Aquarium et la Nation
(The Aquarium and the Nation)
FRANCE, HD, 4:3, COLOR/B&W, 31'18''

[Opening credits, white text on black]
- L'Aquarium et la Nation
- Film by Jean-Marie Straub
- Text extracted from the novel by André Malraux, "Les Noyers de l'Altenburg" ["The Walnut Trees of Altenburg"] © Gallimard
- Actors: Aimé Agnel and Christiane Veschambre
- Image and editing: Christophe Clavert
- Sound: Dimitri Haulet, Sound mix: Jean-Pierre Laforce, Gaël Blondet, La Fémis
- Postproduction: Olivier Boischot, Studio Orlando, La Ruche Studio
- Production: Barbara Ulrich, Belva Film, Andolfi, Arnaud Dommeric
- Thank you Florence Malraux
[End credits, white text on black]
- Excerpt from *La Marseillaise* by Jean Renoir © Studio Canal

- Aquarium: "Chez Ming," Rue Forest, Paris 18ème
- And thank you l'Institut C. G. Jung of Paris

MUSIC: Franz Joseph Haydn, *Die sieben letzten Worte unseres Erlösers am Kreuze* (1738). **PRODUCTION DATES AND LOCATION:** February 2015, Chez Ming, Chinese restaurant, 3rd arrondissement and the offices of the Société Française de Psychologie Analytique-Institut C. G. Jung, 18th arrondissement, Paris. **CAMERA:** Canon 5D. **SUBTITLED IN ENGLISH** by Ted Fendt and Straub, **IN GERMAN** by Johannes Beringer and Straub, **IN ITALIAN** by Giorgio Passerone and Straub. **FIRST SCREENING:** 2015 Viennale (October 30); 2015 Hiroshima Film Festival (November; Mariko Okada Award to actor Aimé Agnel).

2015
Pour Renato
(For Renato)
ITALY/FRANCE, HD, 4:3, COLOR, 8'

Montage of one scene from *Othon* and set photos, made for a celebration of Renato Berta's birthday at Stadtkino Basel on April 1, 2015.

English-language Bibliography

Organized chronologically by publication

BOOKS

RICHARD ROUD, *Straub*, London: BFI, 1971. Reprinted New York: Viking, 1972.

BARTON BYG, *Landscapes of Resistance: The German Films of Danièle Huillet and Jean-Marie Straub*, Berkeley: University of California Press, 1995

URSULA BÖSER, *The Art of Seeing, the Art of Listening: the Politics of Representation in the Work of Jean-Marie Straub and Danièle Huillet*, Frankfurt am Main: Peter Lang, 2004

JEAN-MARIE STRAUB AND DANIÈLE HUILLET, *Writings*, edited and with an introduction by Sally Shafto, New York: Sequence Press, 2016

PUBLISHED SCREENPLAYS

JEAN-MARIE STRAUB AND DANIÈLE HUILLET, "History Lessons – Scenario," *Screen*, vol. 17, no. 1, Spring 1976, p. 54–76

JEAN-MARIE STRAUB AND DANIÈLE HUILLET, "Introduction to Arnold Schoenberg's Accompaniment to a Cinematograph Scene – Scenario," *Screen*, vol. 17, no. 1, Spring 1976, p. 77–83

JEAN-MARIE STRAUB AND DANIÈLE HUILLET, "Fortini/Cani – Script," *Screen*, vol. 19, no. 2, Summer 1978, p. 9–41

INTERVIEWS

ANDI ENGEL, "Andi Engel talks to Jean-Marie Straub," *Cinemantics*, no. 1, 1970, p. 16–24

ANDI ENGEL, "Andi Engel talks to Jean-Marie Straub, and Danièle Huillet is there too," *Enthusiasm*, no. 1, December 1975, p. 1–25

GEOFFREY NOWELL-SMITH, "After 'Othon', before 'History Lessons': Geoffrey Nowell-Smith talks to Jean-Marie Straub and Danièle Huillet," *Enthusiasm*, no. 1, December 1975, p. 26–31

JOEL ROGERS, "*Moses and Aaron* as an object of Marxist reflection," *Jump Cut*, no. 12/13, 1976, p. 61–64

PETER GIDAL, "Straub/Huillet Talking, and Short Notes on Some Contentious Issues," *Ark/Journal from the Royal College of Art*, Jan 1976, p. 89–97

PHIL MARIANI, "An Interview with Jean-Marie Straub and Danièle Huillet," ed. Brian Wallis and Phil Mariani, *Wedge: An Aesthetic Inquiry*, no. 1, Summer 1982, p. 22–29

JONATHAN ROSENBAUM, "Straub and Huillet on Filmmakers They Like and Related Matters," in *The Cinema of Jean-Marie Straub and Danièle Huillet, November 2–14, 1982, Film at the Public* program, ed. Jonathan Rosenbaum, Buffalo: Media Studies Center 1982

BEN BREWSTER, "Too Early/Too Late: Interview with Huillet and Straub. Translation and Notes by Ben Brewster," *Undercut*, no. 7/8, Spring 1983, p. 28–33 [Republished online, *Kinoslang*, August 22, 2014: kinoslang.blogspot.com]

N. N. "Direct Sound: an interview with Jean-Marie Straub and Danièle Huillet," trans. Bill Kavaler, in *Film Sound: Theory and Practice*, ed. Elisabeth Weiss and John Belton, New York: Columbia University Press, 1985, p. 150–153

N. N. *Film Forum: Thirty-Five Top Filmmakers Discuss Their Craft,* edited by Ellen Oumano, New York: St. Martin's Press, 1985

N. N. "There's Nothing More International Than a Pack of Pimps: A Conversation between Pierre Clémenti, Miklos Jancsó, Glauber Rocha and Jean-Marie Straub convened by Simon Hartog in Rome, February 1970," trans. John Mathews, *Rouge*, no. 3, 2004 [www.rouge.com.au]

ELKE MARHÖFER, MIKHAIL LYLOV, "A Thousand Cliffs," trans. John Barrett, in *Standpunkt der Aufnahme*, Berlin: Archive Books, 2014

SELECTED CRITICISM

RICHARD ROUD, "Cut rate cinema," *The Guardian* (London), July 22, 1965

N. N. "London Letter: 'Refugee' film director," *The Guardian* (London), November 17, 1965

N. N. "Interesting New Talents in London Film Festival," *The Times* (London), November 18, 1965

N. N. "The German Cinema," *The Times* (London), November 27, 1965

GIDEON BACHMANN, "Nicht versöhnt," *Film Quarterly*, vol. 19, issue 4, Summer 1966, p. 51–55

ANDREW SARRIS, "Festival Without Fuss," *The New York Times*, July 14, 1968

TOM MILNE, "The Oddities redeem the agony," *The Guardian* (London), September 8, 1968

ALLEN HUGHES, "Bach as Seen in His 2d Wife's Memories," *The New York Times*, September 20, 1968

PENELOPE GILLIAT, "The Current Cinema," *The New Yorker*, September 21, 1968.

J. HOBERMAN, "Report on the New York Film Festival 1968," *Harpur Film Journal* [Republished online, *Film Comment*, September 22, 2014: www.filmcomment.com/blog/nyff-j-hoberman-1968-report]

JOHN RUSSELL TAYLOR, "Enter charm, exit tricks," *The Times* (London), December 7, 1968

HARRIET R. POLT, "Chronicle of Anna Magdalena Bach," *Film Quarterly*, vol. 21, issue 2, Winter 1968/69, p. 55–56

A.H. WEILER, "German Newcomer's 3 Films: Straub's Entire Output Shown at New Yorker," *The New York Times*, February 24, 1969

A.H. WEILER, "'Chronicle of Anna Magdalena Bach' Opens: Composer Seen Through Faithful Wife's Eyes," *The New York Times*, April 7, 1969

RICHARD ROUD, "East is West and West is East," *The Guardian* (London), July 22, 1969

DEREK MALCOLM, "Waiting to be Reconciled," *The Guardian* (London), January 22, 1970

JOHN RUSSELL TAYLOR, "With the animals," *The Times* (London), January 23, 1970

RICHARD ROUD, "Verse against Vespas," *The Guardian* (London), February 11, 1970

RICHARD ROUD, "Petit Tours," *The Guardian* (London), February 23, 1970

DEREK MALCOLM, "Filleted Hamlet," *The Guardian* (London), April 9, 1970

ANDI ENGEL, "Jean-Marie Straub," in *Second Wave*, New York: Praeger, 1970, p. 128–132

RICHARD ROUD, "The Celluloid City," *The Guardian* (London), January 29, 1973

GEORGE ROBINSON, "Straub: Inquiry and Negation," *Columbia Daily Spectator*, February 26, 1973

JOEL GERSMANN, "Review of *Jean-Marie Straub* by Richard Roud," *The Velvet Light Trap*, no. 9, Summer 1973, p. 54

GEORGE ROBINSON, "Straub's Brechtian Lessons," *Columbia Daily Spectator*, October 2, 1973

LOUIS MARCORELLES, *Living Cinema: New Directions in Contemporary Filmmaking*, trans. George Allen, New York: Praeger, 1973

MARTIN WALSH, "Political formations in the cinema of Jean-Marie Straub," *Jump Cut*, issue 4, 1974

RICHARD ROUD, "Golden bull," *The Guardian* (London), February 26, 1975

RICHARD ROUD, "Rotterdam Journal," *Film Comment*, vol. 11, no. 3, May/June 1975, p. 2, 62

GEORGE ROBINSON, "NY Film Festival," *Columbia Daily Spectator*, September 26, 1975

RICHARD EDER, "Straub's Version of 'Aaron and Moses' by Schoenberg Is Uncompromising," *The New York Times*, October 5, 1975

MANNY FARBER AND PATRICIA PATTERSON, "New York Film Festival Review: Breaking Rules at the Roulette Table," *Film Comment*, vol. 11, no. 6, November/December 1975, p. 32–34, 57

ROBIN WOOD, "New Cinema at Edinburgh," *Film Comment*, vol. 11, no. 6, November/December 1975, p. 25–29

DAVID STERRITT, "'Moses and Aaron' – strange, difficult, fascinating," *The Christian Science Monitor*, December 1, 1975

STEPHEN HEATH, "From Brecht to Film: Theses, Problems (on *History Lessons* and *Dear Summer Sister*)," *Screen*, vol. 16, no. 4, Winter 1975/6, p. 34–45

JILL FORBES, "Einleitung zu Arnold Schoenbergs Begleitmusik zu einer Lichtspielscene (Introduction to Arnold Schoenberg's Accompaniment to a Cinematographic Scene)," *Monthly Film Bulletin*, no. 506, March 1976, p. 70–71

GEOFFREY NOWELL-SMITH, "Yeux ne peuvent pas en tout temps se ferms, Les (Othon)," [sic!] *Monthly Film Bulletin*, no. 506, March 1976

JONATHAN ROSENBAUM, "Nicht versöhnt oder Es hilft nur Gewalt wo Gewalt herrscht (Not Reconciled, or Only Violence Helps Where Violence Rules)," *Monthly Film Bulletin*, no. 506, March 1976, p. 60

TONY RAYNS, "Bräutigam, die Komödiantin und der Zuhälter (The Bridegroom, the Comedienne and the Pimp)," *Monthly Film Bulletin*, no. 506, March 1976, p. 69–70

YEHUDA E. SAFRAN, "Geschichtsunterricht (History Lessons)," *Monthly Film Bulletin*, no. 506, March 1976

SUSAN DERMODY, "Jean-Marie Straub and Daniele Huillet: The Politics of Film Practice," *Cinema Papers* (Australia), September 1976

ROY ARMES, "Jean-Marie Straub: Strict Counterpoint," in *The Ambiguous Image*, London: Secker & Warburg, 1976, p. 208–215

MAUREEN TURIM, "'Ecriture Blanche': The Ordering of the Filmic Text in 'Die Chronik Der Anna Magdalena Bach,'" in *Purdue Film Studies Annual*, West Lafayette: Purdue Research Foundation, 1976, p. 177–192

DAVID DEGENER, "Serial," *Miam 2*, June 1977 [Poem dedicated to Straub and Huillet]

MARTIN WALSH, "Introduction to Arnold Schoenberg's 'Accompaniment for a Cinematographic Scene': Straub/Huillet : Brecht : Schoenberg," *Camera Obscura*, vol. 1, no. 2, Fall 1977, p. 34–49

MANNY FARBER AND PATRICA PATTERSON, "Beyond the New Wave I: Kitchen Without Kitsch," *Film Comment*, vol. 13, no. 6, November/December 1977, p. 47–50

MARK NASH AND STEVE NEALE, "Film: History/Production/Memory," *Screen*, vol. 18, no. 4, Winter 1977/78, p. 77–91

GILBERT ADAIR, "Journals: Gilbert Adair from Paris," *Film Comment*, vol. 14, no. 2, March/April 1978, p. 6

DEREK WINNERT, "Exciting cinema shows the way," *The Times* (London), June 27, 1978

EDWARD BENNETT, "The Films of Straub Are Not 'Theoretical,'" *Afterimage*, no. 7, Summer 1978, p. 5–11

MARTIN WALSH, "The Frontiers of Language: Straub/Huillet's History Lessons," *Afterimage*, no. 7, Summer 1978, p. 12–31

GILBERTO PEREZ, "Modernist Cinema: The History Lessons of Straub and Huillet," *Artforum*, October 1978, p. 46–55

DEREK MALCOLM, "The men from the Ministry of Fear," *The Guardian* (London), January 31, 1980

RICHARD ROUD, "Jean-Marie Straub," in *Cinema: A Critical Dictionary*, ed. Richard Roud, New York: Viking, 1980, p. 967–969

JEAN-ANDRE FIESCHI, "Jean-Marie Straub," in *Cinema: A Critical Dictionary*, ed. Richard Roud, New York: Viking, 1980, p. 969–973

GREGORY WOODS AND DANIÈLE HUILLET, "A Work Journal of the Straub/Huillet Film 'Moses and Aaron'/Notes to Gregory's Work Journal," in *Apparatus, Cinematographic Apparatus: Selected Writings* by Theresa Hak Kyung Cha, New York: Tanam Press, 1980, pp. 147-231

MARTIN WALSH, *The Brechtian Aspect of Radical Cinema*, London: BFI, 1981

BRUCE JENKINS, "Adaptation and Ideology: Two Films by Straub and Huillet," unpublished screening introduction, 1981 [Revised and included in *Film at the Public* program, ed. Jonathan Rosenbaum, Buffalo: Media Studies Center 1982]

J. HOBERMAN, "Movie Reviews," *The Village Voice*, November 16, 1982 [Reviews of *Fortini/Cani*, *From the Cloud to the Resistance* and *Too Early, Too Late*]

N. N. *The Cinema of Jean-Marie Straub and Danièle Huillet, November 2–14, 1982, Film at the Public* program, ed. Jonathan Rosenbaum, Buffalo: Media Studies Center 1982

JONATHAN ROSENBAUM, "Transcendental Cuisine," in *Film at the Public* program, 1982 [Reprinted in *Film: The Front Line 1983*, Denver: Arden, 1983]

SERGE DANEY, "Cinemetorology," in *Film at the Public* program, 1982 [Republished online: home.earthlink.net/~steevee/Daney_too.html]

GILBERT ADAIR, "Films by Resnais, Rohmer, and the Straubs", *Sight and Sound*, Summer 1983

JONATHAN ROSENBAUM, "Intense Materialism: Too Soon, Too Late," in *Film: The Front Line 1983*, Denver: Arden, 1983 [Republished online, *Senses of Cinema*, issue 6, May 2000: sensesofcinema.com/2000/retrospective-jeune-dure-et-pure/soon]

MAUREEN TURIM, "Oblique Angles on Film as Ideological Intervention," in *New German Film-makers: From Oberhausen through the 1970s*, ed. Klaus Phillips, New York: Ungar, 1984, p. 335–358

HOLL., "Klassenverhältnisse," *Variety*, February 7, 1984

RICHARD ROUD, "Berlin bows to backstage," *The Guardian* (London), February 24, 1984

HARLAN KENNEDY, "Zoo Parade," *Film Comment*, vol. 20, no. 3, May/June 1984, p. 64, 69–71

J. HOBERMAN, "Once Upon a Time in Amerika: Straub/Huillet/Kafka," *Artforum*, September 1984, p. 75–77

MAUREEN TURIM, "Dice Games: Mallarmé and Straub/Huillet," Ohio Film Conference, October 1984

VINCENT CANBY, "Class Relations is Based on Kafka," *The New York Times*, October 7, 1984

J. HOBERMAN, "Class Relations," *The Village Voice*, October 9, 1984

ELLIOTT STEIN, "Mothers and Milk," *Film Comment*, vol. 20, no. 6, November/December 1984, p. 64–71

DEREK MALCOLM, "Just one damn thing after another," *The Guardian* (London), March 21, 1985

GILBERT ADAIR, "Amerikana: Class Relations," *Sight and Sound*, Spring 1985

MAUREEN TURIM, "Textuality and Theatricality in Brecht and Straub/Huillet's *History Lessons*," in *German Film and Literature: Adaptations and Transformations*, ed. Eric Rentschler, New York: Methuen, 1986, p. 234–245

MARGUERITE DURAS, "*Othon*, by Jean-Marie Straub," trans. Arthur Goldhammer, in *Outside: Selected Writings*, Boston: Beacon Press, 1986, p. 155–157, originally published in French, 1981

DAVE KEHR, "Berlin barometer: International festival shows the state of the art," *Chicago Tribune*, March 15, 1987

JONATHAN ROSENBAUM, "The Sound of German," *Chicago Reader*, December 2, 1988 [Reprinted in *Essential Cinema: On the Necessity of Film Canons*, Baltimore: Johns Hopkins University, 2004]

JULIEN PETLEY, "Etna & Ecology," *Sight and Sound*, Summer 1990, p. 150

GILBERT ADAIR, "Arts Diary: Oh for the wind in the trees," *The Guardian* (London), March 7, 1991

PAUL GRIFFITHS, "Film Festival Review: An Atonal Couple, Muddling Through," *The New York Times*, September 29, 1997

ROBERT HORTON, "New York Film Festival," *Film Comment*, vol. 33, no. 6, November/December 1997, p. 55–59

GILBERTO PEREZ, "History Lessons," in *The Material Ghost: Films and Their Medium*, Baltimore: Johns Hopkins University, 1998, p. 260–335

ROBERT HORTON, "Festivals: New York," *Film Comment*, vol. 35, no. 6, November/December 1999, p. 50–55

PHILIP LOPATE, "Festivals: New York," *Film Comment*, vol. 35, no. 6, November/ December 1999, p. 46–50
STEPHEN HOLDEN, "New York Film Festival Reviews: Talking to Mother and Other Totems," *The New York Times*, September 25, 1999
LOUIS SEGUIN, "Family, History, Romance (extract)," trans. Annwyl Williams, in *Cahiers du cinéma, Volume Four: 1973–1978, History, Ideology, Cultural Struggle*, London: Routledge 2000, p. 132–141, originally published in French, 1975
JAMES QUANDT, "Voyage to Italy: Provisional Notes on Straub/Huillet's *Sicilia!*," *Cinema Scope*, no. 2, Winter 2000, p. 81–83
MARTIN BRADY, "'Du Tag, wann wirst du sein…': Quotation, Emancipation and Dissonance in Straub/Huillet's *Der Bräutigam, die Komödiantin und der Zuhälter*," *German Life and Letters*, vol. 53, no. 3, July 2000, p. 282–302
PAUL ARTHUR, "Essay Questions from Alain Resnais to Michael Moore: Paul Arthur Gives a Crash Course in Nonfiction Cinema's Most Rapidly Evolving Genre," *Film Comment*, vol. 39, no. 1, January/February 2003, p. 58–62
BURLIN BARR, "Too Close, Too Far: Cultural Composition in Straub and Huillet's *Too Early, Too Late*," *Camera Obscura*, vol. 18, no. 2, 2003, p. 1–25
FRANÇOIS ALBERA, "Still Learning at the Louvre," trans. C. Penwarden, *Art Press*, no. 304, 2004, p. 51–54
TAG GALLAGHER, "Lacrimae Rerum Materialized," in *Die Früchte des Zorns und der Zärtlichkeit. Werkschau Danièle Huillet/Jean-Marie Straub und ausgewählte Filme von John Ford*, ed. Astrid Johanna Ofner, Vienna: Viennale and Austrian Film Museum, 2004 [Republished online, *Senses of Cinema*, issue 37, October 2005: sensesofcinema.com/2005/feature-articles/straubs]
FRÉDÉRIC BONNAUD, "Picture Perfect," trans. Dave Kehr, *Film Comment*, vol. 41, no. 1, January/February 2005, p. 6

JACQUES AUMONT, "The Invention of Place: Danièle Huillet and Jean-Marie Straub's *Moses and Aaron*," trans. Kevin Shelton and Martin Lefebvre, in *Landscape and Film*, ed. Martin Lefebvre, New York: Routledge, 2006, p. 1–18
JARED RAPFOGEL, "Stop Motion: Transformation and Stasis at the NYFF's Views from the Avant-Garde," *Senses of Cinema*, issue 39, May 2006 [sensesofcinema.com/2006/festival-reports/views_avant_garde2005]
DOMINIQUE PAÏNI, "Straub, Hölderlin, Cézanne," trans. Sally Shafto, *Senses of Cinema*, issue 39, May 2006 [sensesofcinema.com/2006/cinema-and-the-pictorial/straub_holderlin_cezanne], originally published in French, 1999
ANDY RECTOR, "Danièle Huillet," *Kino Slang*, October 9, 2006 [kinoslang.blogspot.com/2006/10/danile-huillet.html]
DAVE KEHR, "Danièle Huillet, 70, Creator of Challenging Films, Dies," *The New York Times*, October 12, 2006
RONALD BERGAN, "Danièle Huillet: Experimental film-maker who challenged cinematic language," *The Guardian* (London), October 18, 2006 [www.theguardian.com/news/2006/oct/18/guardianobituaries.france]
OLAF MÖLLER, "A Perfect World," *Film Comment*, vol. 42, no. 6, November/December 2006, p. 59–61
EMMANUEL BURDEAU AND JEAN-MICHEL FRODON, "Danièle Huillet (1936–2006): Materialist Filmmaker," trans. by Chris Fujiwara, *Undercurrent*, no. 3, November 2006 [old.fipresci.org/undercurrent/issue_0306/huillet_cahiers.htm]
CHRIS FUJIWARA, "Resistance," *Undercurrent*, no. 3, November 2006 [old.fipresci.org/undercurrent/issue_0306/huillet_fujiwara.htm]
JOHN GIANVITO, "From Yesterday Until Tomorrow," *Undercurrent*, no. 3, November 2006 [old.fipresci.org/undercurrent/issue_0306/huillet_gianvito.htm]

ADRIAN MARTIN, "Curiosity/Exigency," *Undercurrent*, no. 3, November 2006 [old.fipresci.org/undercurrent/issue_0306/huillet_martin.htm]

JONATHAN ROSENBAUM, "The Place(s) of Danièle," *Undercurrent*, no. 3, November 2006 [old.fipresci.org/undercurrent/issue_0306/huillet_rosenbaum.htm]

JENNIFER KRASINSKI, "The Dignities of Dissent," *Modern Painters*, April 2007, p. 50–52

TAG GALLAGHER, "Straub Anti-Straub," *Senses of Cinema*, issue 43, May 2007 [sensesofcinema.com/2007/feature-articles/costa-straub-huillet]

GEORGE CLARK AND REDMOND ENTWISTLE, "We do everything for this art, but this art isn't everything," *Vertigo*, vol. 3, issue 6, Summer 2007 [https://www.closeupfilmcentre.com/vertigo_magazine/volume-3–issue-6–summer-2007/we-do-everything-for-this-art-but-this-art-isnt-everything]

N.N. "No Secrets, Just Lessons: A Dialogue Between Pedro Costa and Thom Andersen," *Cinema Scope*, no. 29, Winter 2007, p. 40–45

OLAF MÖLLER, "Quei loro incontri," *Cinema Scope*, no. 29, Winter 2007, p. 46–47

LARSON POWELL, "Musical Materialism: Straub/Huillet, Brecht, Schoenberg," Panel on the Legacy of Brecht, Modern Languages Association conference, Chicago, December 27, 2007

RICHARD MORRIS, "The Whole and the Sum of its Parts: Reflections on the Nature of Cinema," in *Andrew Bracey: Freianlage*, Manchester: Castlefield Gallery Publications, 2007 [Revised version published online in 2009: www.newwavefilms.co.uk/assets/359/Richard_Morris_on_Straub_Huillet.pdf]

ANDRÉA PICARD, "An Enduring Love Story Composed of 'Cement Blocks & Extraordinary Poetry': Jean-Marie Straub's *Le Genou d'Artémide*," *Cinema Scope*, no. 36, Fall 2008, p. 66–68

RICHARD PORTON, "Amerika the Beautiful," *Cinema Scope*, no. 34, Spring 2008, p. 69–70

DANIEL KASMAN, "Cannes Film Festival 2008: 'Le Genou d'Artémide' (Straub, Italy) & 'Itinéraire de Jean Bricard' (Straub/Huillet, France)," *Mubi Notebook*, May 22, 2008 [https://mubi.com/notebook/posts/cannes-film-festival-2008-le-genou-dartemide-straub-italy-itineraire-de-jean-bricard-straubhuillet-france]

MARTIN BRADY, "Brecht in Brechtian Cinema," in *"Verwisch die Spuren!" Bertolt Brecht's Work and Legacy: A Reassessment,* eds. Robert Gillett and Godela Weiss-Sussex, Amsterdam: Rodopi, 2008, p. 295–308

RYLAND WALKER KNIGHT, "A Glance at Jean-Marie Straub and Danièle Huillet's 'Chronik der Anna Magdalena Bach'," *Mubi Notebook*, April 15, 2009 [https://mubi.com/notebook/posts/a-glance-at-jean-marie-straub-and-daniele-huillets-chronik-der-anna-magdalena-bach]

DANIEL FAIRFAX, "Jean-Marie Straub and Danièle Huillet," *Senses of Cinema*, issue 52, September 2009 [sensesofcinema.com/2009/great-directors/jean-marie-straub-and-daniele-huillet]

SALLY SHAFTO, "Artistic Encounters: Jean-Marie Straub, Danièle Huillet and Paul Cézanne," *Senses of Cinema*, issue 52, September 2009 [sensesofcinema.com/2009/feature-articles/artistic-encounters-jean-marie-straub-daniele-huillet-and-paul-cezanne]

SALLY SHAFTO, "On Straub-Huillet's Une Visite au Louvre," *Senses of Cinema*, issue 53, December 2009 [sensesofcinema.com/2009/feature-articles/on-straub-huillets-une-visite-au-louvre-1]

RICHARD BRODY, "Light Viewing," *The New Yorker*, October 1, 2010 [www.newyorker.com/culture/richard-brody/light-viewing]

JOYCE JESIONOWSKI, "Speaking 'Bach': Strategies of Alienation and Intimacy in Straub-Huillet's *Chronik der Anna Magdalena Bach/Chronicle of Anna Magdalena Bach* (1968)," *Studies in European Cinema*, vol. 7, no. 1, 2010, p. 61–65

CLAUDIA PUMMER, "*Les Passeurs*: Inscriptions of war and exile in Jean-Marie Straub and Danièle Huillet's *Machorka-Muff* (1962)," *Studies in European Cinema*, vol. 7, no. 1, 2010, p. 51–60

MICHAEL SICINSKI, "Reviews of New Releases Seen, January 2011," *The Academic Hack* [academichack.net/reviewsJanuary2011.htm]

KAILAN R. RUBINOFF, "Authenticity as a Political Act: Straub-Huillet's *Chronicle of Anna Magdalena Bach* and the Post-War Bach Revival," *Music and Politics*, vol. 5, no. 1, Winter 2011

ROBERT KOEHLER, "Locarno 2011. Old and New Straub," *Mubi Notebook*, August 9, 2011 [https://mubi.com/notebook/posts/locarno-2011–old-and-new-straub]

THE FERRONI BRIGADE, "The Golden Donkey Locarno 2011," *Mubi Notebook*, September 21, 2011 [https://mubi.com/notebook/posts/the-golden-donkey-locarno-2011]

JACQUES RANCIÈRE, "Politics and Aesthetics in the Straubs' Films," trans. by Ted Fendt, *Mubi Notebook*, November 7, 2011 [https://mubi.com/notebook/posts/politics-and-aesthetics-in-the-straubs-films]

TAG GALLAGHER, "Letter to Helmut Färber," *Lumen*, no. 1, 2011 [lumenjournal.org/issues/issue-i/gallagher]

DENIS LÉVY, "Modern Cinema," trans. Edwin Mak and Nikolaus Vryzidis, *Lumen*, no. 1, 2011 [lumenjournal.org/issues/issue-i/levy]

CESARE PAVESE, "Six Dialogues with Leuco," trans. Gregory Woods, Misha Donat, and Danièle Huillet, *Lumen*, no. 1, 2011 [lumenjournal.org/issues/issue-i/pavese]

CESARE PAVESE, "The Flood, The Beast & The Witches," trans. Tag Gallagher, *Lumen*, no. 1, 2011 [lumenjournal.org/issues/issue-i/pavese2]

CLAUDIA PUMMER, "Elective Affinities: the films of Danièle Huillet and Jean-Marie Straub," PhD (Doctor of Philosophy) thesis, University of Iowa, 2011

LOUIS SEGUIN, "The Beginning of History: 'Class Relations'," trans. by Ted Fendt, *Mubi Notebook*, April 29, 2013 [https://mubi.com/notebook/posts/the-beginning-of-history-class-relations], originally published in French, 1984

MICHAEL SICINSKI, "TIFF 2013. Wavelengths Experimental Films – The Shorts and the Mediums," *Mubi Notebook*, September 8, 2013 [https://mubi.com/notebook/posts/tiff-2013-wavelengths-experimental-films-the-shorts-and-the-mediums]

LARON POWELL, "Straub and Huillet's Music Films," in *The Differentiation of Modernism: Postwar German Media Arts*, Rochester: Camden House, 2013, p. 134–161

RICHARD PORTON, "Topical Malady" [*Fortini/Cani*], *Sight and Sound,* vol. 24, no. 7, July 2014

MANUEL RAMOS-MARTINEZ, "Marx Immemorial: Workers and Peasants in the Cinema of Jean-Marie Straub and Danièle Huillet," in *Marxism and Film Activism: Screening Alternative Worlds*, ed. Ewa Mazierska and Lars Kristensen, New York: Berghahn, 2015, 105–123

GERTJAN WILLEMS, "Longing for politics and dreams: on Jean-Marie Straub's Kommunisten," *Photogenie*, March 2015 [www.photogenie.be/photogenie_blog/blog/longing-politics-and-dreams-jean-marie-straub%E2%80%99s-kommunisten]

TED FENDT, "The Dream of a Thing: Straub's 'Kommunisten'," *Mubi Notebook*, March 17, 2015 [https://mubi.com/notebook/posts/the-dream-of-a-thing-straubs-kommunisten]

BENOÎT TURQUETY, "Orality and Objectification: Danièle Huillet and Jean-Marie Straub, Filmmakers and Translators," *SubStance: A Review of Theory and Literary Criticism,* vol. 44, no. 2, 2015

ANNETT BUSCH, "Universal Pictures: A Dialogue between a Future People from the Desert," in *After Year Zero: Geographies of Collaboration,* ed. Annett Busch and Anselm Franke, Chicago: University of Chicago, 2015, p. 31–36

Contributors

FRANÇOIS ALBERA is a professor of film history and aesthetics at the University of Lausanne, Switzerland, and copy editor of the film journal *1895 Revue d'histoire du cinéma*. He is the author and editor of numerous books on cinema, including *Eisenstein et le constructivisme* (1989), *Albatros, des Russes à Paris 1919–1929* (1995), *Avanguardie* (2004) and *l'Avant-Garde au cinéma* (2006).

HARUN FAROCKI was one of the most important German filmmakers, critics, and theorists. From the late 1960s until his death in 2014, he made more than 120 films, videos, and installations, including *Inextinguishable Fire* (1969), *Images of the World and the Inscription of War* (1988), *How to Live in the German Federal Republic* (1990), *Workers Leaving the Factory* (1995), *I Thought I Was Seeing Convicts* (2004), and the installation *Serious Games* (2009). A friend of Huillet and Straub, he acted in their film *Class Relations* and made a documentary on their rehearsal process.

TED FENDT is a critic, translator, projectionist, and filmmaker. He has translated film criticism by Luc Moullet, Mireille Latil-le-Dantec and Louis Seguin, and subtitles for films by Jean Epstein, Jean-Luc Godard, Marcel Hanoun, and Alain Resnais. He has written on films by Jacques Rivette, William Wellman, and Allan Dwan. Since 2013, he has translated the English subtitles for the films of Jean-Marie Straub.

JOHN GIANVITO is an American filmmaker, teacher and curator. His films include *The Mad Songs of Fernanda Hussein* (2001), *Profit Motive and the Whispering Wind* (2007), *Vapor Trail (Clark)* (2010), *Wake (Subic)* (2015) and the collectively-made *Far From Afghanistan* (2012). For five years he was the curator of the Harvard Film Archive, during which time he acquired prints of two films by Jean-Marie Straub and Danièle Huillet, *From Today Until Tomorrow* and *Sicilia!* He is currently an associate professor at Emerson College in Boston.

JEAN-PIERRE GORIN is a French filmmaker, critic, curator, and teacher. In the late 1960s and 1970s, under the aegis of the Dziga Vertov Group and beyond, he collaborated with Jean-Luc Godard on films such as *Tout va bien* (1972), *Letter to Jane* (1972), and *Ici et ailleurs* (1974/76). Since 1975 he has taught at the University of California, San Diego, where he is now professor emeritus. He is the director of a number of essay films, including the modern classics *Poto and Cabengo* (1979) and *Routine Pleasures* (1986).

CLAUDIA PUMMER teaches courses in Critical Studies at the Academy for Creative Media at the University of Hawai'i at Mānoa. She has a Ph.D. in Film Studies from the University of Iowa and has published on Jean-Marie Straub and Danièle Huillet as well as on the filmmaker Edgar G. Ulmer.

BARBARA ULRICH studied philosophy in Basel and Munich. She met Danièle Huillet and Jean-Marie Straub in 1987, staying with them in Paris. Since 2007, she has been Jean-Marie Straub's closest collaborator. Through her production company BELVA Film, she has produced every film since *Artemide's Knee*. She appears as an actress in *Jackals and Arabs*, *A Tale by Michel de Montaigne*, *Concerning Venice* and *Communists*.

Acknowledgments

Sickle and Hammer, Cannons, Cannons, Dynamite! Danièle Huillet and Jean-Marie Straub in Conversation with François Albera was first published in French, in Hors Champs, no. 7, 2001. An earlier English translation was first published in *Die Früchte des Zorns und der Zärtlichkeit. Werkschau Danièle Huillet / Jean-Marie Straub und ausgewählte Filme von John Ford,* ed. Astrid Johanna Ofner, Vienna: Viennale and Austrian Film Museum, 2004

Stop Coughing! was first published in German: Harun Farocki, "Hör auf zu husten!" in *Der Standard* (Vienna), October 17, 2006

Nine Notes on Where Does Your Hidden Smile Lie? was first published in Portuguese: Jean-Pierre Gorin, "Nove Notas sobre *Onde Jaz o Teu Sorriso?*" in *Cem mil cigarros: Os filmes de Pedro Costa,* ed. Ricardo Matos Cabo, Lisbon: Orfeu Negro, 2009

Photo Credits

BARBARA ULRICH, BELVA-FILM
9, 13, 17 bottom, 19 top and bottom, 28 top left, 31 top left, 35, 41 bottom right, 51, 55, 56, 57 middle, 60, 62, 63 top, 69 top, 71 top, 73 bottom left, 77 top and middle, 78, 80, 82, 84 bottom, 86, 87, 88, 89 top, 91, 93, 94, 129 top and bottom right, 133 top and bottom left, 134 left, 139 bottom, 211

DAN TALBOT PAPERS 44, 45, 143 bottom, 160–184

© BERNARD RUBENSTEIN 4, 47, 96–102

© KARL THUMM 103–108

ÖSTERREICHISCHES FILMMUSEUM
© Richard Dumas: 157; © Berthold Schweiz: Back Cover, 65, 126, 147, 150, 153, 155; 17 top, 19 middle, 23 bottom left, 28 top right and bottom, 31 top right and bottom, 38, 41 top and bottom left, 43 bottom left and right, 49, 54, 57 top, 58, 63 bottom, 67, 69 middle and bottom, 71 bottom, 73 bottom right, 77 bottom, 129 bottom left, 131 top right and bottom left, 133 bottom right, 134 right, 139 top, 143 top

FILMMUSEUM MÜNCHEN
Heiner Roß Collection / Joachim Wolf Estate (Kinemathek Hamburg) at the Munich Film Museum: 24, 25; Frame enlargements by Gerhard Ullmann / Munich Film Museum: 23 top and bottom right, 43 top; Martina Müller, Köln: 89 bottom

VIENNALE
57 bottom, 73 top, 84 top, 92, 131 top left, 131 bottom right, 158, 209

FilmmuseumSynemaPublikationen

Available English Language Titles

Volume 24
BE SAND, NOT OIL
THE LIFE AND WORK OF AMOS VOGEL
Edited by Paul Cronin
Vienna 2014, 272 pages
ISBN 978-3-901644-59-7
An émigré from Austria who arrived in
New York just before the Second
World War, Amos Vogel was one of
America's most innovative film historians and curators. In
1947 he created *Cinema 16*, a pioneering film club aimed at
audiences thirsty for work "that cannot be seen elsewhere,"
and in 1963 was instrumental in establishing the New York
Film Festival. In 1974 he published the culmination of his
thoughts, the book *Film as a Subversive Art*. In the words
of Martin Scorsese: "The man was a giant." This is the first
book about Vogel. *"An indispensable study. If the book is
invaluable for gathering together numerous never-before-
collected or previously unpublished pieces by Vogel himself,
the newly commissioned essays by various scholars are every
bit as welcome."* (Film Comment)

Volume 23
HOU HSIAO-HSIEN
Edited by Richard I. Suchenski
Vienna 2014, 272 pages
ISBN 978-3-901644-55-0
Hou Hsiao-hsien is the most important figure in Taiwanese cinema, and
his sensuous, richly nuanced films reflect everything that is vigorous and
genuine in contemporary film culture. Through its stylistic
originality and historical gravity, Hou's body of work opens
up new possibilities for the medium. This volume includes
contributions by Olivier Assayas, Peggy Chiao, Jean-Michel
Frodon, Shigehiko Hasumi, Jia Zhang-ke, James Quandt,
and many others as well as conversations with Hou Hsiao-
hsien and some of his most important collaborators over
the decades. *"Delicious is a good word for this book, an absolute necessity for every serious cinephile."* (David Bordwell)

Volume 19
JOE DANTE
Edited by Nil Baskar and Gabe Klinger
Vienna 2013, 256 pages
ISBN 978-3-901644-52-8
In the often dreary landscape of Holly-
wood's blockbuster era, the cinema of
Joe Dante has always stood out as a
rare beacon of fearless originality.
Blending humor with terror and trenchant political satire

with sincere tributes to "B" movies, the "Dante touch" is
best described as a mischievous free-for-all of American
pop culture and film history. This first English language
book on Dante includes a career-encompassing interview,
a treasure trove of never-before-seen documents and
illustrations, and new essays by Michael Almereyda,
J. Hoberman, Bill Krohn, John Sayles, and Mark Cotta Vaz,
among many others. *"The closest we currently have to a
full-blown autobiography, the book does an admirable job
as a single-volume overview."* (Sight & Sound)

Volume 17
A POST-MAY ADOLESCENCE
LETTER TO ALICE DEBORD
By Olivier Assayas
Vienna 2012, 104 pages
ISBN 978-3-901644-44-3
Olivier Assayas is best known as a
filmmaker, but cinema makes only
a late appearance in his book. This
reflective memoir takes us from the massive cultural up-
heaval that was May 1968 in France to the mid-1990s when
Assayas made his first film about his teenage years. The
book also includes two essays on the aesthetic and political
legacy of Guy Debord, who played a decisive role in shaping the author's understanding of the world. *"Assayas' voice
is clear, urgent, and persuasive. For him the matter at hand,
the subject that keeps slipping away, is the story of how he
came to know the work of Guy Debord. This is nothing less
than the story of his life."* (Film Quarterly)

Volume 16
OLIVIER ASSAYAS
Edited by Kent Jones
Vienna 2012, 256 pages
ISBN 978-3-901644-43-6
Over the past few decades, French
filmmaker Olivier Assayas has become
a powerful force in contemporary
cinema. Between such major works
as *Irma Vep, Les Destinées, Summer Hours, Carlos* and *Clouds
of Sils Maria*, he has charted an exciting path, strongly
embracing narrative and character and simultaneously
dealing with the 'fragmentary reality' of life in a global
economy. This richly-illustrated monograph includes a
major essay by Kent Jones, contributions from Assayas and
his most important collaborators, as well as 16 individual
essays on each of the filmmaker's works.

Volume 15
SCREEN DYNAMICS
MAPPING THE BORDERS OF CINEMA
Edited by Gertrud Koch, Volker Pantenburg, and Simon Rothöhler
Vienna 2012, 184 pages
ISBN 978-3-901644-39-9
This volume attempts to reconsider the limits and specifics of film and the traditional movie theater. It analyzes notions of spectatorship, the relationship between cinema and the "uncinematic", the contested place of installation art in the history of experimental cinema, and the characteristics of the high definition image. Contributors include Raymond Bellour, Victor Burgin, Vinzenz Hediger, Tom Gunning, Ute Holl, Ekkehard Knörer, Thomas Morsch, Jonathan Rosenbaum and the editors.

Volume 11
GUSTAV DEUTSCH
Edited by Wilbirg Brainin-Donnenberg and Michael Loebenstein
Vienna 2009, 252 pages
ISBN 978-3-901644-30-6
According to Viennese filmmaker Gustav Deutsch, "film is more than film." His own career proves that point. In addition to being an internationally acclaimed creator of found footage films, he is also a visual artist, an architect, a researcher, an educator, an archaeologist, and a traveler. This volume traces the way in which the cinema of Gustav Deutsch transcends our common notion of film. Essays by Nico de Klerk, Stefan Grissemann, Tom Gunning, Beate Hofstadler, Alexander Horwath, Wolfgang Kos, Scott MacDonald, Burkhard Stangl, and the editors.

Volume 9
FILM CURATORSHIP. ARCHIVES, MUSEUMS, AND THE DIGITAL MARKETPLACE
By Paolo Cherchi Usai, David Francis, Alexander Horwath, and Michael Loebenstein
Vienna 2008, 240 pages
ISBN 978-3-901644-24-5
This volume deals with the rarely-discussed discipline of film curatorship and with the major issues and challenges that film museums and cinémathèques are bound to face in the Digital Age. *Film Curatorship* is an experiment: a collective text, a montage of dialogues, conversations, and exchanges among four professionals representing three generations of film archivists and curators.

Volume 6
JAMES BENNING
Edited by Barbara Pichler and Claudia Slanar
Vienna 2007, 264 pages
ISBN 978-3-901644-23-8
James Benning's films are among the most fascinating works in American cinema. He explores the relationship between image, text and sound while paying expansive attention to the "vernacular landscapes" of American life. This volume traces Benning's artistic career as well as his biographical journey through the United States. With contributions by James Benning, Sharon Lockhart, Allan Sekula, Dick Hebdige, Scott MacDonald, Volker Pantenburg, Nils Plath, Michael Pisaro, Amanda Yates, Sadie Benning, Julie Ault, Claudia Slanar and Barbara Pichler.

Volume 5
JOSEF VON STERNBERG
THE CASE OF LENA SMITH
Edited by Alexander Horwath and Michael Omasta
Vienna 2007, 304 pages
ISBN 978-3-901644-22-1
The Case of Lena Smith, directed by Josef von Sternberg, is one of the legendary lost masterpieces of the American cinema. Assembling 150 original stills and set designs, numerous script and production documents as well as essays by eminent film historians, the book reconstructs Sternberg's dramatic film about a young woman fighting the oppressive class system of Imperial Vienna. The book includes essays by Janet Bergstrom, Gero Gandert, Franz Grafl, Alexander Horwath, Hiroshi Komatsu and Michael Omasta, a preface by Meri von Sternberg, as well as contemporary reviews and excerpts from Viennese literature of the era.

Volume 4
DZIGA VERTOV. DIE VERTOV-SAMMLUNG IM ÖSTERREICHISCHEN FILMMUSEUM
THE VERTOV COLLECTION AT THE AUSTRIAN FILM MUSEUM
Edited by the Austrian Film Museum, Thomas Tode, and Barbara Wurm
Vienna 2006, 288 pages
ISBN 3-901644-19-9
For the Russian filmmaker and film theorist Dziga Vertov KINO was both a bold aesthetic experiment and a document of contemporary life. This book presents the Austrian Film Museum's comprehensive Vertov Collection, including many unpublished documents and writings such as his extensive autobiographical "Calling Card" from 1947.

All FilmmuseumSynemaPublications are distributed internationally by Columbia University Press (**cup.columbia.edu**). In the German-language area please also see **www.filmmuseum.at**.